FIFTY YEARS
A FISHERMAN

FIFTY YEARS
A FISHERMAN

*The Autobiography
of John Wilson*

BOXTREE

This book is for my granddaughter Alisha who through another generation will, I hope, come to love the flora and fauna of the countryside and wild open places as much as her granddad.

First published 1999 by Boxtree

an imprint of Macmillan Publishers Ltd
25 Eccleston Place, London, SW1W 9NF
Basingstoke and Oxford

Associated companies throughout the world

ISBN 0 7522 1343 1

www.macmillan.co.uk

3 5 7 9 10 8 6 4 2

A CIP catalogue record for this book is available from the British Library.
Designed by Lovelock & Co.
Illustrations by David Batten
Printed in the UK by Butler & Tanner, Frome, Somerset.

Contents

Acknowledgements

How can I possibly thank everyone who has been influential in my life, which spans more than half a century? It's impossible. Nevertheless I would like to say a big 'thank you' to my parents who gave me immense encouragement and a totally free hand during those all-important formative years. I should also like to compliment James Wadeson for his cartoons, and a really huge badge of merit must go to my long-suffering typist, Jan Carver, who has done the business once again in turning my terrible longhand and 'Wilsonisms' into readable English. Very special thanks go to my wonderful wife and soul mate, Jo, for putting up with a veritable fishing junkie. I wonder if she knew what she was really letting herself in for with those immortal words 'I do'.

Lastly, in addition to seeking absolution from my two children (now adults themselves) Lee and Lisa, who could have seen more of their father during their adolescence but for the fact he was always fishing, I wish to thank all the mates and acquaintances who have become part of my fishing life. I cannot possibly name everyone but the list includes people like John (Jinx) Davey, Terry Houseago, Bruce Vaughan, Andy Davison, Dave Batten, Norman Symmonds, Christine Slater, Susheel and Nanda Gyanchand, John and Veronica Stuart, the late Trevor Housby and the late Doug Allen, Dave Lewis, Sid Johnson, my brother Dave Wilson, my uncle the late Joe Bowler plus his grandsons, Martin and Richard Bowler who have all been greatly influential in what you are now about to read.

BELOW Sunset on Lake Kariba, Zimbabwe.

Introduction

The intention of this book is not to give an intimate and full account of my life, but I trust you will discover enough detail about my love for fishing which has never left me in half a century. To feature each and every special angling occasion and every memorable fish I've caught over the past fifty years is of course an impossibility within the confines of this albeit lengthy volume, and I sincerely hope readers, particularly those who have followed my exploits throughout thirty years of angling journalism, will not in any way feel cheated. For this reason the final chapter contains a complete list of all the largest specimens of every species of coarse, sea and game fish I have ever caught both at home and abroad.

It would take a book in itself simply to cover fully the ninety half-hour *Go Fishing* programmes I have presented for Anglia Television, let alone anything else. What I have tried to provide is a balance of my angling life covering a wide spectrum of interests and subsequent events, be it wine-making, shooting, photography, taxidermy, lake management, or landing the whoppers. My sport has taken me all around the globe to enjoy some of the most exciting adversaries in both fresh and saltwater, from the mighty mahseer in southern India, to the giant lake trout of Canada's frozen Northwest Territories. I've learnt so much along the way and teamed up with some wonderful characters. Fishing has naturally dictated the path of my life and for the past thirty years at least – during my involvement with the tackle trade, television and as a journalist – I have been unable to separate work from play. I enjoy my work so much that they are indeed one and the same thing, which I guess makes me one contented person and a very lucky one.

They say, however, that you only ever get out what you are prepared to put into anything, and following a lifetime's fishing I reckon that's pretty accurate. So, good and bad luck can make all the difference on the day but, overall, things have a way of evening out. No one can always be lucky or always unlucky. For the most part you make your own luck by researching where the fish are, when they feed, and at what depth . . . and then fish accordingly. Sometimes your luck is in and you beat all the odds of landing a monster hooked on ultra-light tackle when you shouldn't have stood a chance. Then on the very next trip the hook will inexplicably pull free from the very fish you've been after, within inches of the waiting net, when you've seemingly done everything right. But that's life!

John Wilson
Great Witchingham, 1999

ABOVE Ponies and
cart horses were a
way of life for rag
and bone trader,
Granddad Wilson.
Although I was just
two years old at the
time, perhaps he
saw me as a
budding Steptoe!

RIGHT As soon as he
could walk, brother
Dave *(left)* was as
fascinated as me by
the sticklebacks and
stone loach we
netted from Hilly
Fields brook.

Early Days

I was born in 1943 in Lea Road, Enfield in the very same flat where my mother and father, Margaret and Denis Wilson, continued to live for the following forty-five years until they eventually moved into sheltered accommodation, also in Enfield. My brother, David – another keen angler and living in Hertfordshire – was born four and a half years later in 1948.

My Dad's father 'Granddad Wilson' was a rag and bone man, 'Steptoe style', who operated a small family business just half a mile away in Baker Street. Some of my earliest recollections are of sitting up there on the horse-driven cart next to him as he yelled out those immortal words, 'Any old iron!' and 'Any old lumber!' My mother still takes great delight in reminding me of the time when I fell foul of such a street trader, by exchanging her best Sunday dress for two large goldfish. But that's how things were in those days. Our bread was even delivered by horse-drawn wagon and any old rags or iron were the conditions by which people traded.

Thus living in a north London flat without a garden or easy access to wild open places until the age of twenty-two when I left home to work abroad, much of my early childhood was spent exploring local park ponds, streams and ditches, first with a net, then with a worm tied by thread to a garden cane and eventually using rod and line. I must have been around three or four years old when Dad first took me netting for sticklebacks at Hillyfields Brook next to Whitewebbs Park in Enfield, about a mile's walk from our home. And it was Nan's old 'Nora Batty' heavy-duty stockings which kept me constantly supplied with nets. A galvanized wire coat hanger was formed into a circle leaving the ends bent at right angles for whipping with Dad's garden string on to a stiff cane, after first threading through the stocking's hem. To finish, a tight knot was tied halfway down the stocking and the remainder below cut off.

Now exactly why I had acquired a liking for frogs, toads, newts and fish at such an early age I can only attribute to Dad, bless him, who being a bricklayer by trade often brought newts home from the old wartime bomb sites where he was working at the time, helping to rebuild Greater London after the war, and as a keen gardener and chrysanthemum grower, encouraged me to potter about looking for creepy crawlies when accompanying him to his allotment at weekends. Apparently I'd play happily for hours on end collecting frogs and toads, but I'm sure those early impressions of fat, silver bellied prickly finned sticklebacks, and especially the red-throated males resplendent in their turquoise livery, lying there glistening like jewels in the folds of Nan's stocking net is what filled my imagination and made me into a life-long angler.

Dad's arms, being significantly longer, could reach far into all the deep, dark and mysterious spots beneath steep banking where young Wilson's could not, to capture the biggest sticklebacks and occasionally a much-prized stone loach or even a bull head. Inverting the net after every scoop, never knowing what was inside, before tipping the catch into the bucket was to me the ultimate in excitement. Netting also gave me a continual lesson in and immediate love of natural history through identifying a myriad of invertebrates like freshwater shrimps, beetles, leeches, dragonfly and caddis larvae, and to a little boy this was far more thrilling than watching chrysanthemums grow. It revealed a wonderful sense of mystery that remains with me to this day and will no doubt continue with me to the grave. My wife, Jo, thinks I would happily fish into a bucket of coloured water providing I

BELOW Mum and Dad with Dave and I at Warners Holiday Camp, Hayling Island in Hampshire, 1950, where I first learnt to swim and row a dinghy.

couldn't see the bottom. And indeed wherever I am beside water, be it a village brook or out upon deep blue tropical saltwater miles offshore, that same sense of mystery prevails. I always want to know what lives down there, what it looks like, how big it grows, what it feeds upon, how it fights and how it reproduces. To me fishing provides the consummate challenge.

As my interest in waterside flora and fauna grew I progressed to garden cane rods and the proverbial bent pin stage. Not that I actually recall using a bent pin. My favourite captures were the smooth newt, occasionally even great crested newts (now an endangered species) and the gluttonous stickleback. They could each be readily lifted from the water once they had gorged half a redworm down their throats. The worm was simply tied on gently around the middle using strong black cotton, with a matchstick float half hitched on two feet above, and the 4–5ft cotton line tied to the end of a garden cane.

Thus a garden cane became my first makeshift rod and with this outfit I explored all the local ditches, brooks, water-filled bomb holes and park ponds with other young kids from my street. I also pursued newts from some of the local boating pools. They loved to hide up within cracks in the concrete just above water level all around the edges. I was always being chased by 'parkies' (the park keepers) for newting, though I can't think why. The old 'jobsworth' syndrome I suppose. This was the late 1940s. There were no computer games, fancy toys, portable sound systems or karate clubs; everyone made their own amusement. And working-class families in many of the council housing estates around London were lucky to have electricity, let alone a television. In fact our flat was not wired up until I was around thirteen years old, mains gas providing everything until then.

In our road only one family had a car parked outside. Today you can barely drive along Lea Road in Enfield for the parked cars. In those days however there was but one, an old dark blue Austin Seven owned by a Mr Lucas, who also owned the only television. At Easter or Whitsun he would kindly take some of us kids to the seaside at Southend or Clacton and at Christmas time he had us all in to watch Laurel and Hardy movies on his black-and-white television. It was one of those old polished wooden monstrosities the size of a washing machine with a huge speaker and a tiny nine-inch screen. Those were the days! Kids went fishing, bird-nesting and happily played football and impromptu cricket matches down the middle of back streets.

I purposely mention bird-nesting (egg collecting) because, abhorrent as it may seem in our conservation-minded society today, it actually gave many kids a valuable education in natural history. While collecting birds' eggs from hedgerows and woodland we soon learned in which trees and bushes to find which nests, and identified countless plants, trees and animals along the way. It got kids out into the countryside, into the fresh air, and fulfilled part of the primal hunting instinct that is in all men and which modern society unfortunately does its utmost to suppress. Now not for one minute am I trying to condone bird-nesting, especially now that numerous indigenous breeds are declining in numbers with some even on the point of extinction. We do however need to recognize why this decline has occurred. It is certainly in no way due to the kids of my generation, and long before, collecting a few eggs. Usually just one egg was taken from a clutch. It was then pricked with a pin at both ends and blown out prior to being displayed proudly upon fine sawdust in a glass-fronted cabinet. We knew that the lighter-weight eggs were maturing inside and so these were never taken, only the heavier freshly-laid ones. Harsh though it may seem it was part of a youngster's education in the countryside.

The fact is, even if a bird's entire clutch of eggs is taken it will simply produce another. But take its habitat away and it has nowhere to breed. Blame therefore can be laid fairly and squarely upon the shoulders of successive governments who, during the 1960s, decreed that British farmers must grow more wheat (for a mountain we didn't need) and in so doing consequently tore out countryside hedgerows in the creation of unnaturally huge, easy-to-plough and easy-to-reap, grain-producing fields. Pop over to Ireland if you wish to see what much of southern England looked like prior to the 1960s. There you will find lovely wind-protected little fields of no more than a few acres apiece, bordered by thick hedges of blackthorn and hawthorn – all full of breeding birds. So the lack of chiffchaffs, chaffinches, greenfinches, goldfinches, hedge sparrows, song thrushes and the like in England today is down purely to government policy through farming practices. Nothing else.

To put it simply, if you destroy its habitat, you ultimately destroy the animal, be it a songbird which has nowhere to build a nest, an orang-utan which finds its rainforest home being felled all around it, or a man without a house. The result is exactly the same. I mention all this because sadly a complete and successive lack of government legislation required to protect our inland waterways has led directly to the destruction of many once fast-flowing and habitat-rich rivers where fish used to breed freely and prolifically. The uncaring actions of Margaret Thatcher selling off to the highest bidder the country's utilities, especially our water companies during the 1980s, was one huge nail in the coffin of British natural history. I have never been in favour of selling off to another something which the country (that's all of us) already owns. But selling off natural resources tops the lot and will no doubt go down in history as one of the biggest blunders ever made by a British government. You can live without a telephone, without electricity even, but you cannot exist without fresh water.

Why should a French conglomerate, Lyonnaise Des Eaux, own Essex and Suffolk water? It is scandalous. The entire subject of water, our most important and valuable natural resource by far, has never been properly addressed by any British government. In the years since the last war both Labour and Conservative administrations have put commercial interests before the existence and maintenance of the country's natural resources. Yes, I do have the bit between my teeth especially as far as water abstraction is concerned, having witnessed the destruction of so many sparkling brooks and streams around north London and in Hertfordshire where I first learnt to fish. This is a subject I shall come back to throughout this book. But let's return to those early years.

Minnows were not silly enough to gorge upon a worm long enough for lifting out, neither were young roach and the likes of gudgeon and dace. So young Wilson, who must have been around six or seven at the time, spent his pocket money on some size 20 hooks tied to nylon, ten yards of green flax linen line and a small tin of 'gentles', as maggots were commonly referred to in those days. I also invested in a brightly coloured 'Day-Glo' bobber float. Few of the fish we caught in those days, though we didn't realize it at the time of course, had the physical strength to pull such bulbous floats under when sucking in our bait. Hence the term 'bobber floats' I suppose, because all they ever did was bob. A cheap and noisy 'clicker' (centre pin) reel was fixed with insulating tape to my designer cane rod which Dad furnished with rod rings made from safety pins. With this outfit I happily caught tiddlers from Whitewebbs Park brook in north Enfield and the New River which then flowed swiftly, sweet and pure, right through Enfield and around the Town Park known as the 'loop'. Created in Hertford with water taken from the rivers Rib, Lea, Mimram and Beane, the New River is in fact north London's drinking supply. Though mostly private and patrolled by guard dogs, certain stretches are fishable and way back in 1907 an eighteen-pound brown trout was caught from the river at Haringey by Mr J. Briggs. It remained the British record for many years and proof to the quality of fish living in the New River.

ABOVE Catching this (then) reasonable roach from the New River in Enfield made me a roach fisherman for life from an early age.

During the late 1940s and 1950s, the New River was my only local river, and many a fat goggle-eyed perch I caught on trotted worm from the dark mysterious water beneath Enfield Town Road Bridge. It was a wonderful training ground for many young anglers. Some bright spark on the local council however decided that the New River could be pumped straight to Winchmore Hill from Enfield Town without flowing around the Town Park, and so part of the very river where I first seriously learnt to fish was actually filled in to become a car park. While the rest of the river that meanders around Enfield has since become stagnant, full of urban rubbish, fishless and a thorough disgrace to the community. Where the children of Enfield learn to fish nowadays I dread to think. Perhaps they simply don't!

Formative Years

One of my favourite locations was the outflow brook which ran from Wildwoods private lake through Whitewebbs Park and golf course in north Enfield. How we kids never got hit by a golf ball I'll never know, but we certainly topped up our pocket money by selling golf balls back to the very golfers who had just lost them in the brook. Though not on the same day naturally. We weren't that silly. We even acquired little curly wire cups which golfers in those days used to retrieve balls from the water, or simply took our boots and socks off and got in to feel around in the silt if we couldn't actually see where their ball entered the brook. By now most of those golfers must surely have passed on into that big 'golden green' in the sky, so I'm sure they'll forgive the white lies of little boys who had them searching all over the place – everywhere except where we knew their balls had really gone. Yes, fishing and ball collecting proved top pursuits throughout those long school holidays.

Fishing for minnows and roach along the Whitewebbs brook also taught me how to obtain free bait. As we couldn't always afford maggots, and what with Matthew's tackle shop in Enfield Town being a mile's walk in the opposite direction on top of the mile walk from home to Whitewebbs, we used worms or caddis grubs most of the time. Complete in their portable homes made of twigs and pieces of gravel, as every angler knows or should know – though I doubt as many as one in a thousand uses them for bait nowadays – caddis can be found easily in shallow water clinging to the undersides of large pieces of flint or crawling along sunken branches. You simply squeeze the rear end of its casing so that when its head and legs appear at the front the greyish white succulent grub (of the sedge fly) can be gently eased out using thumb and forefinger.

Most caddis grubs are longer than the biggest shop-bought maggot and marry perfectly with a size 16 hook. What's more, in half an hour enough can be collected for a morning's float fishing; reason enough, even today, for me to carry on driving if I suddenly realize I've left the bait at home on the way to a summer river session. Caddis are always abundant, and free to those who look. Incidentally, baiting the hook with a large caddis grub or two, whilst loose feeding shop-bought maggots, is a great way of sorting out better quality roach and dace.

It may seem strange to you that here was a young Wilson from the age of six or seven upwards, setting out with other kids of his age and often on his own to boating

OPPOSITE Complete with Elvis haircut, here's me with a catch of chub to 4lb and a trout caught on freelined cheesepaste from the Dorset Stour at Throop Mill.

15

ponds, rivers and lakes unaccompanied by an adult. In today's climate of mega media hype I guess it would appear totally irresponsible; that is if you believe there are more flashers, kidnappers and rapists about now pro rata than there were fifty years ago. Personally I doubt it. I can remember as a young footballer over at the local recreation park always seeing the same so-called 'dirty old men' in proverbial grey raincoats hanging about. But we kids recognized them all on sight and had been forewarned by our parents never to take sweets from or even talk to them, so we stayed well clear. Dad also made sure I could swim at an early age.

When it must have seemed that his young nephew, now around eight years old, wouldn't be too much trouble, my Uncle Joe invited me out for a day's serious fishing at the Barnet Angling Club pit and stream complex in London Colney in Hertfordshire. Here we fished with real Mr Crabtree-type eleven-foot rods comprising three sections: the first two of whole cane and the top of built or 'split cane' to give it its more commonly used name. Reels were centre pins of the 'flick 'em' type and the float rigs we used were all carefully stored on six section wooden winders, having been made up and shotted correctly by Uncle Joe, especially for the smaller river we fished. Auntie Girlie came along because she too liked to fish, but as I recall she spent more time untangling my tackle than fishing herself. From garden cane to a large float rod was too much for young Wilson to accomplish in one day. But the seed was sown and shortly I was tapping Dad for a real rod. My first rod was constructed from an old army tank aerial and though sloppy its nine feet aided line pick-up enormously compared to a short garden cane.

Now aged around ten and armed with my new rod, I visited all the local ponds and lakes, occasionally making a trip by the number 107A bus over to Enfield Lock and the canalized River Lea which became my training ground for several years. To catch roach (in those days the river was full of them) stewed hempseed was the magical bait during the summer months when the fish could easily be seen 'flashing' for the seeds in the clear upper water layers. Using maggots only attracted the dreaded bleak which weren't interested in stewed hempseed. The distinction was such that a handful of hemp resulted in just roach and the odd good dace flashing through the clear water over cabbages, whilst a handful of maggots ensured hundreds of bleak plus small dace hitting the surface within seconds. Rivers were certainly fish full in those days. Even a handful of gravel from the towpath would raise a few roach and I've even had them flashing simply to the movement of an empty hand. Honestly. Broxbourne in Hertfordshire was my favourite venue and the first eight-inch roach I ever caught on hempseed was taken home and fried in batter by Mum, which I ate apparently. Yuk!

I was so keen that, with a rod strapped to the crossbar of my bike, I even used to grab an hour either before or after completing my paper round, depending upon the lake or pond in question. One location was a small man-made lake in front of the old hall at Forty Hill Park in Enfield, not too far in fact from my last paper delivery. During the summer months I just loved fishing there in the early morning before the park keeper got up. It was so stuffed full of common carp – that old 'wildie' strain first brought over by German monks during the fifteenth century and easily identified by a long, lean, powerful body and immaculate scales – that sport was usually both instant and hectic. This was just as well really because I rarely enjoyed more than half an hour's fishing at this shallow, pea-green carp haven before an old gander owned by the park keeper started honking away noisily. Geese are great burglar alarms.

Having hidden my bike amongst the rhododendrons about half a mile away and despite a long walk up a steep hill from the opposite direction of the hall, it was nevertheless always worth the effort. I could usually account for at least three or four carp to around three pounds on float-fished lobworm, before the park keeper could stand it no longer and lights went on in the lodge house opposite. He was a tall man with unusually large ears that stuck out and which were even noticeable from sixty to seventy yards away across the lake, and as he started walking around the lake towards my position I reeled in, returned the carp and disappeared post-haste over the fence and down through the long grass across the field towards my bike.

Though I fished the lake for a couple or three seasons I never did catch a carp from there of over five pounds, something which I couldn't understand. I read all the books, particularly the writings of the late Dick Walker, who was my hero, and those of the Carp Catchers' Club. I tried floating crust during the hours of darkness, plus balanced paste and crust baits, all to no avail. The plain truth however was that, as with many 'wild carp only' fisheries of that era, there were simply no large carp in the lake. This was borne out during the big freeze in the winter of 1963 when the lake remained frozen over for several weeks. Like so many shallow, overstocked lakes that

winter, from which the decomposing gases could not escape, the entire stock of fish, from the smallest gudgeon to the largest carp, perished. The local council collected four lorry loads of bloated carcasses for burial, once the lake thawed out and the grisly facts were revealed. The largest carp weighed barely eight pounds.

I never did fish the lake again following those early morning paper-round days, and was later sad to hear about all the carp dying. But some forty years later, Dad came up with some revealing information about Forty Hill Lake. Jo and I were in Enfield for the day having travelled down from Norwich to see Mum and Dad who now, in their mid eighties, lived in sheltered accommodation. We were enjoying a conversation about the good old times when Dad suddenly said, 'Old Bill Walker passed away last week, John. You know, him with the big ears who used to see you in the morning over at Forty Hill Lake.' Now Dad wasn't aware of my early morning poaching sessions, or so I thought. So I said, 'How did you know I fished there?' 'Well old Bill always told me when you'd been fishing,' says Dad, with a chuckle. 'But whenever he came for a friendly chat you were always gone by the time he'd walked round the lake.' Boy, was I gobsmacked!

One day during the summer holidays of 1954, whilst buying goldfish from a pet shop along Green Street in eastern Enfield, I met a lad slightly older than me, one Tony Morgan, who lived but a few yards from a pretty little lily-covered lake called Lakeside, near Oakwood tube station at the end of the Piccadilly Line. I accepted his invitation to fish for the stunted roach and crucian carp it contained and in a much bigger lake at the bottom of his road called Boxes Lake. I learnt to catch the crafty shy-biting golden-coloured crucians up to almost two pounds using a flour and water paste coloured and flavoured with custard powder which Mum used to make. But I lost touch with Tony after a few years. Then some thirty years later, having arrived at a mutual friend's party in Taverham where I then lived, close to Norwich, the first guest I bumped into was none other than Tony Morgan who to me hadn't changed facially one little bit over the years. I said, 'You're Tony Morgan aren't you? We fished together when we were about ten years old back in Enfield.' He thought it was a wind-up and just couldn't accept what I said for quite some time afterwards. Now we often laugh about the coincidence, though he hasn't fished since those childhood years.

My fascination with fish and other pets continued throughout my childhood, including budgies, pigeons, mice and lizards, and has not waned to this day. I simply adore animals. In fact Jo and I have four dogs, two German Shepherds, a Rhodesian Ridgeback and a West Highland Terrier, plus a cat called Sambo, and Cheeko, an African Grey parrot. Not forgetting all the fish in our two lakes of course. Way back in the 1950s however, living in a London flat merely stretched to a cat and an old galvanized fifty-gallon water tank full of fish on the veranda. I could never have a dog though I was for ever pestering Dad who always said, 'We'll see'. (It was his favourite saying and one which once I grew up I swore I would never use with my own children. But you can guess what was my favourite 'get out of it' phrase when my own two children came along. Exactly!)

Amongst the more regular pets at Lea Road was an assortment of lizards, slow worms and snakes. Young Wilson was always first in putting his hand up when the biology teacher enquired who would like to look after the laboratory's exhibits during the school holidays. Hence poor Mum suffered tanks of frogs, newts, lizards, slow worms, toads and once a large grass snake. Unfortunately this particular snake's life ended rather unceremoniously when it escaped from the makeshift vivarium and wound its way along Lea Road via the guttering of several flats, only to have its head separated from its body by a brave Mr Bullock who thought it was an adder and deadly poisonous. This necessitated Mum accompanying her son to Chase Boys School once the new term resumed to recount the unfortunate snake saga.

It was with much pride that Jo and I accepted an invitation back to my old school a few years ago to give a leaving address and lecture to the sixth formers, most of whom seemed too young and spotty-faced to have gained so many A levels. In my day no one at Chase Boys took A levels, and few were clever enough to pass any GCE examinations. I based my lecture upon a future life where you can either live to work or work to live. Naturally, being a workaholic who loves his work, I recommended the former and by the approving look on the faces of mums and dads present the message got through to both parents and pupils. I emphasized the point that life can be explained by three eight-hour segments each day. You sleep for eight hours and are not conscious so that leaves but two eight-hour segments – or two halves of your life – one for work and one for play. So if you think about it, if you don't thoroughly enjoy your work, half your life could be a lost opportunity.

It would perhaps seem rather strange to the young anglers of today that back in the early 1950s there was little choice of inexpensive fixed spool reels. Threadline and spinning reels were the names given to early top-of-the-range models such as the Ambidex and Mitchell. Those of us using the old 'clicker' centre pins made from cheap bright steel had to pull yards and yards of line from the reel and lay it down on the ground if a long cast was required when ledgering, resulting often in unbelievable birds' nests as bits of twig and leaves clung to the coils as they tried to flow through the rod rings. Trotting in rivers therefore became my favourite technique (and still is) because by now, in addition to owning a three-piece eleven-foot float rod which replaced the tank aerial, I had invested in a quality reel from Matthew's tackle shop. It was an old Trudex centre pin complete with an integral line guard, marked up at the bargain shop-soiled price of £2. 19s. 6d.

This reel lasted for many years and actually started me upon the road to float fishing fulfilment. This also resulted, I am proud to say, albeit over forty years later, in the very same company, J W Young and Sons Ltd of Redditch, producing a modern exceptionally free-running centre pin of my very own design. Named the John Wilson Heritage and marketed through Masterline with whom I have designed fishing tackle now for over a decade, this 4½-inch diameter, ¾-inch-wide model has a multi-position line guard made from stainless steel and the centre pin itself benefits from two ball races.

The first couple of fixed spool reels I owned, because they were cheap, were absolutely awful. Then I decided to spend my paper round money on a Mitchell 300, arguably the world's best ever fixed spool, simply light years ahead of its time (as we all realize now) which cost £7. 19s. 6d by mail order from Bennets of Sheffield. And those eight monthly postal order payments were certainly worth it. That particular reel finally came to grief fifteen years later having served me splendidly all around the world in both fresh and saltwater, when I dropped it on the concrete pier at Dakar in French West Africa and the stem snapped.

I guess fellow anglers over the age of forty will also fondly remember the British-made Intrepid range of reels which, though satisfactory, in no way came close to the French-made Mitchells. It's really all about what's available at the time, and the sheer choice in expertly engineered fixed spool reels currently available is staggering; even more so is their low retail cost.

Much the same can be said about modern rods, especially lightweight carbon float rods. Yet prior to the mid 1970s we all managed happily (or unhappily if you were a long trotting enthusiast and suffered missed bites through arm ache) with hollow fibreglass. Back in the early 1950s however hollow glass was in its infancy and float fishermen used built cane, or Spanish reed rods, which had a built cane tip spliced into the top joint. I can remember mine snapping off like a carrot six inches above the handle when punching a float out too enthusiastically into a strong facing wind.

At the tender age of thirteen, or I could have been a year younger, I attended the inaugural meeting of what was to become the Enfield Town Angling Society. So I was among the first members of a club which, due to its monthly coach outings to lakes and river systems all over southern England, broadened my knowledge considerably.

In the early days there were just four or five of us juniors and some of the older members took us individually under their wings on club outings so we could learn the ropes. Dear old Bill Saville, Bill Poulton and Denis Brown, bless 'em, now all passed on, were each instrumental in their own way in encouraging me. Denis especially, who was the local barber, took my regular fishing pal, Doug Pledger, and me in his old Austin Atlantic to venues not visited by the club, like the River Lark at West Roe and King George VI reservoirs near Chingford where we ledgered during the winter months in the hope of catching specimen roach. We also went to the Suffolk Stour at Bures, Great Henny and Lamarsh, all fabulous roach hot spots if you fished hemp and berry. I can vividly remember taking a catch of roach from the Stour at Bures at the famous 'Rookery Stretch' numbering around 150 fish to around one and a quarter pounds with at least half of them 'goers', meaning they measured larger than eight inches. Sadly I couldn't match such a haul nowadays from anywhere I fish even if my very life depended upon it, such is the extent to which silver shoal species in our rivers have been depleted.

All the clubs in and around the London area fished to London Angling Association size limit rules in those days. Bleak and gudgeon were not even considered worth weighing in at the end of our club outings. So if you didn't have a dace over seven inches, a roach over eight inches, perch over nine inches, bream over twelve inches and so on . . . you couldn't weigh in. Few clubs now bother with these rules which is a pity because it meant that as most of the fish caught were under size, they never spent all day in a keep net and didn't have their tail spread out on a fish rule which we all carried.

Among the great baits in those days were elderberries which I used to bottle when ripe in September (preserved in a weak solution of formalin) specifically for winter use. Fished in conjunction with loose-fed hemp, berries always sorted out the quality fish – just as casters do today really. This was a tip passed on to me by one of the older club members. In fact one of the great advantages of being a club member was that knowledge was freely passed around. We junior members learned so much about a whole variety of alternative baits to maggots.

Another great bait, though only effective during the summer months, was stewed wheat. You put a cupful of wheat into a vacuum flask and top it up only to within three inches of the top with just boiled hot water. The gap was to allow for the expansion of the wheat which could easily shatter the glass insides of the flask. If left overnight, the following morning the now perfectly prepared wheat, with just enough of the white insides showing against the golden corn husk, is tipped out into a bait tin and any surplus water drained off. The nutty aroma of this superb bait is both unusual and attractive, especially to dace, roach, chub, tench, bream and particularly carp. Try it.

Stewed wheat was my favourite summer bait of all and I used it to good effect against the older members on outings to Cambridgeshire's rivers Cam, Granta, Lark, Old West and throughout the Great Ouse. One of my favourite locations was the Old Bedford Drain and River Delph at Mepal, where specimen-size rudd could be readily caught 'on the drop' using a single grain of wheat presented without shots beneath a matchstick float attached to the line with a band of silicon. Using an old bamboo roach pole with the 3lb test line simply tied to the end via a whipped-on loop of

BELOW Yes, I'm the baby-faced teenager on the extreme right of this group of ETAS club members (half of whom have passed on, I'm sad to say) at an annual dinner-dance and prize-giving during the late 1950s.

20lb line (no elastic in those days), the single grain of wheat was accurately lowered into small gaps in the lilies which in parts virtually covered the surface of these narrow drains from one bank to another. If you found a hole the size of your hat or larger, it was a swim. It was a situation where no other technique would work. I remember one particular early morning about half an hour after our club members had settled into their respective swims, a Sheffield club turned up on the opposite bank. Within minutes they deemed the Old Bedford totally unfishable and climbed back into their coach. Where they went I don't know, but I recall coming amongst the 'bob a nob' prize money (everyone put a shilling into the hat) by weighing in several sizeable rudd to nearly two pounds.

Many anglers today probably associate the effectiveness and popularity of pole fishing with European innovation, and as far as the current, super-light super-long carbon models of up to 15 metres long are concerned including internal elastication etc., it is. But pole fishing was born on the rivers Lea and Thames. The famous London firm of Sowerbutts constructed the best bamboo poles made from carefully straightened, tempered and drilled tonkin cane. Most were around 19 feet long and comprising five sections each heavily varnished over black decorative whippings, the top three of which fitted into the 48-inch bottom two. The tip was of spliced-in finely tapered built cane to which a float rig was attached via a small loop. A couple of the old dodgers in the Enfield Town Club incidentally sometimes used an elastic band between loop and rig, if big fish were on the cards. Was this pole elastic forty years ahead of its time? I'm tempted to say it was.

Of course the technique of sensitively presenting a light float rig directly beneath the pole tip on just a few feet of line for maximum control and instant striking is no less valid today than fifty or even a hundred years back. The main difference is one of weight. And with precision-turned brass ferrules those poles of yesteryear weighed an absolute ton. So in no way would I like to turn the clock back. Actually I caught my first ever four-pound tench on a roach pole and it led me a merry song and dance through the weed beds of a Lea Valley gravel pit. I managed to land barbel on the pole too (fixed line remember) and though a walk along the towpath was required to keep in touch with anything over two pounds, it was great fun.

Those early years along the Lea Valley and other rivers like the Thames and Kennet visited by the club on regular monthly outings, always fishing to size limits, certainly influenced me. I found larger fish more interesting to pursue and thus more exciting and satisfying to catch – values that have not changed to this day, incidentally. So wherever possible if bigger and consequently much harder fighting specimens are on the cards, then I want some of the action.

At fifteen years of age I left school and the very next week started an apprenticeship as a ladies' hairdresser at Fior Hair Fashions in Palmers Green, north London. Why a hairdresser? Well, all I can remember is that I'd heard young hairdressers could earn as much as £20 a week – a very good wage back in 1957.

This strange environment with its perfumed shampoo, ammonia-based perm solutions and female gossip was pretty alien to me but I stuck with it nonetheless and, as you will discover, I have much to thank my career in hairdressing for. I had in fact joined a fashion profession immediately before the swinging sixties and I enjoyed everything that came with it, including a regular supply of attractive girlfriends.

My boss, John Horne, in conjunction with an analytical chemist, one Bibby Vine, had perfected a hair-straightening cream for negroid hair which, under the microscope, is one really tight curl after another. One of the most famous piano players of that era, Winifred Atwell, was amongst our customers, together with an exceptionally attractive black jazz singer who I shall not name, because Wilson was responsible for making her bald as the proverbial coot. I had left the (then extremely strong) cream on too long after brushing the hair straight and during the final rinsing the plug hole in the basin started to clog up. Within thirty seconds her entire head of beautifully straightened long hair lay in the sink. It had snapped off within a millimetre of the scalp, leaving her head looking for all the world like a black egg with a day's growth. I guess my hairdressing days could have ended there and then but those were pioneering times. Instead I got a bollocking and our jazz singer got a wig compliments of Fior Hair Fashions.

During the school holidays when the salon wasn't that busy, I was given the miserable job, not a lot of fun for a fifteen year old, of taking John Horne's son, Nicky, a precocious little kid of around five or six years old, to various exhibitions in London's West End including the Schoolboy's Own Exhibition. To get my own back, whenever he came into the salon I used to pick him up and sit him six feet off the floor in the staff room on a shampoo bottle shelf and leave him crying and yelling for his dad.

Nicky Horne is now well known as a DJ and television presenter, and just a few years ago he asked me to appear on his *Tight Lines* angling phone-in programme for Sky TV now hosted by Bruno Brooks. Being too young at the time to remember, he had no idea that he had previously come across me when he was little, let alone been the object of teenage Wilson's adolescent mischievousness. So when I came out with this live on the programme, Nicky was speechless and just sat there open mouthed.

My regular fishing mate, Doug, and I fancied fishing further afield from our local River Lea – where we would stand a chance of catching really big roach and bream. We answered an advertisement in *Angling Times* and had a week's fishing holiday at the Watch House Inn in Bungay, Suffolk which was just a short walk from the then magical River Waveney. We joined the Bungay Cherry Tree Angling Club which controlled much of the fishing and, employing simple trotting tactics, caught mountains of quality roach from both the main river and the many streams using stewed wheat. Even the tiniest drainage dykes were so full of roach it was staggering and I think there and then I vowed one day to live amongst the roach-rich rivers of Norfolk and Suffolk. Now ironically that reason for living in East Anglia no longer exists, thanks to cormorants, abstraction and farming policies, subjects I shall cover shortly.

From the deep and swirling Falcon weir pool in the centre of Bungay I even caught my first ever two-pound roach, also on a grain of stewed wheat. As its massive head-shaking shape came up through the clear water I just couldn't believe roach grew that huge. I can still picture it now lying on the landing net, immensely deep in the flank, with shimmering scales etched in silvery blue and fins of red. It made a fifteen year old a roach angler for life.

During the holiday was also the first time I ever set eyes upon a coypu. This is a giant South American rodent which, having originally been imported for its pelt (though also nice to eat) escaped from the rearing farms to cause destruction throughout East Anglian river systems. The network of wide sub-surface burrows made by the coypu unfortunately created massive bank erosion and you saw them everywhere when fishing, the adults being fully two feet long and weighing between ten and twenty pounds. Quite some rat, believe me. When they dived in the splash they made could have been created by a small dog.

My first encounter was during a break from roach fishing at the Falcon pool when I crept into the old galvanized eel trap, long since replaced with a modern sluice. An old dog coypu was in one corner munching away happily on a clump of lily root (they are totally vegetarian), but when it saw me at close quarters it felt threatened and reared up on its hind legs displaying a nasty pair of long orange-stained front teeth and hissing menacingly. Needless to say young Wilson made a hasty retreat.

Coypus have now finally been eradicated from East Anglia through many years of persistent trapping. Yet in a strange way I miss their busy, early morning and late evening goings on. They were very much part of those early impressionable years spent fishing the rivers of Norfolk and Suffolk.

From the two-mile stretch of the Waveney between Wainford Maltings and Ellingham, both Doug and I took several bream to over five pounds – massive specimens to the young Londoner. Trouble was, the most productive bream swim, a twelve-foot deep bend lined with a thick bed of reed along the far bank, was situated halfway along a field where bullocks grazed. It seems funny now to think we should have been frightened, but whenever the herd started running our way, as inquisitive bullocks do, the two townies grabbed all their gear and high-tailed it over the nearest fence. This completely ruined the chances of our ever amounting any decent bags of big bream.

Then, on the very last morning of our week's holiday, with the bream feeding ravenously, and having again just vacated the swim due to charging bullocks (or so we thought), a couple of kids who couldn't have been more than five or six years old – the farmer's sons in fact – came walking merrily across the field we had just left. We looked on in absolute horror as what must have been forty or fifty Friesian bullocks galloped at full charge towards the helpless children. When the herd was about thirty feet away both kids yelled at the top of their voices and actually ran towards the approaching bullocks, which all instantly about turned and belted off away up the

field. Doug and I looked at each other in absolute amazement. Had we been missing out on the biggest bream catches of our young lives due to a herd of mindless bullocks? We had indeed.

At that time I met a Bungay lad the same age as me, one John ('Jinx') Davey who worked in the local printers and we have remained close friends to this day. Jinx unselfishly put me on to so much superb fishing in and around Bungay that I shall for ever be in his debt. My book *Where to Fish in Norfolk and Suffolk* is dedicated to Jinx whom I cannot ever remember having a cross word with. Except perhaps for one occasion when we decided to drive my Hillman Minx convertible illegally across Bungay Golf Course in the early hours of the morning to avoid the long walk around the common which the Waveney skirts for over four miles. Instead of catching big roach at the crack of dawn we found ourselves well and truly stuck in a bunker. What the first golfer thought who saw us I can't imagine. We were frantically digging for over an hour to get the car's rear wheels moving and by the time we'd finished, the bunker had doubled in size and gave

ABOVE My life-long friend John (Jinx) Davey (*right*) and me with a pike he caught from the Waveney in Bungay. Sorry about the gaff. The word conservation wasn't associated with angling in those days!

the impression that perhaps a dinosaur had deposited its eggs beneath the yellow sand.

Jinx's dad, the late Jim Davey, whose lovely old double-barrelled 'Bond' twelve-bore I have proudly clipped in my gun cabinet, was for most of his life the carpenter at nearby Earsham Mill. Like my own father he was a skilled tradesman of the old school and someone I really respected. I can remember receiving a letter from Jinx (no phones for the likes of us in those days remember) telling me that his dad had witnessed the removal of a colossal chub taken out alive from the eel trap one morning at the mill. It weighed over nine pounds and was returned into the Waveney.

The following weekend saw young Wilson, complete with a bucketful of live bleak from the Lea, driving up to Earsham Mill in order to attempt to lure the monster. Boy, I must have been either keen or fanatical in those days. But neither I nor anyone else ever saw or heard of that huge chub again. I can only assume it was one of the original adult stock fish introduced during the 1950s from Norfolk's River Wissey which had quickly grown fat on the Waveney's rich aquatic food larder. Prior to that era there were no chub in the river, whereas today the Waveney possibly still has record potential, a monster of 8lb 2oz being caught at Bungay in 1993 by P. Heywood.

Today much of the Upper Waveney in these diminutive upper reaches is sadly but a memory of its former self. Entire stretches which were once swiftly flowing roach-rich swims, four to six feet deep with clumps of quivering bullrushes sprouting from clean gravel and long sandy runs, are now half the depth, flow at half the pace and the bottom is for the most part covered in blanket weed. What a pitiful legacy we have left our grandchildren. Only the odd group of, albeit large, chub living over clearings beneath overhanging alders and willows, where light cannot penetrate, seem able to fare well in this over-eutrophic, abstraction-riddled river.

If you think I am exaggerating about the modern scourge of abstraction, compare these two photographs of exactly the same spot on the River Waveney at Bungay. One I took in the early 1960s, the other in 1998. In fact shortly afterwards Jinx and I were discussing the sad situation at a once favourite swim along Bungay Common called

BELOW Here's photographic proof that water authorities kill rivers through abstraction. On the left is the Waveney between Earsham and Bungay in the late 1950s where my brother Dave and mate, Tony Bayford (foreground), are long trotting for roach. On the right, the very same spot forty years on. Need I say more?

ABOVE Appears that
I even favoured
coloured shirts back
in the 1950s; here
netting a tench
from the River
Waveney in Bungay,
Suffolk, with brother
Dave looking on.
Note the yellow
(oiled cotton) keep
net and built cane
float rod.

'Toby's Hole', then a deep junction where a carrier joined the main flow, creating a great eddy and popular swimming spot where all the local kids used to run and dive in. Forty years ago! Funnily enough, despite all the commotion in those days, I always managed to tempt roach to over the pound whilst trotting close to the bottom of this deep eddy. It is now less than two feet deep at summer level and barren.

Part of this modern dilemma is also due to government policy and the over-production of cereals. This leads to over-enrichment of the river from nitrates continually leeching in from the land, encouraging over-prolific growth from the wrong kind of aquatic plants. Blanket weed, in particular, strangles the river, covering and restricting light to runs once inhabited by dace and roach. Now the weed carpets all slow-moving areas of the river bed; not only of the Waveney but every other East Anglian river including my local River Wensum, which during the 1970s produced more specimen roach than any other watercourse in the UK. But that's all history I'm afraid. Blanket weed really is the kiss of death because even if, by some act of God, roach were suddenly reintroduced by the thousand, they would have nowhere to live. Shoal fish will not tolerate blanket weed where sand and gravel should be. It's as simple as that.

Water abstraction however, and the dreadful way in which water authorities have been allowed and allowed others to suck the very life blood from our river systems during the past fifty years, is actually a reversible situation. Ponder for a moment what the consequences would be were government legislation to ban all forms of abstraction along a river's course from source to sea, allowing water to be taken only once it has completed its journey and tips down over the last weir into the tidal reaches. Then, and only then, should the water required by water authorities, farming and industry be abstracted and pumped back along its course via a large bore pipe set beside the river, below ground or short-cutted across farmland, or even sunk in the river itself along one margin. The river would then be as swiftly flowing and as deep as nature intended throughout its entire course. Think seriously about this. Cost apart, I cannot see why such a project or one along similar lines cannot be implemented by government because ultimately water abstraction is the worst killer of all.

Dramatically culling cormorants would help enormously in re-establishing healthy stocks of silver shoal fish throughout clear-watered lakes and gravel pit complexes and certain stretches of rivers. But considering running water as a whole, unless something is done within the next couple of decades to reverse water abstraction we are not going to have many rivers left to save.

During the late 1950s and early 1960s whilst in my teens, I witnessed the start of a slow death to my local rivers in north London and in Hertfordshire, such as the rivers Ash, Ver, Beane, Rib and Mimram, through abstraction. This resulted eventually in my forsaking the south and coming to live in Norfolk. And now I can see it happening all over again here.

In the 1960s if you lived in areas suffering in their river fishing like London or Sheffield, you only contemplated one spot to go fishing on holiday: the fabulous Norfolk Broads. Now in the late 1990s with the Broads sadly in decline and not even a shadow of its former self, those same anglers cross the sea to Ireland or to Denmark if they want to experience prolific sport with roach, rudd, perch and bream. I wonder where we'll all be trotting off to in another thirty years.

Due to the interest instigated by the Enfield Town Angling Society's monthly coach outings to venues further afield, on my sixteenth birthday I purchased my first motorbike. One of the members, Les Minton, was selling his 125cc BSA Bantam complete with a pair of gauntlets and crash helmet for the bargain price of £40. That little bike took me everywhere within a radius of about sixty miles from home. Lying flat on the tank going down a steep hill the speedo just about clipped fifty miles per hour but it wasn't really speed I was after, simply accessibility.

I could then fish many of the same rivers that we had visited on our Sunday coach outings, but during the middle of the week on my day off when the banks were less crowded. Our club fielded a team of six to compete in the then most prestigious London Anglers Association matches which were usually held on the Thames and the Great Ouse. And all were 'rovers', never pegged down. In fact why small clubs insist on pegged-down competitions has always puzzled me. It is much quicker, instead of waiting for a steward to knock a load of pegs in, to put the same amount of numbered tokens into a hat and the angler who draws the highest sees everyone off. He then simply holds the hat whilst number one puts his token in and walks off along the river or around the lake (closely followed by number two and so on) until he stops at a swim he fancies fishing. Then the rest can overtake and select their spots accordingly.

After all, who wants to sit all day in a piece of the countryside they are not happy with? Rovers allow each angler to utilize his skill or watercraft – call it what you will – in selecting his particular swim, as long as he doesn't overtake the man in front. Consequently, everyone starts fishing immediately and there are never any moans about drawing a bad peg or being unlucky.

I caught my very first barbel from the Old Lea at Wormley where the river divides at Kings Weir to become both canal and fast-flowing 'backstream', as it was known in those days. I remember on one autumn afternoon catching no fewer than twenty-two barbel (all small) plus a two-pound chub on ledgered cheese paste from just one swim. I can also remember a painful experience that occurred during the first hour of darkness when I loaded up the BSA Bantam for the ride home.

As a short cut to the 'backstream' I used to drive down a narrow lane and across a farmer's field which more or less took me straight to the lock behind which were some of the best swims. A swift and painful belt across the mouth came from nowhere out of the darkness as I popped along at around twenty miles per hour back along the lane towards the main road. Suddenly I was sitting on the deck in a daze. The bike, which had carried on, was still revving like mad several yards away in a ditch. So I got up to turn it off, when 'Bang!' – something clouted me over the head again (thank heavens

for crash helmets). I fell back to the ground, this time snapping the rod ends protruding from the holdall across my shoulders. My face was one bloody mess, and I could actually feel several bottom teeth protruding through a gaping hole beneath my lower lip but everything else seemed to be in working order. Slowly I attempted to get up again and felt what appeared to be a steel scaffold pole in my way. Indeed it was. Someone – the farmer I suppose – must have put the pole right across the lane about five feet off the ground, to stop the cows from roaming. Trouble was, the totally useless dipped headlight on my old Bantam (no quartz halogen bulbs in those days I'm afraid) had not picked it out and, being more concerned about my tyres and the pot holes, my eyes were of course directed downwards. Had it not been for the perspex windscreen which was completely shattered because it hit the scaffold pole first and instantly slowed the bike down, I might well have been decapitated. There but for the grace of God, eh?

Whilst contemplating strange occurrences, it was around this time when young Wilson experienced one of the most embarrassing moments of his life. One day, with the Bantam hidden amongst roadside shrubbery, I was enjoying an afternoon's freelining for trout along a strictly private beat of the lovely little River Ash, near Ware in Hertfordshire. The banks were marvellously overgrown with bushes and mature trees and as I always crept about stealthily exploring each likely-looking hole and deep run with a lively lobworm, with my ex-Army parka blending into the greenery perfectly, nobody ever saw me.

On this particular afternoon, I'd already accounted for a couple of pound-plus brown trout and a deep-bodied roach of fully one and a half pounds (a superb catch for such a little river) when I saw a car pull up alongside the hedge where my Bantam was hidden. Suddenly the doors flew open and out climbed three women all around their early thirties who passed through a gap in the hedge and ran straight across the ploughed field towards the huge weeping chestnut, whose lower branches almost touched the ground and beneath which I stood leaning against the wide trunk as though a part of it. The deep run beneath was in fact one of my favourite roach swims. Surely it was impossible for them to know I was hidden there poaching (though I always returned everything I caught of course) so why were they making a beeline for my tree? Suddenly and without more ado, certainly before I could clear my throat and say, 'Er, excuse me ladies', it was a case of knickers down and them peeing and farting away to their heart's content, not yards from where Wilson was doing his best impression of a chestnut tree trunk.

But my ploy didn't work. Quite suddenly the closest woman fixed her eyes upon mine and let out an excruciatingly loud manic scream, whereupon all three pulled up their knickers and were running across that field as fast as they could. Can't say I ever want to experience anything like that again!

From the BSA Bantam I progressed first on to a 225cc James and then to a lovely old British motorbike (now a classic of course), a BSA 350cc single called the B31. Lavishly appointed in maroon and chrome, it had double crash bars through which

ABOVE Loading up after a day's fishing on the Great Ouse at Godmanchester. Our BSA 350 motor bikes took my friend, Doug Pledger (*right*), and I to rivers and lakes all over southern England.

my rod holdall passed, enabling me to sit astride the rods as opposed to having the strain of the strap across my shoulders.

I visited many southern rivers on the BSA like the Kentish Stour near Canterbury, the Kennet at Burghfield, and numerous spots along the Thames from Appleford all the way downstream to the tidal reaches at Richmond. I very nearly came a cropper one morning, though, on the way to Richmond for a roaching session. I was heading for a spot just in front of the ice rink where, from between the moored boats, superb bags of winter roach could be taken on trotted maggots. On this particular foggy morning (those living and working in London during that period will indeed remember them with little sense of affection) I was chugging along through Enfield Town at around six o'clock opposite the Roman Catholic church, when completely from nowhere a nun walked across the road right in front of my bike. One minute she was there, the next she was gone and disappeared from view in the grey fog. It happened too quickly for me to brake, swerve or react in any way. And had I not been opposite the church at that time I might have even considered the event a hallucination!

I would also regularly trundle the hundred or so miles from Enfield to Bungay, even during the winter months, just for a day's roach fishing. And I'm sure that old bike would still be ticking over now with that lovely throb of a big single, had I not chopped it in for my first car, the Hillman Minx convertible.

Despite the slow decline of my local rivers, I learnt a tremendous amount from stalking individual fish from one small haven in particular – the River Rib at Wadesmill in Hertfordshire. It passes beneath the A10 road bridge at the bottom of a long steep hill at Thunderidge just outside Ware (though don't bother walking its course today, it's heartbreaking) and whilst my mates could be fishing in next to no time by visiting their local River Lea, I chose the extra distance of the River Rib because I knew the fish I would catch there were far larger than those of the Lea. I guess I had a leaning towards specimen hunting even then at the age of seventeen. Due to the overgrown banks and crystal-clear water, however, extracting sizeable specimens from the diminutive River Rib took much cunning and creeping about stealthily on all fours. Once I had seen the inhabitants' reactions to a careless footfall or my shadow over the water, I soon developed a cautious approach which of course I use to this day wherever I fish. Those days were a wonderful education for me.

This was also the time I became seriously interested in colour transparency photography. I had been disappointed with the quality of black-and-white photos taken using Dad's old pre-war Brownie box camera and by several equally useless cheapies. I therefore purchased a 35mm Halina camera from Boots. This was later superseded by a German Super Frankarette, and then a few years later by a single lens reflex, a Minolta SR7 with a Tokina 135 telephoto lens in addition to the standard 55mm. I enjoyed immensely recording all the locations visited and regularly gave slide shows to the Enfield Town Angling Club.

Full of crayfish, brook lampreys, huge dace, roach to over two pounds and prolific in chub between two and three pounds, the sparklingly clear River Rib was a joy to fish. I freelined breadflake, large lumps on a size 8 hook direct to a 3lb line to lure the roach and dace, and fared best with the chub by using crayfish, though big lobworms and cheese paste also produced. So rich in crayfish was this charming little river that my brother, Dave, and I decided to start the new season at Wadesmill on 16 June after chub and actually left home without any bait. Who would have the bottle to do this nowadays? But we did, and in an hour of darkness prior to dawn breaking, using a powerful torch each, we gathered enough two to three-inch crayfish from beneath large pieces of flint and sunken logs to keep us in chub baits until we headed for home in the late morning, having accounted for close on twenty sizeable chub and walked over three miles of river. Being five years my junior I was until now rather reluctant to take Dave fishing. But from around the age of thirteen he started to become quite serious and we have been regular partners to this day.

For several years the River Rib became my training ground for practising the art of concealment, stealth and observation, where through polarized glasses I was able to watch most of the fish I caught actually suck in the bait. Such close-range stalking of a diminutive, overgrown river also demanded the utmost skill in tackle control, using the flow to work a freelined bait downstream into a certain lie, or skate casting fat slugs or crayfish beneath overhanging branches to the chub hiding below, using nothing more than an underarm flick of the rod. I learnt to crawl on all fours where necessary and always to keep my silhouette low to the ground. I carried the absolute minimum of tackle and thus roamed happily for miles learning a new trick or overcoming a particularly difficult swim or problem around each and every twist of this enchanting little river.

One incident in particular portrays how shy and sensitive to bankside movements those fish were. I had taken fully several minutes on all fours to worm my way beneath blackthorn bushes into a position high above a deep bend. There I plopped in a fat slug a couple of feet upstream from where five nice chub, the best pushing three pounds, were enjoying their afternoon siesta beneath an old willow whose lower limbs shaded the surface on the opposite bank. I knew I hadn't made any detrimental movements, but, with the slug in mid flight and yet to touch the surface, those chub suddenly turned tail and shot downstream as though scared by the devil himself. Had the sun hit the varnish along the rod and created a 'flash'? Had my arm movement caught their attention? No, neither. A minute later all was explained as a large man, sweating profusely from the heatwave conditions, carrying a wicker basket and rod holdall plus rod and landing net already made up, crunched through the undergrowth, uttering those immortal words . . . 'Any luck, mate?' For him I doubt the penny ever dropped, despite a pitiful look in his direction from the teenager

ABOVE One of the numerous barbel I caught from the River Lea at Enfield Lock, touch ledgering during the hours of darkness.

emerging from the marginal entanglement. The point is, those chub had heard the vibrations of this seventeen-stone 'chuck it and chance it' long before I did and it's a lesson I've never forgotten.

I often used to fish on into darkness during the summer and autumn, because when the light has all but gone, that's when bites from the biggest roach and dace become extremely confident. Sensitive quivertips and luminous betalight elements were not around in those days of course and I simply touch ledgered by pointing the rod tip more or less directly at the bait, with the line hooked over the tip of my forefinger. It's such a super-sensitive way of feeling for bites in the dark whilst ledgering or freelining at close range. I even use the technique when I am float fishing for big fish like carp and tench during the daytime when my eyes might, for a few seconds, wander away from the float. It's that sudden tightening of the line over the ball of the forefinger that brings an instant response with a hard strike. Try it yourself and see. This can only be accomplished, however, if you hold the rod handle with your four fingers split around the reel's stem. Your right forefinger will then be perfectly placed to pick up the line directly from the bale arm roller which should be wound close up to the rod handle. The same finger will then also be ideally positioned to apply pressure to the side of the spool when playing big fish.

Touch ledgering is of course equally effective whilst holding a quivertip rod in a strong current with barbel and chub in mind. Again that tightening over the tip of your forefinger instantly puts you on 'red alert'. Whilst in my late teens I spent many a dark evening touch ledgering for barbel on a lovely streamy and weedy stretch of the Old Lea at Enfield Lock behind the Royal Small Arms Company factory. In fact I rarely ever arrived until an hour after dark because by then the barbel had usually left the weediest, snaggiest swims and moved immediately upstream to feed upon the shallows where less than two feet of water covered the clean gravel. After loose feeding in a few lumps of cheese paste, it wasn't long before a barbel snuffed up mine and tore off downstream virtually hooking itself. So I needed neither torch nor rod rest, simply the line hooked around my forefinger. The sheer suspense of waiting for a bite in the dark is electrifying, especially when a fish rolls in the swim or approaches the bait from the side creating a gentle 'plink' on the line as its pectoral fins momentarily catch it.

My rod then was an old eleven-foot, three-piece built cane 'Octofloat' which, though it bent alarmingly in conjunction with a 6lb reel line, managed to subdue barbel to just over nine pounds. I never did succeed in catching a double from the Lea, and had to wait over twenty years to achieve that goal with a 10lb 14oz fish from the River Wensum at Drayton, near Norwich, in 1981. This very same fish incidentally (easily identified by fin disfiguration) I caught again a few years later from the very same deep run immediately downstream from an overhanging willow, weighing exactly 12¾lb, which remains my largest barbel ever. Another coincidence is that on both occasions I was float fishing stret-pegging style. Yes, those teenage years were much inspired by the barbel and chub of Izaak Walton's old River Lea, the wonderful Waveney in Suffolk and through crawling along the overgrown reaches of Hertfordshire's River Rib, not to mention countless lakes and rivers all over southern England visited through the Enfield Town Angling Society's monthly coach outings. Reading the *Angling Times* (the only paper of its kind then) also fired my imagination, especially the articles written by my hero of the day, the late Richard Walker, surely the motivator of many a specialist angler today whether they are too young to remember him or not.

BELOW Outside 32 Lea Road in Enfield, North London where I was born and spent the first twenty-two years of my life, with the perfect fishing jalopy of that era – an A35 van.

The Swinging Decade

The swinging sixties, as they are affectionately named by those of us fortunate enough to have experienced young life during this period, were indeed a revelation. It seems now as if I went from the age of seventeen to twenty-seven in a flash, though on reflection a great deal happened to affect my personal life and fishing during this impressionable decade.

Sadly it started with me not being able to afford the steep monthly payments on the Hillman Minx convertible and so I took Dad's advice and, in 1962, chopped it in for what turned out to be a far more practical fishing vehicle – an Austin A35 van. This left me with no outstanding debts, though I had indeed paid the price for trying to look flash as youngsters do (image came at a price even then) and it's a lesson I've never forgotten.

Together with my cousin, John, who had a Morris Mini van, I fished all over southern England and from then on over the next three to four years we took it in turns using each other's vehicles both at weekends and summer holidays to visit the Broads, the Dorset Stour at Throop Mill and many spots along the Great Ouse system. We even combined courting with fishing by driving up to Norwich and spending Saturday night at the Samson & Hercules – the night club of the area – followed the next day with some roach fishing on the River Waveney at Bungay or flattie fishing in the harbour at Great Yarmouth if we didn't score!

I have already mentioned that it was my Uncle Joe (John's dad) who started me fishing seriously, but John never became an ardent angler and within a few years had sold all his gear. Ironically two of his four sons have become extremely fine anglers. In their early teens, Martin and Richard Bowler used to come and stay with me in Norfolk to catch carp from my two lakes (Martin has since caught more big carp than I've had hot dinners), and nowadays I like to join them every so often along their local stretches of the Great Ouse above Bedford after big perch. With their help I have, during the mid 1990s, accounted for rudd to 3½lb, perch to 3¾lb and barbel getting on for double figures live on camera during the filming of my *Go Fishing* television series. So you could say it's taken fifty years for an angling family to go full circle since I first gave their granddad's tackle a bashing. Dear old Uncle Joe.

OPPOSITE Cousin, John Bowler (*left*), and me on Bournemouth Pier in the early 1960s. Though John never became a serious angler, thirty-five years on I now regularly fish with his two sons, Richard and Martin.

During the early 60s, in my later teen years, I used to relish all-night bream bashing sessions on the middle reaches of the Great Ouse. By today's standards they were very modest-sized bream, averaging perhaps two to three pounds a piece with the occasional two-pound-plus hybrid thrown in for good measure. But what the Ouse lacked in quality it made up for in quantity. By ledgering bread paste or flake eels were avoided and in favourable conditions bites could be expected consistently throughout the hours of darkness, following heavy ground baiting with a mixture of mashed bread and bran.

The St Neots to Little Paxton beat was my favourite, particularly St Neots Common where a flood dyke joined the main stream. I have a precious memory of something hilarious that happened one morning when a group of us young Enfield Town Angling Club members trudged wearily back to our old bangers (all of them classic cars today of course) after a good bream haul. It seems crazy now but we regularly descended upon St Neots in the early hours after a Saturday night's bash at the Locarno in Stevenage. With all the breaming gear and a change of clothing stashed in the cars, we simply drove to the Ouse whenever the dancing finished, with a warming fry-up at an all-night transport café *en route*. Anyway, there we were all covered in bream slime, weary but happy and hoping, as always, that the cars would start. An idiosyncrasy of the 60s was that ignition systems were not always obliging in damp foggy conditions.

One of our gang, Howard, a tall slim lad, spent week upon week painstakingly hand-painting – yes, hand-painting – his old Morris Oxford. He made a really nice job of it too, carefully smoothing out all the brush strokes with cutting-down compound and finishing off with Brasso and then polish. It really did match any baked-on spray job at a fraction of the cost, though it took hundreds of hours to complete. Trouble was, nobody told the bullocks on St Neots Common. They obviously liked the taste of Howard's paint because that herd of Friesians almost completely licked his car paintless during the latter part of one night. We just didn't know what to do – laugh, cry or look the other way and pretend we hadn't noticed. So we did the sort of honourable thing any gang of mates would do and split our bellies laughing. Poor old Howard!

At the tender age of twenty I became engaged to my first wife, Barbara. We had met as hairdressers at Fior Hair Fashions and planned within a year or so to move to Norfolk where I would eventually seek employment in the printers where my friend John (Jinx) Davey worked. Detached, three-bedroomed bungalows backing on to farmland were at that time selling for between just two to three thousand pounds in East Anglia, and we so much wanted to vacate the claustrophobia of foggy London for the charm of the countryside. So in 1964 I made a career change, having become somewhat disgruntled with hairdressing, and started as a trainee lithographic printer at Waltham Abbey Press in Hertfordshire. Then after a year of being engaged we drifted apart and Barbara found someone else (although we did meet up again and eventually marry four years later) and I found myself in a trade without a reason, which although I stuck at it and became quite proficient, was not what I really wanted.

However I struck up a firm friendship with my boss in the printing department of Standard Telephones and Cables (my third and last printing employer incidentally within a two-year separation from hairdressing), one Les Wright. He got me really interested in sea fishing. During the next two summers we regularly drove south to Beachy Head in Sussex in search of bass and picked our tides carefully so we could dig for lugworm and collect peeler crabs from Eastbourne, before making the long pilgrimage along the steep cliffs to Birling Gap where we climbed down. We then fished all of the flood tide up and some of the ebb throughout the hours of darkness before we could safely leave our chosen ledges and climb back up again for the arduous walk back to where we'd left Les's old Morris Countryman. One of the tricks at Beachy Head, where long fringes of rocks reach out to sea, was literally to place your bait by hand in a sandy area amongst a cluster of rocks at low tide and then walk backwards up the beach paying out line as the tide came in. This sometimes produced a good bass, once the bait was covered by several feet of water. Generally however, having gone through all this palaver, a fat pouting would find it first.

BELOW Yes, that's me on the left, young Wilson the printer, with two workmates at Waltham Abbey Press during a short career change from hairdressing.

I also did a bit of beach fishing for cod during the winter months at Dungeness, which was *the* south coast hot spot at that time, and enjoyed boat fishing out from Bournemouth after thornback rays and tope. Had I been living closer to the sea I would have gone more often I'm sure. But I later made up for this, as you will discover.

Career-wise printing was finally kicked into touch and in 1966 I made a return to hairdressing at a salon in St John's Wood High Street in north-west London, called 'Boris and Andre'. It was only a short walk from the London Zoo where I frequently spent my lunch hour admiring the late Dick Walker's then record 44lb common carp caught from Redmire. Though decidedly lean in the body, after so long in captivity, its huge frame literally dwarfed all the other specimens in the long tank and had a mesmerizing effect upon every angler who paid to see it. I doubt Dick ever received a penny from the Zoo but he certainly should have been on a lucrative commission.

My new workplace had amongst its influential clientele numerous top flight models from the fashion industry. It was an exciting world which Wilson now found himself playing – sorry – *working* in, with regular invites after work to way-out bashes in London's West End including those thrown by Harrison Marks, one of the top nude photographers of the day. At these parties it was not unusual to rub noses with many of the fashion world's top models, some of whom were wearing nothing else but painted-on illustrations from head to toe, which left absolutely nothing to the imagination. My part in the 'swinging sixties' had indeed begun. I'd traded the old van in for a sporty new Mini and was at the time dating an airline hostess who worked for Pan Am. Life in the fast lane was fulfilling, hectic, extremely demanding, but above all exciting. Yet strangely there was still something missing – I felt footloose despite my enjoyable everyday commitments.

There was in me at this time what I can only describe as an explorer trying to emerge, and travelling abroad to work, play and fish seemed the obvious course. Within a year of answering adverts in foreign hairdressing magazines I was given the opportunity of a position in a busy salon in the USA in Kansas City, Missouri. What the fishing was like I never found out unfortunately because I was then advised that anyone entering the United States on a work permit would be first in the line-up for drafting out to Vietnam!

Along with several other London stylists I then put in for what seemed like a fantastic position in Dar es Salaam in Tanzania, managing the salon in the famous Kilimanjaro Hotel, only a cast away from the Indian Ocean on Africa's prolific east coast. What with a large salary, my own apartment in the hotel and big game fishing boats on tap close by, this was the job of all jobs. And hey presto! Within a few days the agency confirmed that I had been selected for the position and suggested I book flights immediately as the hotel wanted someone within a few weeks.

Well, talk about being excited! I was absolutely over the moon and quickly sold the car, then booked a one-way passage to Dar es Salaam. The Enfield Town Angling Club presented me with an engraved reverse taper Moncrieff-style beachcaster and I said farewell to all my friends. However as it turned out, I was counting my chickens. I was not particularly politically motivated at this time so I didn't know that the Tanzanian government had decided to break off diplomatic relations with Britain out of sympathy for Rhodesia (now Zimbabwe). This was because our prime minister, Harold Wilson, would not pressurize Rhodesia's prime minister, Ian Smith, into giving the country black majority rule. This meant that this Wilson could not obtain an entry visa and work permit, even though I had a job arranged. I even pestered the Tanzanian staff at Australia House into which their embassy had retreated. But it was all to no avail: Wilson wasn't going big game fishing on Africa's east coast after all.

Actually as it turned out, I rather think being unable to get that work permit changed my life for the better because just a few years back whilst researching the Rufigi River in Tanzania for the catfish and tiger fish with fellow angling journalist, Dave Lewis, I found myself in Dar es Salaam with time to kill between flights. So Dave and I had lunch at the Kilimanjaro. It was not what I had expected at all, now being rather run down and not at all the glamorous colonial-type hotel I had imagined!

Anyway, let's return to the latter part of 1966 because whilst in town trying unsuccessfully to secure an entry visa I decided on impulse (you know the slogan – 'Run away to sea with P & O') to pop into the Peninsular and Oriental Steam Navigation Company's offices to see whether there were any hairdressers' jobs going aboard their passenger liners. It was no secret amongst hairstylists that working on the ships and seeing the world unlocked enormous possibilities because you were likely to meet all the 'right people'. I was interviewed by a Mr Crawford, who must have been impressed because he put me on P & O's list of future possibilities for cruiseship work. He suggested that I take a medical there and then in case a position suddenly arose but as he couldn't guarantee anything, it was still a case of 'don't ring us we'll ring you'.

So it was back to racing across north London every morning and evening from Enfield to St John's Wood and back again, which are only slightly more than ten miles apart as the crow flies. Yet rarely could I make the journey in less than an hour and a quarter. It all changed for the better however when, around three months later and barely a month before Christmas when the salon was getting madly busy, I received a telegram. It read: 'Hairdresser leaving SS *Oronsay* when it berths in two weeks. You can sail New Year's day. Urgent reply required. Mr Crawford, P & O lines.' Incidentally, all shop and hairdressing staff were contracted to sign on 'articles' for one voyage at a time, most of which were mail-run sailings going west to east lasting three and a half months, plus the occasional five-month trip which incorporated either Australian or Mediterranean cruising. As it turned out I loved the life so much I was to stay on board for two years.

Wilson's door had been opened at last, but there was so much to arrange. For starters I'd told Crawford that I could handle both ladies' and gents' hairdressing and, despite what your local unisex stylist tells you, the two skills are entirely different. If you doubt what I'm saying, ask your ladies' hairdresser for a crew cut. Although on

second thoughts – don't! So I asked my cousin, Terry Webb, who ran a barber's shop in Enfield, to give me a crash course. He sold me some Forfex electric clippers complete with three different cutting heads and I arranged for a group of my Dad's mates to come round to our flat for a free 'back and sides'.

Then I attended a shaving course in the West End at a hairdressing training school, as the credentials from P & O lines insisted on their hairdressers being able to shave their passengers if they so wished. Not once during the two years I spent on SS *Oronsay* did anyone ever ask for a shave. Frankly who in their right mind would ask for a shave with a cutthroat razor on a rocking ship? But I wasn't to know that then, and together with several female would-be barbers – lady barbers were just starting to become fashionable in the West End – I joined a one-day shaving class. This included the entire works, from preparing hot scented towels to working up a good lather of soap in the shaving mug and of course sharpening cutthroat razors. Our training started with balloons which were blown up to head size and well lathered, then shaved. All went perfectly well in the morning but after lunch it was the real thing – human skin. A number of unsuspecting, filthy dirty drunks had been brought in straight off the street. Though eager for a clean shave, they were about to experience rather more than they had bargained for. On lathered balloons the girls had no qualms. Yet once they approached real flesh, their razor hands started to shake visibly. Within seconds the drunks' faces started to look for all the world like strawberry truffles, with blood welling up through the pure white shaving lather in a glorious whirl of colour. It was modern art almost, and when the girls had wiped off the remaining lather each drunk owned an amazing array of bleeding slits, cuts and slashes, plus missing moles and warts. Even sizeable chunks of skin had been gouged out!

Together with several mates from the Enfield Town Angling Club I spent New Year's Eve enjoying a riotous send-off in London's West End, in and out of the fountains at Trafalgar Square and getting completely paralytic. I cannot ever remember being so drunk, either before or since. I can recall one of the lads, on leave from the Marines (so I guess he had to look tough) who stood up on a table in one of the numerous bars we visited, peed into an empty pint mug and downed the lot in one. And how I made it on time the following morning to join SS *Oronsay* I'll never know.

Dad drove me to the dismal Tilbury docks for eight o'clock in the morning on 1 January 1967. Everything was various shades of grey, grey and grey; even the weather was foggy and drizzling. Dad parked right beside the towering presence of the steamer ship SS *Oronsay* and said, 'Well John, see you in five months'. I looked upwards and wondered what lay ahead. We shook hands and I staggered up the crew gangplank with suitcase and beachcaster into an entirely different world.

Named after a Scottish island, SS *Oronsay* amounted to 28,000 tons, had seven decks, a crew of 600 (half European and half Goanese Indians) and, with both first- and second-class accommodation completely full, had a capacity for 1,600 passengers. Some were on short voyages to a particular country, some were on a lengthy cruise or round-the-world tour, whilst others were on their way to a new life in Australia via the then ten-pound assisted passage deal. To say that the ship was similar to a village, or small town even, with its associated galaxy of social problems,

LEFT P & O Liner SS *Oronsay* (my home for two years) berthed in Sydney Harbour, Australia, allowed me to travel the world and really enjoy the swinging 60s.

indiscretions, joys and aspirations is an understatement. It was a travelling institution and the biggest learning curve of my life.

I was introduced to the shop and hairdressing staff including Shops Manager, Roy Lee, and spent the following week going nowhere humping heavy cardboard boxes around from where a crane had deposited them on the forward deck, to lockers all over the ship. Shop staff, under which I came with the strange title of Junior Leading Hand (whatever that meant), had to be back on board five days prior to sailing in order to load up with confectionery, toiletries, medicines, clothes and soft goods – in fact everything passengers would buy during our five-month voyage. No one had told me that part of my job when I had finished hairdressing each day – which I did from eight in the morning to six in the evening – was to replace all that had been sold in the shops that day from various lockers. I was about to work the hardest I have ever worked in my life, often not finishing until gone ten o'clock or sometimes much later. But then I made certain I played hard too.

This first voyage – which was the longest I ever made – included Australian cruising for six weeks out of Sydney to such exotic places as the Great Barrier Reef, Fiji, Tonga and the Samoan Islands. Even better, for one of those cruises a convention of no fewer than 300 female schoolteachers was on board. So with half the crew being Goanese and not permitted to mix with the passengers and half the 300 European crew being rampant gays, that left us heterosexual males outnumbered by young schoolteachers at a ratio of 2:1. Need I say more!

As shop staff we did not have officer status like the engineers and electricians, so we didn't have our own cabins at passenger deck levels. This made womanizing a continual problem, because we had to dodge back and forth, up and down decks from tourist to first-class accommodation in the early hours of the morning to evade the two Masters at Arms. But on the positive side we did eat extremely well on our own table in the passenger dining rooms and had virtually the same amount of time off in port as the passengers.

I initially found all the rules and regulations difficult to handle, like having to wear 'whites' when in the tropics and 'blues' when in temperate climates. I'd often climb the numerous staircases from my cabin five decks down, up to the hairdressing salon for instance, only to find I was in whites and the order of the day was blues, or vice versa. And a change to the correct colour was mandatory. (Quite simply, as *Oronsay* cruised at over 20 knots and could cover 500 miles in a day, we passed from one temperature band to another very quickly.) I soon learned to keep my head down and realized that as a barber a free haircut could get me almost anything on board, from an empty first-class cabin for the night when wanting to wine and dine, to enough blood and best raw steak from the butcher to enjoy a day's shark fishing.

This brings me to a particular occasion in the Mediterranean when *Oronsay* had anchored well offshore in deep water at Palermo. Most of the passengers had gone ashore via the life-boat shuttle service together with most of the deck crew who enjoyed nothing better than irritating the local mafiosi, so I decided on a quiet session at the aft end of the ship just above the laundry. This was actually an isolation deck, with a lock–up cell where anyone extremely infectious or aggressive was put, and so rarely used. And it became my favourite spot when fishing from the ship at anchor or in port, despite the deck being twenty feet above the waterline. Anyway first things first, and a visit to the fish chef was required but he was nowhere to be seen. So I helped myself to a few whole herrings and a tray of large peeled Pacific prawns, no doubt prepared for first-class starters that evening.

To cut a long story short, after liberally scattering all the prawns into the deep blue void and watching them spiral straight down to the bottom during slack water, I lowered a whole herring on a wire trace to the bottom and was rewarded an hour later with a conger eel of around thirty pounds, which put up a great scrap. The Goanese Indian crew, some of whom were keen anglers themselves and ardent fish eaters, were always around whenever I caught anything. Whatever it was – and I've eaten curried sailfish, stingray and conger to name but a few dishes – was instantly taken down to the galley and cooked. My conger was therefore immediately grabbed and I never saw it again, though there were strange and dire consequences.

Whilst down in my cabin getting ready for dinner once we had pulled anchor and were under way (the ship's screws turning over became a noise as familiar as one's front door bell ringing) there was a loud knock on the cabin door. I opened it and there stood the imposing figure of Ship's Chef, Lou King, with an angry look on his red face. From behind his back a huge hand appeared and slowly opened to reveal three partly digested peeled prawns. 'Can you explain how my peeled Pacific prawns got into the stomach of a Mediterranean conger?' asks the chef. All I could think of saying was, 'Er, how about a couple of free haircuts, Lou?' He smiled and said 'Yeah OK! But keep your bloody hands off my starters in future!'

The rod I used to catch that unforgettable conger eel was in fact the top joint of my beachcaster fitted into a short handle I made up, having purchased a duplicate set of ferrules before joining the ship. Though it seems strange now, it was all brass reinforced ferrules in those days. Together with the full-length beachcaster plus a two-piece nine-foot ABU heavy spinning rod, I could cope with most situations wherever *Oronsay* docked around the world.

I landed several silver catfish to over ten pounds whilst we were tied up for refuelling in Aden, followed by a small guitar fish and a sixty-five-pound stingray from the shore in Adelaide in South Australia. I looked forward to catching leopard sharks to around the thirty-pound mark whenever SS *Oronsay* berthed in San Francisco opposite the old prison on the island of Alcatraz. Which, incidentally,

looked just as foreboding as in the Clint Eastwood movie *Escape from Alcatraz*. I also once unintentionally foulhooked a dolphin when *Oronsay* was berthed in Bombay harbour and because of the religious value of these friendly mammals I nearly caused an international incident. Workers were running about screaming and gesturing in my direction all over shoreside. Fortunately for me the small hook pulled free before I was lynched. That's how I read the situation anyway.

Which brings me to Italy, and Naples in particular where, for the price of 200 cigarettes, you could walk back on to the ship with an armful of wrist watches. These were then swapped in Bombay for leather suitcases which were sold on to passengers at a later date. We worked a similar ruse with coloured coral which could be bought by the basketful quite cheaply in Fiji, but only in Fiji. The white, sunbleached pieces of coral were put into hot springs full of various coloured dyes and the result looked most exotic. We could have got our money back purely on the raffia baskets the coral was sold in. We waited until Fiji was not on *Oronsay*'s itinerary before getting the coral out for sale. There were other money-making schemes, of course, that I shan't go into. So back to the fishing.

Every now and again, usually when tied up in tropical deep-water harbours and presenting fresh fish baits on the bottom, I became attached to unseen monsters which just kept on going, despite all the pressure I could apply with a 40lb reel line. When nothing was left on the Penn Long Beach multiplier, one of two things usually happened. Either the hook snapped or the brass ferrules on my beachcaster bent at right angles immediately prior to the line cracking off like a pistol shot. Whilst fishing from the rocks in American Samoa on the island of Pago Pago, however, I watched my rod break in half for the last time as an unseen shark or ray made off for the horizon. I finally decided to do something about landing these unstoppable monsters.

I wanted an outfit with real big-time stopping power, or at least slowing-down power, and so in Honolulu, where I repeatedly lost leviathans in the harbour, I purchased a six-foot, 130lb class, hollow glass marlin tip together with an extra-strong boat rod screw-reel fitting in heavily chromed brass, plus top-quality roller tip and butt rings, and enough intermediates to construct an eight-foot custom whopper stopper, once I had added a two-foot hardwood handle. I also purchased the ideal partner in a Penn 9/0 Senator reel which held around a quarter of a mile of 80lb monofilament. I still have that reel and occasionally use it in warmer parts when sharking.

On our next voyage when berthed in Auckland in New Zealand, where I usually enjoyed charter boat fishing for red snapper and yellowtail twenty-five miles out near the heads, my new outfit was well and truly put to the test. *Oronsay* was berthed alongside an old wooden pier under which I had, on previous visits, lost huge, unstoppable stingrays fishing from the aft end, and I was more than keen to see one of the monsters at close quarters. There are in fact many different species of stingray around the globe and the two species liable to be caught from British shores, *Dasyatis pastinaca* and *Myliobatis aquila* (eagle ray) are typical of the two shapes which seem to dominate the stingray kingdom which, incidentally, even includes freshwater species such as those found in the mighty Amazon river system in South America.

That stringrays attain monstrous proportions there is no doubt. But because comparatively few anglers bother to specialize in catching them, even on a worldwide basis, very little is known of their ultimate weight potential. Something approaching a thousand pounds is far from unrealistic in my opinion, and what an awesome creature that would be.

Anyway, back to North Island, New Zealand and to Auckland harbour with *Oronsay* tied up to the pier. One afternoon I lowered half a fresh herring mounted on a strong 5/0 tuna hook to 100lb test-wire trace down to the bottom beside the aft end. Due to there being next to no tide I used just an ounce bomb above the trace and, allowing a little slack line from bait to rod tip, put the 9/0 Senator out of gear after flicking the ratchet on. After about an hour or so, the reel suddenly clicked a couple of times (just like the big-game reel in the film *Jaws*) then screeched into life like a stuck pig, as something powerful made off, fortunately not towards the pier (something I was afraid of) but across the wide harbour in the direction of where *Oronsay*'s sister ship, SS *Orsova*, was coincidentally also berthed.

I stuck the rod's long handle under my crotch, steadied myself against the handrail and flipped the reel into gear having already preset the clutch to a firm setting. Yet still I was not prepared for the awesome animal power which came vibrating through the arched marlin tip, as the hook made purchase. It was like connecting my line to a lorry on the M25. The ray, and somehow I instinctively knew that this was a huge stingray by the way it kept close to the bottom, instantly doubled its speed and roared off across the harbour going deeper and deeper. And there in the middle of the harbour between the two ships, first kiting one way and then the other, it stayed for what seemed an eternity. The 80lb mono sang loudly in the

BELOW Considering the prices of the wine list on *Oronsay*'s Christmas menu, everyone certainly ate and drank well whilst travelling the world as the ship's itinerary also illustrates.

wind, while I strained every muscle in my body to pump back line whenever I could. I was much lighter in those days – I can remember weighing in for one of the boxing matches, regularly held on the crew deck up forward, at just 10 stone 13lb. So I had little weight to lean against this obviously huge fish. For close on two hours the ray battled away, but my stand-up big-game outfit eventually proved its worth and I was able to pump my adversary back to directly below the ship where it sulked for a while, until it finally lay exhausted on the surface close beside SS *Oronsay*.

It was absolutely monstrous, as wide as a car, two feet thick and with a tail root as large as a man's calf, thrashing its sting positioned halfway along the tail frantically from side to side. At this stage I was shaking with nervous exhaustion and pumped up on pure adrenaline, though quite near to the point of not caring whether I landed it or not, which is a period anyone who has ever experienced blue-water game fishing always goes through. The light was fading fast and the time was getting closer to the *Oronsay*'s departure from Auckland. Because of this the captain, generally a most obliging chap to those of us who fished, couldn't really hold up the scheduled departure by putting a lifeboat down just because one of the crew had by far the largest fish of his life waiting on the surface to be gaffed. After all it was a passenger ship.

Anyway the best I could do was to let some mates try and rope-gaff it, but from over twenty feet up this proved impossible and not a little dangerous. Then suddenly there came a real chance of turning the now ridiculous situation around, which unintentionally had become a flood-lit spectacle for both passengers and their loved ones on the quay waving goodbye. Thankfully a tug had arrived alongside early in order to push us off and the obliging crewmen, realizing my predicament, picked up the two gaffs thrown down to them. Unfortunately they couldn't hold the beast even with a gaff in each wing and once it started to dive one of the gaffs bent straight, leaving the ray thrashing about on the other. The trace was then severed below the swivel as it became tangled up in the confusion, leaving two New Zealand tugmen trying to haul something like five hundred pounds over the side of their craft on one gaff head. Needless to say they didn't make it, which brought a pained 'oh' from the gallery of spectators on the upper decks.

A rope was then dangled down to the tug to retrieve my two now useless gaffs and I slowly packed up the big-game outfit, numb but thankful that the ordeal was over. In a way I was glad that my ray was not killed simply to ascertain what it weighed. But I still wonder – even now.

I once spent what turned out to be a most infuriating day fishing in Kobe harbour in Japan. Despite a good supply of fresh bait in the way of prawns and sardines, compliments of the fish cook, not a single twitch or nibble did I have with all three rods out over the side. But the penny quickly dropped in the late afternoon when our local English-speaking agent asked the Shops Manager why I was bothering to fish in a harbour that had been polluted for years. Boy, did I feel stupid!

It was upon leaving Japan on one of our many visits there, with the next port on the itinerary being Hong Kong, that a most harrowing experience came to all those working and travelling aboard SS *Oronsay*, somewhere in the middle of the Taiwan Sea. At the time I was relaxing next to the swimming pool on the tourist sundeck at lunchtime. I overheard a woman asking a young officer what was the fine trail of smoke coming from a hole in one of the hatch covers. He opened it slowly and whoosh, up it all went. A huge hold that you could drive dozens of double-decker buses into was full of toys, radios and other plastic goods that apparently had been smouldering away for a couple of days since we left Japan and suddenly ignited into a veritable fireball.

All colour instantly drained from the officer's face as he slammed the cover down and ran off to hit the alarm. Within the next couple of hours complete pandemonium had broken out. All of both E and F decks in tourist accommodation, which amounted to several hundred cabins, were flooded with sea water to stop the bulk heads from melting, leaving most passengers owning little more than what they had been wearing on deck. Cameras and hi-fi systems purchased in Japan, plus money, valuables and everything else left in their cabins became immediately irretrievable to hundreds of passengers.

SS *Oronsay* was within a short space of time put on 'abandon ship alert' and, in truth from those in the know, I was given the impression that for a day or so at least

it was indeed touch and go whilst crews worked unceasingly to prevent the intense heat from spreading. My mum must have had a fit when listening to the news back home. Most newspapers ran the headlines 'SS *Oronsay* ablaze in Taiwan Sea'. The truth however was that visible flames were never seen by the majority of both passengers and crew.

My most vivid memory of the occasion, bizarre though it may seem, was that within a few hours of crew alert, at every embarkation lifeboat station, there suddenly appeared from the bowels of the ship hundreds of sewing machines and bicycles, property of the Goanese Indian crew who, laden down with these valuables, were all life-jacketed up and ready to go. Where they thought they were going I'm not sure, but they sure as hell weren't going to let their prize possessions go down with the ship.

Fortunately the internal fire was kept at bay and the old man made the decision of going into our next port of call, Hong Kong, with SS *Oronsay* still technically on fire. It was quickly made safe on arrival however and everyone enjoyed an extra week's leave in this truly magical city while Lloyds insurance delegates flew in from London to estimate the cost of the damage.

Much of the damaged cargo was in fact simply heaved over the side in Hong Kong harbour but a quantity of salvageable goods, novelty radios in particular, somehow found their way into the cabins of *Oronsay*'s wheeler dealers. No, not me, but my fishing buddy, Phil the plumber (with whom I have kept in touch ever since), came by an assignment of these which were dried out and sold a few weeks later on the west coast of Africa when we berthed in Dakar. Saltwater had achieved the obvious, however, resulting in those who bought them only ever hearing a crackle and buzz, regardless of battery strength. Phil handed out a cock-and-bull story about not being able to hear anything in port due to *Oronsay*'s aerials interfering with the radio channels, which seemed to pacify his unsophisticated customers. And he promised that once *Oronsay* had departed, the radios would work perfectly.

Needless to say the next time we tied up in Dakar several months later, where the fishing can be exceptionally good from the harbour entrance piers, there was a reception committee all on the look-out for Phil. This didn't stop us fishing though, because we smuggled Phil out with a hood over his head down the galley gangway straight into a waiting taxi. But it was a bit hairy. Those tall, French-speaking West Africans in their fezzes would have lynched him given the chance.

Phil and I fished together all over the world once the screws had stopped and SS *Oronsay* was tied up. Australian ports were amongst our favourite and when on leave in Sydney we'd sometimes get a taxi up to the Hawkesbury River at Bobbin Head and hire a twenty-foot boat on which we lived for a couple of days whilst exploring the fascinating maze of saltwater channels north of the city. One night Phil swore I was snoring so loudly that a wild boar up in the hills close to where we were anchored in a deep channel was answering me. What codswallop! At night the deep, crystal-clear water was continually lit up by millions of moving particles of luminous green phosphorus. It was indeed an eerie experience whilst fishing when anything could turn up from flatheads to sharks.

Mention of the wonderful city of Sydney reminds me of an occasion when *Oronsay* was tied up at Circular Quay and I was fishing from the rocks at famous Bondi Beach. It almost ended in tragedy – mine. I was casting from a high rocky plateau way out beyond the waves crashing on to the rocks below, hoping for grouper, and holding my beachcaster up high to stop the line from being ragged in. I had just asked a mate standing a fair way back behind my precarious perch what he thought of the two birds sitting upon a large rock around a hundred yards away (which were actually bronze statues and a local landmark) and as I turned back to watch the rod tip all I could see was a gigantic column of water accompanied by a loud roar. It was one of those freak waves (every forty-ninth some say) and it completely engulfed me. For what seemed like an eternity it was as though I had been put in a washing machine.

I was in fact being bowled backwards head over heels, over and over the jagged, limpet-covered rocks from which I had been casting by the enormous force of water.

I managed fortunately (and this probably saved my life) to hold on to my beachcaster with both hands. When the sea receded the draw was immensely strong, and had it not been for the rod sticking fast amongst the crevices I would have been drawn over twenty feet down and smashed against the lower rocks.

Then came my only experience of the famous Australian lifeguards, a group of whom were posing with muscles pumped up at the top of the beach by the main road. When I came hobbling along in a half-concussed state, sporting numerous rather nasty open wounds on my back, elbows and legs which were all bleeding profusely, I received a curt 'There's a chemist down the road, Mack'.

Whenever *Oronsay* was berthed for a week or more in Sydney, probably the most picturesque natural harbour in the world, I took the opportunity of travelling inland and seeing something of Australia. One of the relief Australian hairdressers, Fred, invited me back to share a few days with his wife and kids in the town of Yass close to the Burrinjuck Dam near the Blue Mountains. Here on spinners we caught brim (a brownish, unstriped version of our perch), rainbow trout and small Murray cod, in a most enchanting flooded valley where only the bleating of grazing sheep could be heard in an otherwise completely silent environment.

In one of the rivers, called the Goodradigbee, we fished for rainbow trout and I actually set eyes upon a duck-billed platypus in the wild – which is something even most Australians haven't experienced. It suddenly popped up to the surface right beneath my rod tip, all black and shiny with that strange-looking flat head and tail combination, and was actually much smaller than I had imagined, being no more than twenty inches long. It looked directly up at me for a couple of seconds and dived out of sight in a flash. Every so often along the valley we caught sight of sulphur-

BELOW Having nearly been smashed to death by a freak wave the previous day, here I am patched up, fishing from the same rocks at famous Bondi Beach, near Sydney, Australia.

crested cockatoos and huge flocks of budgerigars. It actually seemed kind of strange to see them in the wild.

The rainbow trout were totally preoccupied feeding on grasshoppers which, due to a strong wind, were continually landing upon the surface of this extremely fast-flowing river (it reminded me of Derbyshire's River Derwent). They would look at neither worm nor spinner, so Fred and I set about catching some live hoppers. For a container we used an empty beer bottle and following an hour's toil chasing these unusually large and fast insects through waist-high grass, we were streaming with sweat and close to exhaustion, having captured just two. Sadly even one of these appeared dead. It mattered not however to those rainbow trout, for we caught an unbelievably hard fighting rainbow apiece, both over three pounds, within mere minutes of trotting our hoppers downstream beneath a bubble float.

Judging by the number of aggressive swirls on the surface, the river was full of trout and all of them were large, wild rainbows. When I think back to that day the memory still frustrates me because we packed up shortly after that brace of trout, unable to capture any more grasshoppers. We needed to be on our way in any event due to the long drive back into Yass, and before we left the river where the track veered upwards and across the next valley, I saw an old man with long grey hair flapping either side of his bush hat, in the middle of a meadow beside the river behaving in a most unusual way. Fred stopped the shooting-break and we sauntered through the long grass to say 'hello', passing a trailer van in front of which was a large pile of prime rainbow trout in the 3–6lb class all ready for gutting. At least someone had the answer to catching enough grasshoppers for bait.

This canny bushman was not chasing after them however. Once he spotted the grasshopper he wanted (and he politely showed us exactly how to do it) he raised his hands above his head and from a few yards back simply waved them about in a sort of mock karate display, slowly moving closer and closer. This he said confused the grasshopper's two long antennae which could then not focus on any one point (rather like a modern auto-focus camera lens hunts when it is aimed at a moving object) and simply by swaying his hands from side to side he could quietly walk right up to any grasshopper and pick it up. Fred and I looked at each other in

BELOW My first set of jaws, a black-tipped spinner shark caught from a ski boat hired whilst *Oronsay* was berthed in the beautiful waters off Fiji.

despair at what might have been. A drawstring cotton bag around the old man's neck was twitching away, full of dozens of live insects, so he wasn't kidding us. And I can assure you that this ruse works all over the world for catching grasshoppers. You can literally see their two antennae crossing over each other trying to obtain an accurate bearing. But of course by then they are bait.

I caught my very first shark, an eighty-pound black-tipped spinner shark, whilst Pacific cruising out from Sydney in the warm blue waters off the islands of Fiji. A Swiss passenger and angling fanatic, Jacques, and I had struck up a firm friendship and we hired a fifteen-foot water-skiing boat for the day with a local guide. Upon returning to the marina with the shark, which unfortunately had swallowed the hook and three pounds of raw steak (compliments of the butcher), its belly suddenly started to move. Although this female was well and truly dead on arrival, the four live pups inside, complete with umbilical cords connected to food sacs, swam straight away when returned to the sea. This, in part I like to think, vindicated my catching it on rod and line.

Later that trip when berthed in Acapulco, Mexico, Jacques and I teamed up again and talked David, a young hairdresser, and Barry, who worked in the ship's shop (both non-anglers), into sharing the expense of a big-game boat for the day to see if we could catch a sailfish. With pelicans following overhead we left the harbour and allowed the two non-anglers to sit on the rods, thinking that nothing would grab hold until we hit blue water. What a mistake! Within minutes out whizzed one of the outrigger lines presenting a fresh whole mullet, and non-angler Barry was fast into a bloody great sailfish, which went absolutely berserk, repeatedly jumping all over the place on a ridiculously inadequate rod and reel combination. Consequently it took ages to bring to the boat.

Fortunately the ocean off Acapulco was at that time a veritable sailfish haven and we boated no fewer than three, despite our inexperience at blue-water trolling. Each was around eighty to ninety pounds, and one of these we took back to the ship and from the fishing boat hauled it up the side of *Oronsay* by rope to the afterdeck. After the photographs I'm ashamed to say that this magnificent creature was subsequently curried. But in those days conservation was a rarely used word.

We were taking a big risk as it was, because if the old man had seen an eight-foot sailfish being hauled on to his ship, we'd all have been in deep trouble. Sadly Jacques was the only one of the group who didn't hit a sail, but he made up for it by boating a big bull dorado.

Acapulco was a most colourful resort which typified third-world countries at that time. Plenty of showcase, plush hotels and westernized facilities, but always just away from the commercialized sector people lived in squalor, literally on the poverty line in houses made from cardboard boxes. On the face of it, it seems little different from tourists coming to London and seeing the down-and-outs and winos dossing down for the night along the Embankment and in shop doorways. Again, in makeshift cardboard shelters. But in third-world countries, for such a large proportion of the

RIGHT (*Left to Right*) David, Barry, yes I smoked in those days, and Jacques with one of the sailfish we caught trolling off Acapulco in Mexico, and decided to haul 20 feet up the side of the *Oronsay's* stern for a photo.

population, it is their way of life, and I think witnessing this all over the globe whilst SS *Oronsay* took its passengers to some of the most elegant resorts really opened up my eyes to the reality of life in third-world countries and made me feel both humble and thankful for my own roots. It also blew my childish belief that British was always best. I guess being brought up in London just after the war, at a time when we still had colonies and much of the world atlas was subsequently coloured in pink and under British rule, this belief was perhaps excusable. Naturally I also gained a clear impression of what the rest of the world thought of us, which really opened my eyes – for it was not always complimentary.

I have already hinted at the swinging sixties attitude towards sex on SS *Oronsay*. It was indeed one floating hotel for the hot-blooded folk of the world and I can only explain this by the way in which the so-called fairer sex totally change for the better, as far as rampant males are concerned, particularly the young Wilson, as soon as they are taken away from a socially controlled environment where their family and friends know both them and their position within the local community. To say inhibitions go straight out the window would indeed be a gross understatement!

Even the most chaste of women change from demure, hard to chat up housewives and lovers and turn into vociferous predators, after a few days out on the ocean waves. Scientists no doubt put a label on this phenomenon, but the young Wilson never tried to understand what was happening, he simply enjoyed it.

As tourist hairdresser for the greater part of my two years aboard SS *Oronsay* you could say that just about every female travelling tourist class, plus some of those who filtered down from first class, passed through my hands. Perhaps mention of that immortal film *Shampoo* starring Warren Beatty might provide an idea of what life as a hairdresser on board a P & O liner was like during the latter part of the 1960s. Suffice it to say that I always felt knackered. I hope memories of the following two clandestine meetings give a sufficient clue.

I became particularly involved with a first-class passenger, an attractive blonde in her late twenties, whom I shall call Carol from Oregon. I first met her in the salon whilst *Oronsay* was in Fort Lauderdale, Miami (all the hairdressers took it in turns to be on duty for the morning only whilst in port). Each evening Carol would leave her cabin door on the latch while she drank with some of the young officers, all of whom were dying to get her into the sack, so I could let myself into her first-class cabin up on A deck once my duties were finished and wait for her return. To be frank, she was a bit of an artist, probably worse than me, and usually three parts to the wind, but was a wonderfully warm person and once I'd belted down a few whiskies (she would always leave a bottle and some ginger ales on ice in her cabin) we were soon on the same level. Anyway one particular evening Carol didn't arrive back in the cabin at the usual time of around midnight and I must have dozed off. Because at 2 am crash bang went the door and into the cabin fell Carol completely bombed. Great, I thought, no nookie for Wilson tonight, and pushed the door shut (still on the latch) before heaving her from the floor on to the bed and removing her clothes. She threw up a couple of times and immediately started dry retching. Nevertheless I dragged her completely naked from the bed towards the shower, supporting her dead weight with my arms lightly locked around her waist and was just in front of the cabin door when solid footsteps and gentle but concerned words from the tall, ginger-haired officer whose voice I recognized, whispered, 'Are you alright Carol? Are you alright?'

There I was a junior leading hand (the lowest of the low) and not supposed to be anywhere near passenger accommodation, particularly first class, doing my best to stop the woman that same officer had been plying with drinks all night and thinking no doubt he had cracked it, from sliding to the floor. I'd also stripped off to hold her up in the shower, so was standing stock still, bollock naked, just two feet from the mahogany door which separated us, still on the latch, unable to free a hand to put the lock on.

Fortunately at that precise moment, which seemed like an eternity (I could picture Wilson being hanged from the yard arm), fate took a positive turn in the form of a couple of passengers who must have returned to their cabin nearby, because there was a polite exchange of words and the lanky young officer walked away slowly down the passageway.

About a week later Carol decided to risk the journey (passengers were not allowed to walk from one class to another class, and would be asked to return to their own section if caught) and visit me in the tourist salon for a hairdo. Now to cut a long, complicated story short, I ended up in a strange situation with three women under dryers all at the same time, each of whom I had been carrying on with during the preceding weeks. My problem was how to get the first out from beneath the dryer, brushed out and away from the small salon before the other two switched off their dryers. Women cannot hear under the dryer (though some were masters at lip reading) due to a headful of rollers covered in a net with cardboard covers over their ears so they don't burn. I worked frantically away simultaneously trying to look nonchalant, whilst arranging the next rendezvous with one, while the other two exchanged curious glances every so often. It was indeed a most precarious tightrope I walked in those days. But I loved every minute of it.

I did however get my come-uppance a few months later whilst trying to woo a particularly attractive woman from America's Deep South, called Mary Lou. Just about everyone had tried it on with this striking woman whose high cheek bones and vivacious looks were not totally unlike those of the actress Mary Tyler Moore. But in no way was she getting into the sack with anyone not holding out a wedding ring. She was, you might say, the exception to just about every unattached young woman travelling on board SS *Oronsay* at that time, and as such posed a magnificent challenge. In fact to Wilson it was the ultimate challenge and I decided on the 'cool' approach by suggesting we play chess one evening, to which she actually agreed. Yes, chess!

My good pal, Geoff Wedge (now settled in Melbourne) who worked in the purser's department, nicked a key to an unoccupied cabin (as he regularly did) in tourist accommodation on F deck for the occasion. In truth Mary Lou and I spent a really pleasant evening – she was a cute chess player – but I got absolutely nowhere. I was in fact on the point of calling it a night and conceding defeat at around two o'clock in the morning when there was a loud authoritative banging at the door. I kneeled down and looked up through the grill at the bottom of the cabin door to a most unwelcome scene: there were the Staff Captain, Chief Steward, the Master at Arms, plus several young officers who each no doubt relished the chance of doing Wilson down and being along at the kill. A bedroom steward must have heard our voices or seen the light on in what should have been an unoccupied cabin and reported it.

By the following morning stories of the fiasco had spread throughout the ship like a forest fire and I was a laughing stock. My penance included a dressing-down from the old man himself who tried to keep a straight face while I stood in his office upon the Union Jack (an obligatory act) lined on both sides by sniggering young officers. I also lost a day's pay with the inevitability that Crawford in London would get to hear about my wrongdoings, which could result in Wilson not joining *Oronsay* on its next voyage. (Actually Crawford was informed but being a good hairdresser with a clean record save for this one indiscretion I suffered his caustic remarks and innuendoes in silence when *Oronsay* docked in Southampton, and that was the end of it.)

Several months after this little episode Geoff Wedge said 'goodbye' to us all on board and emigrated to Australia where, as far as I know, he still lives. But before he departed he threw a party at his parents' large house in Brighton (they were on holiday). This necessitated hiring a car from a firm based just outside Southampton Docks where *Oronsay* was berthed. Being younger than me, both Geoff and Jeremy, the ship's chemist, rented a new Ford on my licence and took turns in gunning it along narrow coastal roads between Southampton and Brighton where we picked up three obliging young ladies from Geoff's local pub to take back to the party. On the way back during the early hours of the morning (we had to get back to *Oronsay* for departure that day) I experienced the weird dream of spinning round and round, followed by falling heavily. In fact I *had*, straight on to the floor from a prone position on the rear seats, while Geoff completely lost control at the wheel and promptly razed to the ground the low front walls of at least two terraced houses. He then crashed back on to the road and continued the journey as though nothing had happened.

As the mangled Ford was taken out on my licence I had to drive it the last couple of hundred yards back into the car hire compound, which was in fact the only occasion I sat behind the steering wheel. The blonde behind the desk should never have been sweet-talked by Geoff into hiring it out on my licence (but she fancied him) and I saw her clutch her head in disbelief and horror as I chugged the forlorn-looking Ford around the corner into the yard. But there was more to come.

Unknown to us at the time, although we saw them at the party, a spanking new pillar-box red Hillman Imp taken out by Bruce, a self-confessed driving wizard who was said to be on first-name terms with Lotus boss, Colin Chapman, and Kevin, the laundryman, arrived back a total write-off. Somehow they had managed to wrap it around a tree on the outskirts of Southampton and then just about limp back. At least ours only needed a new front end plus passenger and driver's side doors!

Hiring cars whilst on leave between trips was never my strong point. Take for instance the Triumph Herald convertible I hired from Edwards of Epsom in Surrey. It was a lovely little car to drive. It was white with a black hood, and the soft top was a real boon in the particularly hot weather we were experiencing that week.

I had chosen to visit a favourite haunt on the Great Ouse in Holywell where for several years I regularly rented a punt during the winter months for piking from the late Tom Metcalf Arnold – one of the few people at that time still making eel traps from reeds. Only being midsummer, my thoughts were with the tench and bream inhabiting the deeper water about half a mile downstream from Tom's house, and he kindly opened the farm gate allowing me to drive right down to within ten yards of the river. It was a lovely spot with a raised bank behind to break the wind and comfortable swims cut into thick beds of sweet rush and reeds. There was a good depth close in and I quickly got amongst the bream by laying on with breadflake over a carpet of groundbait. I had left all the hustle and bustle behind, and my mind was completely relaxed by the serenity of being alone and at peace with the river.

Then I heard a most peculiar sound. It was quite indescribable really, but I can remember thinking at the time that it sounded like heavy munching. It went on for several minutes before curiosity got the better of me and I stood up to look over the high bank from behind which it seemed to be coming. Nothing out of the ordinary, from my angle of view; just picturesque open countryside and the Triumph convertible with a horse's head inside.

Inside the car! What the bloody hell was a horse's head doing inside the car? What happens to my own jalopies is one thing but what happens to a hired car is something else. I'd lose my deposit for a start. I flew up the bank clutching the landing net. The entire car shook and off bolted the horse leaving behind a gaping two-foot hole right in the middle of the black leatherette roof. When I rang Edwards of Epsom that afternoon enquiring about mitigating circumstances in insurance claims, I first said to the girl on the phone, 'now you're not going to believe this, but . . .' 'Try me,' she said. After my story she said, 'You're right I don't, it's a bit far fetched isn't it? I am afraid you will have to forfeit your deposit, Mr Wilson.'

By far the largest thing I ever hooked during those two wonderful years on SS *Oronsay*, which included several east-to-west mail runs around the globe lasting three months apiece, was a police launch. How? Well we were lying at anchor in deep water off Bermuda at the time with most of the passengers having been taken ashore in the lifeboat shuttle service. This was the perfect combination of circumstances for Wilson to partake in a spot of serious shark fishing which necessitated collecting a big drum of fresh blood from the butcher (who saved it up for me) and emptying the lot over the side from the afterdeck by the isolation hospital. One of the shop's staff, a likeable Geordie called Andrew, fancied a go at fishing and so I made him up a light outfit baited with thin strips of raw steak in the hope of him catching a reasonable-sized snapper or grunt to use as live shark bait. (Incidentally wherever you find yourself in tropical blue waters around the world without bait, remember that strips of raw steak will catch most species from catfish to sharks. It's the blood which is the attractor of course, and this soon washes from the steak, necessitating regular bait changes.)

Then I put together my heavy whopper-stopper outfit with the Penn 9/0 reel, and on to the cable laid wire trace and duo of size 10/0 hooks went a huge slab of best beef steak simply dripping with blood. A balloon was tied on the 80lb reel line several feet above the 10-foot trace and this I used to drift the bait slowly down tide with the ratchet on and the big multiplier out of gear.

Emptying blood over the side usually resulted – and often in a ridiculously short time – in several sharks following the trail up to the ship. But this time action came from an entirely different quarter. I suddenly heard Andrew croak loudly and turned around to see him crash backwards against the steel door of the isolation hospital gripped firmly around the throat by a pair of large black hands reaching through the iron bars. Unbeknown to us a Goanese crew member, who was delirious and completely off his trolley, had been locked up for the night in the isolation deck cell. He was ranting and raving exactly how you would expect a madman to with Andrew's face turning redder by the second.

He was on the point of passing out when I finally managed to prise the lunatic's fingers from around his throat and we settled back down to the fishing again, several feet in front of the cell door with the incarcerated man still shouting and raving. With the amount of blood spreading below I was expecting a shark to show up at any minute. In the distance there came the sound of a motorboat. It was the Bermuda police launch circling *Oronsay*, no doubt to see that no one was engaged in any kind of smuggling. Trouble was it was heading straight towards my shark line, so I yelled at the top of my voice and waved exaggeratedly at the copper to get out of the way and gestured towards my balloon float. But he obviously could not hear and simply waved back cordially.

By now there was insufficient time for me to retrieve the shark rig, and so the inevitable happened. Suddenly the put, put, put of the engine stopped as the wire trace wound around the propeller. Wilson was fast into a twenty-foot police launch drifting downwind begrudgingly against a heavily set drag on the 9/0 and slowly taking line. The copper came out of the wheelhouse, looked at my 80lb line angled up from his stern to the rod I was holding and shook his fist angrily. It was no time to argue whose fault it was and without further ado he stripped off to his underpants and, grabbing a pair of pliers, plopped over the side beneath the boat. With so much blood in the sea (if only the passengers knew what went on) the farce could well have turned into *Jaws 4*.

I couldn't look, I simply bent my back into the police launch trying to stop it from going further down tide with the 80lb line so tight that it sang in the wind. After what seemed an age that included several dives beneath the launch, the copper finally managed to unwind the 200lb wire trace from his prop and clambered wearily on board, again shaking a fist in my direction. But Wilson was long gone, having packed up in record time to make a hasty retreat back to the sanctuary of his cabin before the

irate copper could kick up a fuss with the Master at Arms at embarkation deck level. An hour after we pulled anchor, a bell boy knocked on my cabin door and said, 'here's your trace back, compliments of the Bermuda Police Force.'

I honestly think I could fill a whole book with weird and wonderful tales experienced on board *SS Oronsay*. I could relate the time in Horseshoe Bay, Vancouver, Canada, for instance, when my hired boat was nearly mowed down in thick fog by the Victoria Island ferry, and on the very same day how I almost became attached to a sea eagle which grabbed a fish bait in full flight during the cast. Fortunately the hooks came clear. I could provide more womanizing stories but I was really no different from any other red-blooded unattached male in his early twenties. Besides there then came a complete change in direction for me when, on leave between trips back in north London, I met up again with my former fiancée, Barbara, in a local night club.

Having sown my wild oats, I was ready to settle down and get married. During the intervening years since we last met Barbara and I had both lived life to the full. With the prospect of marriage there also came the additional opportunity of starting a new life, managing a chain of hairdressing salons together in the West Indies on the island of Barbados.

I had been informed of this position by one of my clients on board *Oronsay* and when I was next on leave, Barbara and I went to see (our eventual bosses) John and Veronica Stuart at their house in south London. We struck up a friendship immediately (which lasts to this day) and at the beginning of December Barbara and

I were due out in Barbados to take on the extra workload in the hairdressing salons at the start of peak tourist season which ran through until April.

It was certainly a whirlwind December for us in 1968. Within five days of saying farewell to all my friends and two fantastic years on board SS *Oronsay*, Barbara and I were married in a church close to where she lived in Muswell Hill, north-west London, and two days later the VC10 from Heathrow touched down in Bridgetown, Barbados. Another chapter of life and fishing had begun.

Measuring just twenty-five miles long by seven miles wide, Barbados is the most easterly of all the Caribbean islands. The rugged east coast receives a constant battering from the full force of the Atlantic whilst the quieter west coast faces the Caribbean Sea, lined with hotels and condominiums. As the population at that time was ninety-seven per cent black, living on the island as a resident as opposed to a holidaymaker – two entirely different things – gave me first-hand experience of what it feels like to be the minority race. And the West Indians and Asians living on the outskirts of London, or any ethnic minority living in any country, have my sympathy.

Although Barbara and I worked in the Mirimar, Colony Club and Discovery Bay hotels on the west coast and in the Holiday Inn, catering for a westernized clientel

BELOW This picture taken in 1970, is the beautiful tropical shoreline of Barbados near its capital, Bridgetown, between the Hilton and Holiday Inn Hotel, where I ran the hairdressing salon, skin dived and spear fished every day for three years.

(the largest segment coming from the USA's eastern seaboard, particularly New York), we lived in a small wooden house on the beach surrounded by local people. Coconut and banana trees grew wild around the house – which in Britain would amount to little more than a garden shed – from which a pebble could be thrown underarm into the warm, clear blue Caribbean Sea. So we went to sleep with the restful sound of the surf rolling up on to the white coral sand. It was that close, and for a while it was absolute paradise, just like the Bounty Bar television adverts. With best-quality local cane rum costing just £1.50 a gallon (yes, a gallon), how could you not be happy? We enjoyed numerous parties in that little cottage, with bottles of Coke being the most expensive items.

For the first time in my life I had my own house (albeit rented) and a garden, so we bought a pair of young Labrador puppies, one black and one golden, which we named Bonnie and Clyde. It seems strange, I know, but there were so many coconuts in the palms high above the garden all around the house that I regularly had to pay a young local lad to climb up and cut them down, in case they fell on the dogs.

Before long I started to explore all the local creeks and tidal channels entering the Caribbean Sea between the numerous hotels. I can remember vividly my first encounter with a tarpon one morning when I was armed with a spinning rod and small diving plug.

The sixty-foot wide swamp was festooned along both banks with impenetrable mangrove roots and ran inland for about 200 yards into dense tropical vegetation. It was in fact separated from the gently sloping beach of white coral sand by a giant mound of grass-covered sand with the Caribbean Sea no more than thirty yards away. I was later to find out that most of these drainage swamps and dykes were actually flooded open once a year by high spring tides, allowing the fish they contained, which had grown fat on a rich diet of crabs and small fishes, to swim out and a new consignment of both young snook and tarpon to swim in.

Anyway back to my first tarpon. The only spot I could comfortably stand to make a cast without sinking up to my knees in black, foul-smelling mud was at the sea end. And as I crept up several long, dark, slow-moving shadows could be seen just beneath the surface of the decidedly green water. This was such a vastly different world from the sparklingly clear ocean only a stone's throw away. I was tingling with excitement as I threw the small yellow plug out under the bushes to my right, not really knowing what to expect.

That very first cast made me a tarpon fan for life, because as the plug jittered and fluttered along the surface at the start of the retrieve, there was an instant bow wave in its wake. I reeled in faster and faster as the bow wave followed until, quite suddenly, there was an almighty 'boil' at my feet and a giant silver fish of forty-pounds-plus and fully five feet long cavorted six feet into the air, shaking its huge head from side to side, soaking and almost hitting me before it crashed back into the swamp snapping the line like cotton. I stood there dumbfounded, plugless and shaking like a nervous fruit jelly as the tarpon went charging along the dyke, leaping every few yards to rid itself of the plug which was stuck in its jaws. It was still jumping and thrashing about some minutes later when I finally regained my composure and tried to puzzle out what had actually happened.

My next visit to the little dyke later that evening proved more fruitful and although I couldn't induce a take by lure fishing, I managed to tempt an eighteen-pound fish into accepting a soft crab twitched below a bottle cork which put up one hell of a scrap on the 10lb line. I immediately noticed those bevelled jaw hinges, abrasive and sharp, and thought myself lucky that the monofil had not parted. It is the hard bony jaws and sharp hinges that make hooking and landing a tarpon so difficult, because as it leaps and shakes its head while tail-walking, even a stout wire trace is sometimes severed, unless you can quickly lower the rod tip and give line instantly.

After taking a dozen or more fish up to nearly thirty pounds from the little dyke, I soon managed to locate other such swamps on the island. One in particular was not

BELOW Using my old Minolta SR7 35mm camera I actually managed to photograph this 40lb tarpon tailwalking and crashing through a shallow inland swamp, whilst playing it.

unlike the Norfolk Broads where much of my present-day fishing is done. It was quite extensive – about forty acres – and completely covered around the perimeter with huge irregular beds of marsh grass and reeds, which sometimes formed little bays and lagoons. I came across this veritable tarpon and snook haven whilst exploring along the southern coast.

In an eerie way it was a piece of colonial Barbados forgotten by time. All around were the dilapidated remains of duck-shooting hides built on wooden stagings that reached through the reedy margins into open water (they made great fishing platforms) and in the centre of the swamp, reached via a gravel track, was an old wooden pavilion with a galvanized sheet roof. Inside were wartime posters of dance bands and coming events still pinned to the walls. I could almost hear the music of Glenn Miller come whispering through the rotting tongue-and-groove planking. I felt a little uneasy even being there on my first visit. But the gate was open and as I walked down to the pavilion all along the site of a creek to my right was the chicken wire framework of duck breeding pens.

In an old sink sunk into the ground to provide a drinking trough were a dozen or so tilapia of ideal size which I took for bait. However unbeknown to me they were observed and fed daily by an old boy from the village who had been paid a pittance for many years, via a UK account, to look after the entire swamp complex. Now it is a posh marina – a fishing swamp no longer. But then, in 1969, it became my favourite tarpon location once I had the approval of its curator. Every so often I bribed him with a fish for his supper, and he finally forgave me for taking his family of tilapia to use as livebaits.

It was at this time I purchased and learnt to use a cast net which procured enough tilapia for bait in mere minutes. I also made fish traps from one-inch diameter chicken wire that I baited with bread scraps and lowered into several of the dykes close to our beach house. Thus I was never short of bait.

The water in the swamp was never more than four feet deep or less than two feet, being connected to the ocean via drainage locks, and was always gin clear. Due to their extreme caution in such clear, open water I could only catch tarpon by carefully stalking (carp-fishing fashion) through the reeds. As soon as a group of fish came patrolling round I offered a six-inch tilapia on a small treble to 2ft of 18lb wire, reel line being 12lb on my battered old Mitchell 300 on a 10ft carp rod. When the lead fish saw or sensed the bait it would make a beeline for it, sometimes engulfing the fish in those huge jaws and occasionally even batting the bait right out of the water and grabbing it in mid air. They really are the greatest acrobats among fishes and quite unpredictable. Tarpon can twist, somersault, swap ends, leap while running and run hard whilst leaping. They make the most agile trout look positively senile. They can wallow in shallow water like a bream, run faster than a tope, hit a livebait harder than any bass but sometimes – and thank goodness it is only sometimes – they can be as discerning over a fly or an artificial lure as the salmon.

I have had them jump high into bankside trees, go crashing through the branches and make off the other side with a free line. One good fish, I remember, actually jumped out on to a hard bank and snapped the line over a rock as it jumped back in again. There are even stories of huge tarpon – which can weigh anything up to 300lb – jumping into the boat on top of the angler playing them; and, in two known incidents, actually killing the angler in the process. I can well believe it!

Tarpon are members of the 'bony' fishes family to which the herring is related and perhaps the best way to describe one would be to imagine a colossal herring, or better still a six-foot-long bleak. They are deep bodied, with compressed flanks covered in vast silver scales just like a mahseer. (It is customary in fact, should a scale come adrift, for the angler to write on it the fish's weight and date of capture, once dried between the pages of a book. Incidentally, I would put these two species at the top of my all-time best fighting fish list, with mahseer first and tarpon second – although perhaps I am being unfair to the tarpon for I have yet to catch one in flowing water.) Tarpon are also equipped with large, extremely powerful fins and a huge extendible bony mouth which, together with very abrasive jaw hinges, makes hooking them extremely difficult.

It is a great pity that tarpon are such warm water lovers and could not tolerate our colder climate, for they would suit the beachcaster, the boat angler, the salmon spinner, the fly-fishing fraternity and the livebaiter. They are just about every fresh and saltwater fisherman's dream fish rolled into one. Mind you, it's perhaps just as well we haven't got them in our waters. Who'd fish for salmon?

Though I accounted for snook to around ten pounds and tarpon to over forty pounds from the swamp, I soon realized that to contact those fifty-pound-plus tarpon I would need to leave the swamps – interesting though they were – and fish in the ocean proper. Due to the shallow, incredibly clear water this necessitated fishing from the beach at night despite irritating bites from sandflies. I smoked in those days however, which usually kept them under control. But from the sand jiggers there was no respite. These tiny burrowing worms lived in the dead sand just above high-water mark and all too easily penetrated your feet. You could even follow their route around your foot by a fine white line just beneath the skin. Usually a hatchet job with a razor blade had the desired effect. Even so I still had a jigger in my big toe when we returned to the UK – but it didn't last in our colder climate.

When fishing at the top of the highest spring tides I usually found a pod or two of nomadic big tarpon working close inshore. But when one came along – just like my first encounter in the swamp – it was really more by chance and it happened most unexpectedly. One evening I was concentrating my efforts on stingrays using a whole, fresh flying fish (cheaply bought from the markets). I lobbed fifty yards into a gulley between two reefs at Discovery Bay Hotel which was as far as my metal-spooled Penn Delmar would allow with 18lb line without overruns and with just a one-ounce bomb to hold the bottom (there are no real tide problems inshore in the Caribbean). Having taken stingrays on this set-up to over a hundred pounds a few weeks before, I felt

confident of beaching almost anything. It was surprising what the average British reverse-taper beachcaster (popular at that time due to the lay-back casting technique developed by shore-fishing guru Leslie Moncrieff back in the sixties) could handle.

Then I hit into something which ran and ran and ran, and then jumped high into the air. I could see its shape caught by the hotel spotlights which shone out over the bay and at once I knew it was a really big tarpon – perhaps 150lb plus. Unfortunately I never stood a chance with that fish and after just two more jumps I reeled in a frayed 50lb wire trace. So up in strength went the trace wire to 80lb (cabled) and I swapped the Penn Delmar for a Long Beach 67 holding 350 yards of 28lb mono, still keeping my 12ft reverse-taper 'Dungeness Special'. Being a keen spear fisherman I speared fresh squid and octopus (tarpon delicacies) a few hours before dark and swam out to place them in the sandy gulley for the tarpon to find (little tides, remember). Few other predators would take these free baits except tarpon and stingrays because I fished midway between the two reefs and nuisance fish like moray eels and lobsters rarely left the reefs, even at night. I found the fairly high spring tides most productive (if you can call a rise and fall of around five feet high) and usually at high water, which gave me a depth of about nine feet where the bait was lying, I expected runs!

Perhaps 'run' is the wrong word to use. I know how hard tarpon hit a plug, or a big streamer fly like they use in the Florida Keys, but they pick up a deadbait like it is the only one left in the sea. If you connected your hook to a speedboat you might understand the velocity of the take. Unfortunately you always lose far more than you land. In fact in two and a half years of serious big tarpon fishing from the beach at night I had more than sixty good runs, hooked into about forty for a few seconds (and occasionally for a little longer) and beached the grand total of three! The best was pushing a hundred pounds but I lost several fish of twice the size. One such fish caught me off balance as I ran back up the beach to keep in contact as it sped towards the shore. It suddenly changed direction and made for the horizon, dragging me down on to the sand. Can you imagine anybody being towed on his belly through the sand whilst trying frantically to release the drag, with the sickening sight of a two-hundred-pound tarpon leaping away on the end of his line some one hundred yards away? I soon learned to accept such times as part of the crazy world of tarpon fishing.

Earlier I mentioned stingrays, for which the warm shallow beaches along the west coast of Barbados were a real haven. Although I haven't sought stingrays since I left the West Indies nearly thirty years ago, I was once a stingray fanatic. I am therefore a little puzzled why the British record stingray of 68¼lb has not been increased substantially, as the same species in the Mediterranean reaches weights of around 500lb. I cannot accept that only small stingers frequent our coastal waters and I rather suspect that the main reason for hundred-pound-plus stingrays not being caught is because they are simply not landed. They are most certainly hooked, if all the stories you hear of immovable, unstoppable fish from beach anglers – who had their reels stripped of every yard of line before parting company – are true.

OPPOSITE The sandy bays between coral reefs along the west coast attracted big stingrays which I caught at night to over 200lb. This one weighed 110lb and was beaten following an hour-long battle on my reverse taper beachcaster.

Such encounters are invariably attributed to seals or oversize tope, conger or even sharks. An argument against the presence of large stingrays might be put forward on behalf of the charter and keen offshore boat anglers. They would expect to encounter the odd big one among their usual thornback and tope hauls, especially on the generally heavier gear used for boat work and where running out of line like the shore men is a rare event. However, as stingrays in general prefer quite shallow water over a sandy bottom, which is not the usual boat angler's choice when he leaves harbour, it is hardly surprising that few big rays are taken offshore. Unless of course someone has been keeping very quiet! No, big stingrays are certainly present around our shallow coastlines and I predict that if enough thinking anglers seek them out on gear sound and man enough to beach something of seventy to eighty pounds plus, the present 68¼lb record could be obliterated.

There are actually two separate species of ray to be caught around British shores although both are considered to be sub-tropical and tropical species. The first, *Dasyatis pastinaca*, is usually called the plain stingray and is the most commonly caught Atlantic stingray. It is of a uniform shape following, if anything, the thornback lines, but in complete contrast to the thornback it is immensely thick in the body (at least twice as thick as any other ray) and has a long, thickish tail. Its back colouring can range from grey-green to brown (depending on the ground over which it is caught) whilst underneath it is a dirty shade of pale grey. There are a few denticles along its mid back travelling towards the tail, and here, halfway along, lies the lethal serrated spine or sting. The *Myliobatis aquila*, or eagle ray as it is frequently called, differs vastly in its appearance from the plain stingray. This ray has a pronounced hump-shaped head and long triangular wings, which in fact render it almost a miniature copy of the giant manta ray of the family *Mobulidae*. But here the similarity ends, for whilst the manta is a plankton eater, the eagle ray, being true of all stingrays, is a flesh and crustacean muncher. Coloration is generally on the dark side and there are often many lightish flecks or spots over the wings. A tiny dorsal fin is situated at the junction between tail and body and immediately below this protrudes the sting, which is a rather weak affair considering its location compared to most species of stingrays. The tail is very long and quite round, rather like a whip.

The sting, which can cause acute pain accompanied by hallucinations and possibly temporary paralysis, is a hard, porous, stiletto-shape bone projection covered in a dark, jelly-like poisonous secretion. This bevelled spine has mini serrations along both edges which are actually barbs that grow downwards towards the base where it is literally part of the tail. These would make the sting's removal from a victim excruciatingly painful and would cause much flesh-tearing, but the sting itself is rarely left behind. Usually only the poisonous jelly remains.

The truth is that few sea anglers outside Europe really consider fish like congers and rays worth catching. Or rather, I should say the International Game Fishing Association (IGFA), based and organized in the United States, does not consider them game enough. Why anybody worries about claiming records from the IGFA, which is geared just about one hundred per cent to accepting fish only found off the USA coastline as worthy adversaries and everything else to be just trash fish, amazes me. (British Record Fish Committee, please note: you are not the only record body to be knocked.) However there are a few Americans who show a little interest in the stingray. Down in Florida, for instance, where they hunt them across the shallow flats with bow and arrow. Who knows, perhaps they have bow-and-arrow records for rays! But catching rays by this method has nothing on how a friend of mine once beat one. Have you ever heard of a stingray landed by a Mini-Moke? Then read on.

It was during our stay in Barbados that a friend of mine, George Lyons, an American who owned a scenic water-front property near Bridgetown, invented a unique way of long-lining stingrays from his patio which overlooked a beautiful clear-water shallow bay. Day and night George always had a handline over the patio wall baited with a whole dead flying-fish for anything that happened along and as the depth alongside the wall was usually between six and eight feet (little tide drop in the Caribbean, remember) almost everything did. We occasionally saw a pair of eyes which we took to be sharks and once a huge manta ray flung itself clear of the surface just a hundred yards out from the house. It was at a party round at George's however that I first found out about his craving for handlining.

A crowd of friends was gathered on the patio in the warm evening air, talking quietly over the local rum cocktails, when all of a sudden the drinks table lurched forward a foot or so and then went careering across the patio and nearly over the wall before there was a loud 'crack' somewhere out in the ocean. George went charging after the runaway table, swearing about losing another ray. This was the point where I joined in the hunt, becoming firm friends with George as soon as I mentioned my mania for catching stingrays from the beach at night, only half a mile down the coast from his beach house.

From that moment on Barbara and I were weekly guests of George in a sort of drinking-cum-stingray-fishing way, and week by week George increased his tackle strength from a 200lb handline to a huge drum of nylon cord with a breaking strain of 750lb to which was added twenty feet of 500lb cable laid wire and an 8/0 hook, should a fish reach the reef before he could slow it down. For several evenings it seemed that every stingray (attracted to George's bait by a wicker basket full of rotten flying-fish rubby-dubby slung over the wall into the sea) must at some time or another have been hooked and lost. It appeared that even sea fish learn not to repeat their mistakes and the only action for quite a while was my being bitten by a large centipede whilst sitting on the patio wall waiting for a run. Within minutes my left leg started to feel very warm indeed and blew up to at least one-third larger, but George came quickly to the rescue with half a bottle of whisky which he poured over the bite. What a waste! Anyhow it had the desired effect and within a few hours my leg resumed its usual size, so we carried on the long wait. (Incidentally, having been bitten twice by scorpions in India whilst mahseer fishing, it's worth mentioning that the bite of a centipede is far more painful. Both, however, are not recommended – believe me.)

George had the most unusual arrangement of bite detection in the form of two empty tin cans tied on the line and resting on the patio wall. (He discarded his table idea after nearly losing it.) Above these were more cans as the line swept upwards over a pulley which was rawl-plugged into the wall just below the bedroom window on road level, high above the patio. Then the line ran around another pulley below the adjacent garage and finally disappeared through a drain pipe to be tied to the bumper bar of his Mini-Moke.

This probably sounds like the best cock-and-bull story you have ever heard but I swear that it is all perfectly true. There were several yards of slack line from bait to bumper bar used in the hope that a ray would hook itself and be stopped when it had straightened out the line. Funnily enough George was right, and late one evening the phone rang and an excited voice blurted out that a ray had been landed – or driven perhaps. For when I arrived at George's the following morning after breakfast there, dangling from the garage wall, was his first stingray – a female of about 160lb.

A few weeks afterwards while night fishing, I landed an even larger ray – which I estimated at over 200lb – from my favourite sandy beach behind Discovery Bay Hotel. Fortunately it had sucked up the fresh flying-fish bait on my whopper-stopper rod – Penn 9/0 reel outfit loaded with 80lb test and it took a good forty-five minutes to subdue. Small wonder a ray of similar size cannot be handled on a standard British beach outfit. Its power was phenomenal, even without any appreciable tide to help. It was so immensely thick, a good twenty inches or more, with a pair of substantial

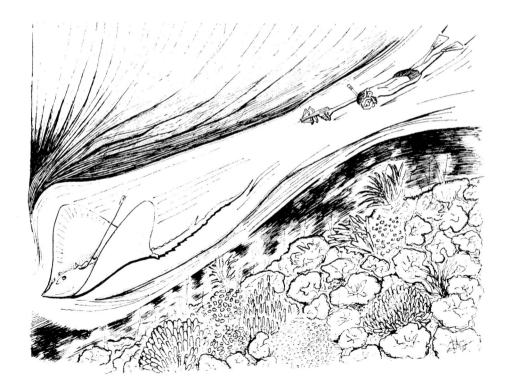

serrated bone stings halfway along its tail, and after a few photos I dragged it back into the gentle surf. I did in fact hook into a much larger, far more powerful creature one evening but I rather think it was a big shark.

Holiday-makers were known to go skinny dipping at the very spot where I placed my bait (in just five feet of water) once they were full of rum cocktails and in partying mood following a late dinner. They were obviously completely unaware of the dangers. How no one was ever ravaged whilst bathing after dark along the west coast amazes me.

Anyway, I stuck into what I thought initially to be a big ray. This monster – whatever it was – had not the slightest intention of slowing down against a firmly set clutch with fully two hundred yards of line gone from the reel. It never jumped, which ruled out a big tarpon, and simply kept on heading out to sea against everything I piled on, in long powerful surges. There was simply no way I could slow it down and I guess the end was inevitable. When it reached the first large coral reef with over a quarter of a mile of 80lb line on the 9/0 now gone and just a few turns remaining, two things happened in quick succession. The hardwood rod handle snapped just below the reel and a split second later (otherwise I would have lost the lot and been left with a stump) the 80lb monofilament severed over the reef. The word 'awesome' simply cannot describe the power of that huge fish which could only have been a very large shark – probably a tiger shark, the predominant big boys throughout the West Indies.

There is a rather gruesome postscript to this encounter which came about through my love of spear fishing along the west coast. In fact there was hardly a day for the best part of three years when I didn't spend at least two or three hours exploring the colourful coral reefs either directly in front of our cottage or out from the Holiday Inn Hotel near Bridgetown, where I ran the hairdressing salon. Apart from the occasional local client there was little to do until around three in the afternoon when the ladies started to leave the beach or pool and have their hair done in readiness for the evening entertainment. So Wilson made the most of the best job he had ever had by skin-diving and returning with spear-caught squid, octopus and lobsters.

I made the mistake of spearing a big stingray once, which actually towed me for some distance over the reefs into a deep blue void. So discretion being the better part of valour, I let go of the spear gun. On another occasion, probably the closest shave of all – and I have experienced a few – I nearly drowned through spearing a big moray eel that lived in a huge clump of brain coral. Unfortunately the spear went through both eel and coral and so I dived down to unscrew the removable head in order to pull the shaft free. Trouble was I needed to come up for a gulp of air midway through due to the tight fitting spear head. However when my head was within just a foot or so of the surface, my ascent was stopped abruptly. Looking down I could see that the strong nylon cord connecting spear gun to the eel and clump of brain coral had somehow knotted around one ankle. I carried no knife then, so at the point when my lungs were about to burst and craving for air, I had to exhale and dive down to undo it. The very next day I went out and purchased the best diving knife I could find.

One of my regular diving companions was a local Bajan of around my own age called Frank who worked as maitre d' at Discovery Bay Hotel where Barbara ran the hairdressers. He was so fit he could free dive and sit on a clump of coral fifteen to twenty feet down on the sea floor and actually wait for up to a minute for a grouper or parrotfish to come out of its hole, while I trod water above wondering how on earth he could hold his breath for so long. When diving alone Frank's little terrier would follow him along the beach as he methodically worked his way through various routes in the never-ending maze of coral reefs, spearing rockhind, trigger fish, lobsters and octopus for the pot.

Then one afternoon, only two days after I had lost the huge shark and just an hour or so before Frank was due to put on his tuxedo for the evening's restaurant duties, he did not return when expected. His wife went down to the beach and found their terrier standing rooted to the spot, looking out to sea and whining continually.

At this point I must say there was another factor to consider. A lot of quarrying was done on the island to produce blocks of white coral stone for building, and as a result far too many people had access to explosives. It was common knowledge that indiscriminate poachers used explosives to obtain basketfuls of marketable reef fishes. In fact inshore sport with sizeable reef fishes was virtually non-existent all along the west coast due to years of constant dynamiting – hence my preferring to fish after dark when big fish ventured close into shore.

Was the fact that Frank could stay so long underwater the very cause of his disappearance at the hands of indiscriminate fish poachers? They might have thought the area was clear of witnesses when they threw in their detonators. And if so, surely they must then have concealed the body. I have already mentioned that there is little tide flow inshore on the west coast, so a body would not drift far overnight. Then again had Frank been unlucky enough to meet the same marauding shark which (as I was later to find out) had been spotted on several occasions within that same week? It was skirting the reefs between Sandy Lane Hotel and the Colony Club – a distance of only a few miles.

By the following morning everyone in the hotel business was aware of Frank's disappearance, and there was soon a police launch from Bridgetown patrolling up and down the west coast. As I knew Frank's route along the local reefs better than anyone I eventually persuaded Trevor, assistant manager to Mike Beckley at Discovery Bay Hotel, to accompany me on a wide search of the area as the police launch had come up with nothing.

Now I am not by any means over glorifying the situation but once we were out there, several hundred yards offshore in water so deep you could hardly make out the coral on the bottom, we were absolutely terrified – we felt completely vulnerable to attack. We only had my one spear gun, a powerful three rubber champion model, but it was no match for a man-eating shark. Initially we covered every route inshore through a network of coral reefs that Frank might have taken. Then we ventured seawards over depths of fifty to sixty feet, but all to no avail.

ABOVE The late
Charles Angelus on
whose sportsfishing
boat I crewed once
a week, with a hard
battling blackjack
caught trolling on
the west coast of
Barbados.

The idea of suddenly coming upon a friend's dismembered body is bad enough, but when you think you could well be the next victim, your nerves get the better of you – believe me. Boy, was I glad when we eventually entered shallow warm water again after two hours of searching. But just before I pulled off my face mask I saw a head rolling about on the sand in the little furrows made by the waves. For a minute I thought I was going to be sick, then reality sank in. It was only a doll's head, and it had blue eyes and blonde hair – nothing at all like Frank! Everything appears around one-third larger than it actually is when viewed through the glass of a diving mask, but for a split second my heart was in my mouth.

I am sad to say there is no happy conclusion to this story, but the incident was hushed up so the tourists didn't become alarmed. Immediately following Frank's disappearance six of us got together for a 'retribution fish in'. We decided to stage an all-night vigil from a thirty-foot yacht owned by one of the hotel managers, moored in forty feet of water a hundred yards offshore from the Colony Club, in the hope of contacting the rogue shark. We rowed out in the yacht's tiny plywood dinghy late in the afternoon complete with my big game outfit, extra-strong commercial long lines, several gallons of fresh blood compliments of Bill the chef at Discovery Bay, and enough food and booze – obligatory in the Caribbean – to last until dawn.

Little happened during the night, other than everybody getting paralytic, and by two o'clock in the morning, having caught nothing but snappers on our light outfits, with not a murmur coming from the shark baits, general opinion was for us to call it a night seeing as all the booze and food were gone. Then the reality of the situation dawned upon us. With so much blood around the yacht, to risk the six of us paddling back in a tiny dinghy with just a few inches of free board was not such a good idea. So we stayed until dawn. The shark was never seen again and neither, I am saddened to say, was my friend Frank. Some said he had just left everything and gone to live on another island. But with the financial security that his job provided, plus a lovely wife and a young son whom he adored, it was most unlikely and completely out of character. In fact nothing of what happened that afternoon ever surfaced, right up until we left the island a year or so later, but I'm convinced a big tiger shark was responsible for Frank's disappearance.

Strangely, something occurred several months later which got me thinking how vulnerable you are when snorkelling alone. A whole group of hairdressers, hotel managers and chefs were larking about on the east coast near Bathsheba on a Sunday, using foam boards to body surf in the strong waves, having taken a barbecue along for the day. I was standing waist deep and laughing at someone falling off their board when suddenly I couldn't breathe. I could neither inhale nor exhale. It was as though my throat was paralysed. I indicated to Barbara to bang my back which she did and eventually, not long before I passed out, I was able to cough, be sick and breathe again. Now had this freak occurrence happened whilst snorkelling over deep water – bingo! I went to the doctor who said that just a single drop of water had hit the tip of my larynx and literally paralysed it. So if it ever happens to you while swimming, get your feet on to firm ground immediately.

In addition to my lunchtime spear-fishing jaunts and at least one weekly night-time fishing vigil from the beach after stingrays and tarpon, I crewed each Thursday on my afternoon off aboard a 42ft sports fishing boat owned by an ex-pat, Charles Angelus, who had settled in Barbados many years before and opened a furniture factory near Bridgetown.

We trolled up and down the west coast following the outer reefs using drone spoons on monal metal line (horrible stuff to fish with but it got the lure down fast and kept it there) in depths of forty to sixty feet and took some good hauls of jacks, plus barracudas and the occasional wahoo. On several occasions we hooked sailfish (and once a small marlin) on flying-fish presented away from the boat on outriggers but for various reasons we never landed any. In fact it was always a joke at parties that Wilson seemed to catch bigger fish from the beach than when out in Charles's expensively imported sports fishing cruiser. And the truth was they were right!

Daily life on the island at the end of the swinging 60s was, I suppose, as close as you could get to the perfect existence. By then Barbados had the best infrastructure of all the Caribbean islands. It was the place to be seen. We ate extremely well and drank a great deal, we played hard and we received invites to all the best parties going. Hosts usually incorporated grass into some of the dishes, so we couldn't help having a great time, and quite often various celebrities of the day would show up. These included people like the late Natalie Wood, and the late Oliver Reed, plus David Bailey, who at that time was producing some unusual photography for *Vogue* and *Tatler* magazines with the help of an equally unusual-looking model, Penelope Tree. Being fashion hair stylists, Barbara and I were in the thick of it and enjoying our life tremendously. Barbados then was indeed the up-and-coming island, still with an old-fashioned charm all of its own. It is certainly different today.

A Tropical Start

After a while we thought about starting a family and began looking at life on the island of Barbados as a permanent thing. Returning to the cold winters of Britain was not appealing at all. Though eventually, and it seems strange now, I know, but heading up towards when we finally left I used to crave a pint of cold milk (no fresh milk on the island) and really missed the seasons.

With her first pregnancy Barbara unfortunately miscarried at five months. However after much rest, life carried on and a year later on 28 October 1970 our son, Lee Stephen Wilson, was born. I still remember sitting up all night in the waiting room listening to the wailing and screams of several dozen local women (I was the only husband there) until one of the nurses suggested I rest on a spare bed until they called me.

At sometime between three and four in the morning I was woken up, told to put on a green gown and face mask and led into the delivery room. My instant reaction was 'I don't want to be here'. Ultimately the whole experience was and remains one of the most wonderful moments in my life.

With a family now started Barbara and I were considering investing in a plot of land and having a house built, preferably on the beach overlooking the sea, just like our little rented cottage. Our boss, John Stuart, had hinted he would like us to think about a partnership and our future on the island seemed to have a ring of permanency about it. But within a short space of time two events were to change the way we felt about settling down in paradise.

The first was when I picked up the phone in the salon one morning to take what I thought was a hairdressing appointment. The male caller said, 'Is that John Wilson?' and I replied 'Yes'. He then said in a flat tone, 'I'm going to put a bullet through your head' and then put the phone down. Instantly the hairs on the back of my neck stood up and that cold sweat feeling of fear came over me. It obviously wasn't a joke and I discussed the situation with John Stuart who immediately called the police. Following a few sleepless nights and days of constantly looking over my shoulder, the call was traced back by the police to the disgruntled boyfriend of one of our female staff, a girl whom I had had the displeasure of sacking only a couple of weeks before because she was stealing.

This event quickly blew over however and life returned to normal. But then something happened which instantly made our minds up about returning to Britain

OPPOSITE Dragging a huge tarpon back into the sea from St James beach on the west coast of Barbados, where I caught them, took almost as much out of me as playing them.

and deciding against raising our family in Barbados no matter how idyllic life appeared to the holiday-maker. John and Veronica Stuart who owned a superb property on Bamboo Ridge, near Holtown, along with other beautifully designed ex-pat homes, asked Barbara and me if we would move into their house for a few weeks and look after it while they went back to Britain on holiday – which we agreed to do. What they forgot to tell us was that this would be the only occupied house in the entire group of several luxurious designer properties during their absence, everyone having gone back to Britain for their summer holidays whilst trade in their island boutiques, hairdressers and hotels was extremely quiet.

On the second night after moving in, just when we were starting to enjoy the facilities provided by John's cook, Viola, and a house girl who came in for a few hours each day, I suddenly noticed through the dense canopy of trees surrounding the house that the courtesy light in one of the cars had come on. Now I don't know why, but I instinctively felt very uneasy. It was pitch black outside and Barbara and I were in the master bedroom (where John Stuart's safe was installed) which, like all the other spacious rooms, was independent of the lounge and kitchen, being secured with louvre doors and connected only by gravel pathways and mock Spanish wooden screenwork densely overgrown with tropical palms and vines.

As no one ever locked their cars on the islands (the furthest a thief could go was twenty-five miles) I wasn't worried about the car being stolen but word had obviously been passed around – possibly via one of the house servants – that we were alone with all the week's takings from the hairdressing salons and boutiques in the house. Quickly I locked the four louvre doors and then the phone rang. Barbara answered and by the look on her face it was an obscene caller – who wouldn't hang up. This was obviously a ploy to keep us occupied because while Barbara was lying back on the bed trembling with fear and totally incoherent, I could make out the noise of several feet walking around the bedroom towards the louvre doors. I tried slapping Barbara's face to bring her back to reality but it was no use. I picked up the phone and could understand why she had entered into a nervous stupor. The guy at the other end had no intention of stopping his foul-mouth intentions nor of putting the phone down which would allow me to ring the police. I was on my own. I even feel shivery now, thirty years on from that night, just writing about it.

I sat on the end of the large double bed sick with fear, tingling with pure adrenaline with my powerful three rubber champion spear gun loaded. What was going round in my head at the point was that I was going to take the first bastard out regardless, knowing full well that afterwards I could have been killed and Barbara most certainly raped, not to mention what could have happened to our newborn son, Lee, who was fast asleep in his cot. For what seemed like an eternity, though it could have been no more than a minute or so – during which time I could see in the light from the patio eyes peering up at me through the lower half of those flimsy louvre doors – it was as though our idyllic world stood still. I could hear much shuffling about and low murmuring whispers but I couldn't make out what they were saying. I expected the

doors to be kicked in at any moment. And then, as if by some miracle, the dark menacing figures melted slowly away into the humid night air and we were left with just the sound of the crickets. Perhaps they saw my spear gun and didn't fancy four feet of quarter-inch steel through their gut after all. I tried the phone again. Now it was free and within minutes we saw the headlights of two police cars racing up Bamboo Ridge towards the house.

Whoever they were, they were never caught. But they convinced me of one thing – that we should return to England. Barbara and I together with our son, Lee, now just six months old, were going home. Consequently it wasn't long before I wrote to John (Jinx) Davey back in East Anglia (I had kept in touch with him throughout my years abroad both in the Merchant Navy and whilst in the West Indies) asking him to send me the local Norfolk and Suffolk newspapers. Barbara and I had discussed whether we should sink our savings into a hairdressing salon when we returned home, or a fishing tackle shop which had been my life's ambition. As Barbara would be restricted at home for some while (we wanted more children) and I really didn't fancy being a hairdresser for much longer, a tackle shop it was – preferably somewhere in Norfolk where property was still affordable and where I had enjoyed such wonderful roach fishing during my late teens.

Week after week of thumbing through Norfolk and Suffolk papers, kindly sent out by Jinx, produced just one possibility: an old existing tackle shop in Bridewell Alley in the middle of Norwich run for thirty years by the late Bill Cooper. Unfortunately it had also been run right down and there was little stock left because Bill was about to lease it out (he owned the freehold) to a delicatessen. This transaction could only be halted by my cheque to put down a deposit by post from Barbados. Bill, bless him, obviously wanted it to remain a tackle shop and I figured that he couldn't have been losing money for thirty years. So off went the cheque and we booked our flight home. We had purchased our first business, site unseen. I wouldn't want to do that now, but I was just twenty-eight, and the thought of failure didn't even enter my mind.

During those last few weeks prior to our leaving the island, many of our friends made during the previous three years wanted to take us out for farewell dinners. The trouble was I suddenly started to suffer chronic stomach pains and so we could not take anyone up on their kindness. My doctor said it was nerves. I thought it was far more serious than that, but he was obviously right because once on the plane I suffered no more.

John and Veronica Stuart, who had been both employers and wonderful friends, came round to the cottage early on the morning of our departure with a gift of a cine camera. I still have the footage John shot of my last walk along the beach dipping six-month-old Lee in and out of the waves. Many years have passed since that walk and now he is the exact age I was then, six foot two inches tall and fifteen stone of muscle due to his sport of bodybuilding.

I can remember our homecoming extremely well for two reasons. We were met by Mum, Dad and brother Dave at Heathrow and I asked to drive Dad's Morris Traveller home. It promptly stuck in first gear at the first set of traffic lights. 'What did you rest your hand on the lever for?' said Dad, as if I was to know about his car's peculiarities! So we drove the entire way home to Enfield in north London in first gear. How strange it was to be back in the old country again. The first thing I did at Mum and Dad's was down two pints of milk straight from the fridge.

BELOW This shop at 18A Bridewell Alley may well have been the most narrow in Norwich, but it was my beginning as a tackle dealer.

The second event came two days later when, having purchased a second-hand Mini van, Barbara and I drove to Norwich. As we walked slowly up Bridewell Alley the shops seemed to be getting narrower and narrower. And there it was, Bill Cooper's (or rather our) tackle shop. The width of a London cigarette kiosk. It was tiny. I think, had we not put money down, we would have happily walked away there and then but while we were wondering what we had let ourselves in for Bill's wife, Terry, came from behind the counter and said, 'You must be John and Barbara Wilson.' She put the kettle on and in a very short space of time, judging by the number of customers asking to purchase items which weren't in stock, I realized that we were going to be able to make a success of it. If you stood in the middle of the incredibly narrow sales area (which is now a cake shop) and stretched out both arms, you could touch both walls, honestly. But it was our first stab at the retail trade and I was going to make it work, though what happened when we took over the shop two weeks later made me wish I had never got involved. After paying the deposit of a month's rent on a small terraced cottage along the Aylsham Road (which is now Smarts Auto Parts), we had slightly less than £2,000 left to purchase the goodwill and what stock Bill had left, which was not a lot. To say money was tight was indeed an understatement. In fact, during those first few months, I can remember actually covering a dozen of the tall, round maggot tins with wallpaper to form supports for chipboard (also covered in wallpaper) to make bookshelves for an alcove in our cottage.

So now for my favourite maggot story. Late Friday afternoon before our first Saturday of business, I took delivery of sixteen gallons of both coloured and white maggots in sawdust. Bill said I probably didn't need anywhere near that many but the last thing I wanted in a new business was to refuse custom. So they were all taken out back to the coolness of a stone floor where Bill said they should be fine until the morning (he only had a small fridge anyway). OK, so I know it was the first week in July and I should have known better, but I didn't. Next morning I arrived early at the shop – now called John's Tackle Den – at around half past eight and eagerly unlocked the door in readiness for what I hoped would be a busy Saturday. I immediately caught sight of a couple of maggots on the floor as I switched the light on, followed by another and another as I walked through the shop. Before I had time to go out the back to see if many more had escaped there was a loud banging on the thinly partitioned wall and an angry voice from the barber's shop next door. Bill, the barber, had seemed such an amiable fellow when Bill Cooper introduced me to him only a few days earlier, but as I opened his front door he was like a man possessed. 'Look at this place,' he screamed at the top of his voice. 'I've never had anything like this

before. I'm getting the public health people in to sort you out.' Great, I thought, though he did have a point. There were maggots everywhere – big time. In fact probably the greater part of my sixteen gallons were now the wrong side of the partitioned wall which was constructed from tongue-and-groove planking. (Apparently the two shops had been one many years back and the carpenter hadn't been too bothered about ensuring a tight fit with the floor.)

There were maggots in Bill's soap dishes, in his gowns and towels, in his shaving mugs and between magazines. They were coming out of his shampoo nozzle and the floor was one seething, wriggling carpet of white, red and yellow. (Bronze maggots weren't popular as yet!) As maggots always travel towards the light and Bill had left a bulb on overnight, he virtually had the lot. I rushed back into my shop and ran outside to the sixteen tins. All were empty save for foul-smelling froth all down the sides, proving conclusively that maggots can easily climb vertical sides once they start to sweat in their own juices. Talk about a stink of ammonia!

Fortunately I managed to calm Bill down after a while and stop him from ringing the environmental health people. I think the mention of a free rod and reel did the trick (him being an angler too) and I set about the task with dustpan and brush of reclaiming my maggots. I actually recovered less than half of the sixteen gallons, and boy, were there some wonderful hatches over the following weeks.

Only a few weeks after this Bill Cooper popped into the shop to see how I was getting on and to collect some old things he had left in the shop's attic. 'Terry's asked me to take her mother's china home,' said Bill and without more ado climbed the narrow stairs. Now I just knew there was going to be a problem because during the weeks in between, friend Jinx had come up to Norwich to look over the shop. While rummaging through a load of junk in the attic (which I had naturally assumed was mine to dispose of), we came across a stack of old blue patterned plates and jugs. Jinx asked if he could have them for his front garden wall, a mammoth project started by his father: two feet thick and completely fronting their large roadside property in Bungay (friends actually referred to it as the Bungay Wall). This wall incorporated all sorts of strange building materials such as flowerpots, pipes, sinks, even old loos, and crockery. Once it was grown over by rockery plants like aubretia it looked attractively different.

Bill came almost running down the stairs with a look of horror on his face. 'Where's all that china gone to, John? It was in that old galvanized bath. It belonged to Terry's mother and it's priceless.' 'Oh dear,' I said, 'I am afraid it's now in the Bungay Wall.' Bill, I am afraid, never really saw the funny side of the story. Nevertheless his influence and good will of running the shop in Norwich for three decades were of enormous help in those early years. I never guessed then, however, that I would be a tackle dealer for almost as long.

With the help of a few friends, I organized a kids' fishing match along the River Wensum in the middle of Norwich, and with just a couple of small ads in the local paper, I arrived at Foundry Road bridge opposite the railway station to find over two hundred young anglers eagerly awaiting the match. How I wish it could be the same

today. But with the wealth of televized and computerized distractions at their disposal, small wonder only a small proportion of today's youngsters get to experience the joy of angling, which is rather sad.

With every penny ploughed back into stock (so extensive advertising was out) I set about making a name for myself by catching specimen fish, which I hoped would draw fresh custom into the shop. I revisited many parts of my old stomping ground along the intimate, roach-rich parts of the Upper Waveney around Bungay that were so productive during the late 1950s. I hoped that things hadn't changed too much and I was excited at the prospect of using light float-fishing tackle again. I was disappointed to find that certain favourite swims had visibly shrunk in both width and depth, as I have described earlier, but others were thankfully as prolific as ever. I quickly familiarized myself with the bream again along the two-mile reach between Wainford Maltings and Ellingham, taking some fine hauls with specimens to over seven pounds – big bream in those days.

By walking the Waveney's clear-flowing upper reaches extensively that first summer we were back and searching for roach shoals through Polaroid glasses, I was able to pinpoint the whereabouts of numerous shoals of quality fish, each of which contained specimens to over two pounds. I then set about catching them on trotting tackle during the winter months, capturing several beauties, the best scaling 2lb 7oz. This opened up opportunities of writing about my exploits both in the local paper, the *Eastern Evening News*, and in the *Angler's Mail*, which had in fact published a story I sent whilst in Barbados called 'Stingrays in the Moonlight'.

At around the same time Jarrold Publishing, which is based in Norwich, enquired whether I should like to bring up to date a 'where to fish guide' written by Bill Cooper and now hopelessly out of date. I agreed on the condition that I would write a totally new book complete with photos and diagrams. So that's how a Londoner came to write his first book with the imaginative title *Where to Fish in Norfolk and Suffolk*. I really worked at that book. At weekends and before opening the shop, I visited and photographed everywhere I wrote about. I literally walked all the upper reaches of my local rivers – the Tas, Tud, Wensum, Yare, Bure and Waveney – from source to their tidal reaches and fished as many meres, lakes, gravel pits and Broads as I could. I wore Barbara's patience and tolerance down to the bone, often leaving her and young Lee alone for long periods each Sunday in order to gather the information required for the book. Friends like Bill Cooper and Nobby Clarke of Norwich, now both sadly gone, and my old mate Terry Houseago of Dereham helped enormously on local issues and, when seeking details about fisheries deep in Suffolk, George Alderson and Len Head came to the rescue in addition to Jinx Davey.

Eventually many local anglers who had probably jeered behind my back when I first arrived on the scene, started coming into the shop and asked me where to fish. I felt that I had indeed arrived. That same book has now been in print for twenty-seven years. It has been updated and reprinted five times. It must be one of the longest-surviving angling books in the UK.

Once settled in Norfolk, with the shop doing well, we managed to obtain a house mortgage. I borrowed the deposit off Dad, and Barbara and I left the cottage for our own property, a detached three-bedroomed bungalow (costing just £6,500, which seems ridiculous now) in Taverham, a nice little village on the point of expanding (it has now fully exploded) on the outskirts of Norwich, just six miles west of the city.

RIGHT Start 'em young, that's what I say. A recent (1999) photo of my daughter, Lisa, and granddaughter, Alisha, and me, enjoying the rudd fishing on our own lakes in Norfolk.

Within a year of enjoying my own house at last, with a garden in which I quickly built a pond, Barbara gave birth to our daughter, Lisa. She grew up to become more interested in going fishing with Dad than Lee. Now twenty-five years on I take great pride in taking her own daughter fishing. In fact my four-year-old granddaughter, Alisha, is even more fascinated by water than her mother. So unless either of my children eventually produce a grandson to continue the craze, I'll put all my bets on her. With just a little help from Granddad, Alisha has already caught numerous small roach and rudd on float tackle from our own lakes. She is absolutely mustard.

Unfortunately I made the cardinal mistake when taking young Lee fishing in allowing him to catch the specimen-size roach, bream and tench that I was enjoying at that time. So he virtually bypassed that bent-pin-cum-mystery stage in which I served my apprenticeship amidst the park lakes and brooks of north London. With Dad, Lee for instance actually struck and landed single handedly tench to almost six pounds when only six years old. That was a big tench back in the mid 1970s. I should have weaned him on sticklebacks and two-ounce roach. But so it goes.

It was around this time, the mid 1970s, that another interest became important to me. Allow me to refer back to Barbados for a moment, because it was there that I first became interested in taxidermy. This came about through my spearing really large puffer fish and handing them over to an old lady in the village for preserving. This she did simply by making a slit from throat to vent, removing the insides which, considering their size (between sixteen and twenty-four inches long) amounted to just a handful of guts, and stitching them up again. She then made a cardboard funnel and filled the entire puffer fish up with dry sand through its mouth. This stretched the puffer out to the expanded size it reaches as a defence mechanism against predators. Finally the entire sand-filled fish was sprayed with formalin, to preserve and harden the skin, and hung out in the sun to dry.

About a week or so later the sun had done its work and the sand could be emptied out. And hey presto – you had a unique lampshade complete with puffer fish prickles fully erect. It was taxidermy at its most basic but I was intrigued and bought a book on the ancient art. This resulted in my buying a few of the basic chemicals required and actually setting up some of the weird and wonderful fishes I speared over the coral reefs. These I brought back to the UK and arranged in a display case along with pieces of coloured coral (from Fiji, collected during my two years on SS *Oronsay*) and various sea fans, shells and sea urchins. The arrangement looks down at me from my office wall as I write this and is a wonderful reminder of those exciting three years skin diving the reefs along the west coast of Barbados.

I was so pleased with the result of my Caribbean display that I decided to have a go at freshwater species, my first attempt being a seven-pound zander. This was followed by a pike, then a carp from Redmire that was found dead. I later restored a big pike found virtually falling to bits in someone's damp garage, originally preserved by the famous firm Gunns of Norwich, followed by a brace of unwanted grayling from a chalk stream trout fishery and then a couple of two-and-a-half-pound perch which died through being hooked in deep water. These I found three days after catching and releasing them back into a large clay pit near Newmarket. Had I not returned and come across them dead in the margins I would have sworn they were released none the worse for being caught. I was so concerned that I rang the late Dick Walker, whose catches from the depths of Arlesey Lake during the 1950s were legendary, and asked him if he had ever noticed repeat catches, before sport with the big stripies inexplicably dropped off after just a couple of productive seasons. Dick said no and hinted that he too suspected many he returned could have suffered what scuba divers know as the bends. The fish have excess air in their swim bladder that cannot escape and which can lead to their death unless they are taken immediately back down to the depth at which they were caught.

In recent years I have experienced similar problems with the huge Nile perch inhabiting Lake Nasser in Egypt, where certain fish hooked on the troll in depths of thirty feet or more have 'blown', or 'gassed up', to quote the phrase best used to describe their problem. Using a heavy weight to lower these monsters back down to somewhere approaching the depth at which they were holding has achieved a high success rate, incidentally. Quite how you get big British perch back out into the middle of a deep clay or gravel pit without the use of a boat is another problem. I guess it can only be solved by not fishing for them at great depths in the first place. This brings me back full circle to the brace of perch which I decided to preserve so they were not entirely wasted.

Not for one moment am I suggesting in today's world of catch and release that specimen fish should be killed to be stuffed. There are precious few whoppers to go

RIGHT Here I'm using my original outline and colour notes while painting a 39½lb pike caught from a gravel pit trout fishery at Lyng in Norfolk.

round as it is. A colour photo on the wall can provide equal memories, and the fish like it better too.

However as jumbo-size rainbow and brown trout are now bred in such vast quantities to be caught and killed for the table, no one is going to give you a hard time for preserving the skin of a particularly large or beautifully marked specimen as an art form. Similarly should you come across a well-proportioned, freshly dead specimen of any species that has died through natural causes (everything has to die at some time) what's the harm in having a go at preserving it for others to enjoy? There are several specialist books available covering the fascinating art of taxidermy, and it's surprising just how quickly these new skills can be aquired, particularly for those who are artistically minded and enjoy modelling or painting.

The last fish I preserved was a monstrous 39½lb pike caught locally in the village of Lyng from a then gravel pit trout fishery (now a carp fishery) by an old friend, Dan Leary. I didn't really want to take on the responsibility of such a magnificent specimen but Dan talked me into it nevertheless. Two years later, following goodness knows how many hours of painstaking work, particularly in colouring and constructing the bow-fronted glass case, I felt rather proud finally presenting Dan with his trophy. But it's not something I want to take on ever again.

Around 1973–74 I started writing for the prestigious *Angling* magazine edited by Brian Harris, which was later sold to Burlington Publishing to become *Coarse Fishing Monthly* edited by Sandy Leventon and Bruce Vaughan. Since then Bruce has been one of my best fishing buddies. The same magazine was then sold on to Emap and became *The Coarse Fishing Handbook*, then later *Coarse Fishing Today*. All in all I survived too many editors to name and ended up writing for more or less the same publication (despite its four different titles) for over twenty years when Emap finally stopped the last title in the early 1990s.

But back to those early *Angling* days. The magazine was much loved by traditionalist anglers such as me who enjoyed all three disciplines of game, sea and coarse, plus fishing in foreign parts. In fact some of what I have already mentioned about my exploits in the tropics with stingrays and tarpon appeared within the pages of *Angling*, plus my experiences when scuba diving my local lakes, gravel pits and rivers. Though I had skin dived virtually every day whilst in Barbados, I had in fact never scuba dived before. Then one day Sid Johnson popped into John's Tackle Den to buy a new float rod and happened to ask if I fancied joining him diving for bottles in a few of the local mill pools. Being a commercial diver in the North Sea, Sid was a great teacher and I soon became fascinated by being able to appreciate many of my local clear-water fisheries from a sub-surface viewpoint.

Sid and I quickly became firm friends, as we are to this day, and we dived regularly together during the summer months for over ten years. Initially I borrowed one of his old neoprene wet suits, but once the bug had got a hold I bought my own single-phase demand valve, an aluminium bottle and a lead belt. I even decided to make my own wet suit.

A company in Southampton specialized in DIY wet suits made from top-quality 6mm neoprene and cut the required pieces exactly to fit, once body dimensions had been measured and sent off. All I had to do when a parcel full of numbered pieces arrived two weeks later was glue them all together and then glue yellow tape over and along each join. Everything was provided including several heavy duty zips plus a large screw-top tin of black, evil-smelling adhesive. I can remember Barbara saying,

'You're not going to do that in the middle of the carpet are you?' But I was. Besides, I had spread several old newspapers all around the lounge over which I laid all the numbered parts. It was kind of like painting by numbers really and I soon had my new wet suit resplendent with a rich red lining taking shape. You simply butted the two edges together after coating them in adhesive and then left them for a minute until almost dry. Then you couldn't pull them apart. I took great care in assembling the wet suit and finally adding the yellow (easy to see under water) tape over each join.

I was almost on the home straight with just a few lengths of yellow tape left to glue on, when I accidentally knocked over the tin of adhesive. I looked round in horror to see a football-size patch of black Evo-Stik slowly spreading out even further over the gold-coloured carpet. Barbara was not a happy bunny.

With my new DIY wet suit complete, and not a bad fit, I was raring to go. As a specimen hunter opting then to study the quarry from beneath the surface whilst scuba diving in addition to bankside fish spotting, I was often asked how diving could help to catch more and larger fish. The obvious answer, of course, was that within a short dive it's possible to assess the potential of most small waters fairly accurately, providing visibility is good. However seeing and even being able to touch, say, a three-pound roach in the water bears no comparison with putting that same fish on the bank via a baited hook. Yet many people are under the impression that if you have located a big fish under the surface, catching it is a mere formality. I wish!

Actually I was often amazed whilst diving a section of river which, from bankside experiences, I thought I knew well, that there were far fewer fish around than I had imagined. This is a common occurrence, because we all prefer to believe there are far more, and far larger, fish in a water than have ever come out of it on rod and line. It's part of our inherent eternal optimism as anglers. Yet it's surprising how much water (and this applies to most fisheries) is, for the most part, totally barren of fish. We nearly always assume fish are 'off' the feed when a biteless session occurs but the reality is that they are often simply just not there. Miniature, shallow, weedy rivers are probably among the few exceptions and, to the square foot of water, invariably contain a larger proportion of specimen fish than any other type of water.

After diving dozens of my favourite swims at varying times throughout a period of over ten years I was surprised on just a very few occasions. The surprises were usually fish which shouldn't have been there, like a double-figure brown trout in a pike hot spot, perhaps finding plenty of crayfish in a tidal river, or the sheer number of eels in a big weir pool which would reach a bait long before the tiny percentage of specimens present. This was a real eye-opener which swayed my attention from rivers as potential big eel locations.

Understanding the fish's silent underwater world from its own point of view with regard to fluctuations of water flow, displacement of silt throughout the year, gravel bars, weeds, snags and predators is the reward when diving. Furthermore you can choose angling tactics accordingly and decide where a bait should be placed for optimum results.

When seen from the bankside, surface movement – especially that of running water where much of my diving was done – can be very misleading. You may often pass by a boiling or turbulent swim, such as weir hatches and sluices, and overshoot pools, simply because the surface deviations suggest the current is far too powerful to hold fish or to present the tackle easily. Yet immediately you dive a few feet below the 'white water' visibility increases and in nearly all cases – particularly if there is a goodish depth below – the current is quite slow, providing a larder for both the fish and the food they eat. With a little more forethought all but the most turbulent of swims may be fished, provided you present enough line over-depth to allow the bait and lead to rest on the bottom of the hole, while the float (capped top and bottom) lies flat and sways alongside and within inches of the bank – stret pegging style.

Fishing twelve feet deep in a five-foot hole may seem out of the question, but for the float man it is the way to succeed in turbulent water, for a float will create that valuable 'slack', particularly when fishing directly downstream – something the ledger cannot do. Even non-turbulent, purely fast water glides, requiring several swan shot to float fish, are so much slower close to the river bed. Here lies the reason why excessively light tackle so often fails in such a swim: the bait is whisked away along the bottom, much faster than the loose feed around it, whereas the heavier float and lead allows the bait a more natural passage. I often think that if anglers could only see their terminal tackle in action below the surface they would pay much more attention to its design and be more inclined to experiment if bites were not forthcoming.

All anglers appreciate the advantages of having that all-important tinge of colour to the water prior to fishing. To the diver, of course, it works in reverse and I always hoped for good visibility whenever I dived. I was often amazed, however, just how clear beneath the surface even apparently quite coloured water actually is. Even in near flood water conditions, given a fairly bright day, the diver has some eighteen inches of good visibility. This being the case, the fish must have it too and so are quite capable of seeing, for instance, the bait, line and shot, or an angler walking too close along the banks of a flooded river. The angler, remember, is looking down into darkness whereas the fish is looking up into brightness.

A phenomenon I sometimes encountered, particularly in the summer time and especially in tidal rivers, was that at the point of entry the river appeared heavily coloured and until I neared the bottom it was, but the last two feet down to the bottom were curiously really clear. Silt washed up by water craft, for example, appears suspended in the warmer upper water layers. For the angler this means problems if he has geared his tackle and tactics to the apparent colour of the water he can see. This is indeed a point well worth remembering,

Now on to monofilament lines which, despite the makers' claims to the contrary, are seen only too easily by our quarry. Even to my eyes a 5lb line looks like a hawser beneath the surface and, in clear-water sunny conditions, the shadow of it thrown on the river bed is giant-size. Indeed I deem it a blessing, whether it is through sight or their radar system, that fish are aware of our lines at night as well as during daylight. Just imagine the number of frustrating line bites that would occur if the situation were otherwise! As it is we usually only suffer from line bites when bream are in a feeding frenzy or when some species, such as carp or tench, are spawning and oblivious to everything else.

However you can minimize the number of line bites when freelining or ledgering by soaking the line with washing-up liquid so it sinks quickly and clings to the contours along the bottom. Because fish are used to weed fronds bending as they swim into them, they are in turn frightened by anything which is stiff and doesn't give to their body or fins, or the flow of water. Hence the lighter the line the more it gives, and it subsequently imparts a more natural appearance to the bait. Obviously the softer and the more supple the line the better – when fish are shy it produces more bites.

The most important lesson learned whilst diving some of my favourite river haunts was how vastly different most undercut bank swims actually are compared to how I imagined them to be. Take, for instance, those typical chub swims where overhanging alder bushes shade the surface. I once thought there simply existed a big cavern into which the chub retreated when danger seemed imminent, and I rather pictured the cavern stretching from just below the surface right down to the river bed. But how wrong I was! Certainly a little way under the surface the bank has usually eroded away inwards a little into a sort of half circle, but in nine cases out of ten the cavern itself is a long, low, flat tunnel starting from the bottom up some six to twelve inches, and often reaching far into the bank.

Several swims into which Sid and I regularly dived had caverns cutting as much as ten feet into the bank, with entrances so narrow that the chub and barbel inhabiting them were forced to lie over on their sides to swim in. There is obviously no good reason to expect a ledgered hook length to drift into these undercuts and even if it did I doubt whether the bait would be taken, because it always seemed to me that those caverns were resting places, the darkness being such that even with a powerful diving torch you only caught glimpses of bodies slowly, sleepily and almost aimlessly drifting about. The occupants always seemed to be anything but in a feeding mood.

It is the very existence of these caverns that gives the impression that a river is devoid of fish when the water is gin-clear and everything or nothing may be seen through Polaroids from the bankside. Even to the diver there sometimes appear to be few fish about, and one such occasion – when Sid and I were diving Trowse Mill pool on the River Yare on the outskirts of Norwich – really had us puzzled. Visibility was excellent, helped by a nice sunny day, as we entered the deep pool from the shallow water downstream with the sun's rays filtering down through the unbelievably clear water. However there appeared not to be a single big fish present, apart from a huge shoal of roach in the middle of the white water in the operative sluice. We knew that big chub, trout and barbel inhabited the pool and we were at a complete loss to their whereabouts until we stumbled upon the one and only resting place in a cavern under the roots of a huge chestnut tree.

To view its occupants I had to lie flat on the river bed, moving as little as possible lest the silt clouded the water, and stretch my arm plus torch into a six-inch crevice. The cavern opened up inside to about the size of a coffin and there, all in a semi-dormant state, were three barbel to about eight pounds, a huge brown trout looking all of seven pounds plus and a dozen or so chub from three pounds upwards. A lone biggish perch was resting suspended on its side between two exposed roots and there was another smaller brownie at the far end of the hide-out, which must have gone back for a least seven feet into the clay bank. All the fish seemed to be in a semi-torpid state and the largest barbel actually allowed me gently to pull him backwards out through the entrance, but once outside in the light he soon woke up and promptly shot off.

Barbel certainly are by far the most amiable of fishes that I have experienced underwater anywhere in the world – and that includes both salt and freshwater. With the exception of the prickly pufferfish which blows itself up as a defence mechanism and so cannot get away fast, I have yet to come across anything comparable to the closeness one can experience with barbel. Through diving I discovered why it is that you often get a 'sandpapery' feeling up the line just before a bite. The explanation is simply that the barbel's barbules 'pluck' over the line as it gently swings its head from side to side – but in an agitated fashion – to locate the bait with its underslung mouth. The barbel cannot quite see what it is about to eat right at the last moment, so it feels for it instead. We humans have relatively flat faces so we lose sight of our food only a split second before it enters our mouths. Just hold a cup to your lips and then imagine a mouth situated beneath the cup. This should help you appreciate just what a snout the barbel has to put up with! No wonder it was blessed with such enormous barbules.

I think the most fascinating sub-surface encounter Sid and I shared whilst diving was when we were exploring beneath one of the huge rafts covering an overhanging goat willow immediately downstream from the mill pool at Costessey, near Norwich on my local River Wensum. As we moved slowly and carefully between the entangled roots and accumulated debris, keeping our bodies at an angle of forty-five degrees, the water pressure kept us pressed to the bottom. I clung to the handle of an old bucket lying on its side buried in silt. We waited, perfectly still, while our pupils grew accustomed to the low light values, then we noticed the barbel swimming all around us. There were a dozen or so sheltering among the roots, several with markings or peculiarities well known to us, for we had shared their dark, silent world on many occasions in the past.

Ever so slowly we moved our free hands to touch the barbel grouped in twos and threes and resting on the bottom between us and the point where the silt shelved up to the bank. Sid watched while I gently lifted a fish of around nine pounds off the bottom and cradled it in my arms like a baby. I twitched its whiskers slowly. The barbel sensed no danger but I encouraged it to return to the others as the current washed me downstream and almost out of the cavern. I crept slowly back, half swimming and half pulling myself upstream along the water weed. Sid was making friends with the barbel too. They allowed him to stroke their fins and run his hand along their flanks and backs, their eyes restful, their dorsal fins lowered.

In this mood, provided your movements are slow and friendly, barbel will remain approachable for as long as you care to stay. I am even tempted to say that they enjoy friendship. On this occasion we spent a full fifteen minutes with a pair of fish, taking it in turns to caress and hold them in our arms. My emotions as an angler had been stirred as never before. We had shared a rare and quite remarkable encounter and come as close, perhaps, as it will ever be possible to come to the fish in its wild environment. It was an unforgettable experience and afterwards, when we came up for a breath of fresh air and a quick rest, Sid pulled a long hank of blanket weed from his mask, took out his mouthpiece and said, 'How on earth do you explain that?' He didn't even swear – most out of character.

Whilst learning where some of the largest specimen-size roach, chub and barbel used to hide up in several stretches of our local rivers, the Bure, Yare and Wensum, Sid and I simultaneously enjoyed collecting old ceramic beer bottles and marmalade jars, some of which had lain in the silt undisturbed for fifty years or more. I guess it's a similar buzz enjoyed by those who go metal detecting and subsequently find ancient coins and other items. Then one evening whilst diving one of our favourite locations at Hellesdon Mill pool where the Wensum starts to enter the city of Norwich, we really thought we had struck gold. The bottom of the pool was quite literally littered with hundreds of little red jewellery boxes containing rings, earrings, necklaces etc. I could see Sid's eyes lighting up even through the thick protective glass of his diving mask and like me he instantly assumed someone had dumped the spoils of a robbery in the pool to avoid being caught.

We filled the inside of our wet suit jackets with booty until the zips could cope with no more and swam over to the private side of the pool to surface beneath a canopy of overhanging willow branches to inspect our haul. Sid was smiling like a Cheshire cat. But when he rubbed the pearls the paint immediately came off. We had simply come across the dross of a heist, so it was back to barbel and bottle spotting until our compressed air ran out.

I was not the only angler/diver putting pen to paper about sub-surface experiences during the 1970s in *Angling* magazine. Polish angler/diver, Tadeusz Andrzejczyk, was also filling in many parts of the underwater puzzle and years later, in February 1998 to be exact, I had the privilege of actually meeting 'Ted' whilst attending a tackle exhibition in Warsaw. We had so very much in common to talk about and a signed copy of his excellent book, *Wedkarsturo Jeziorowe*, covering every aspect of Poland's vast lakelands, stares down at me from a bulging bookcase as I write. First written in 1978, it contains many superb underwater photographs that would more than do justice to any magazine printed today.

During the heatwave year of 1976 I wrote a book entitled *A Specimen Fishing Year* which was a factual diary-type account of my fishing for that year whilst in pursuit of specimen fish within Norfolk and Suffolk. The book started as a labour of love but by the end of 1976 I found myself more than looking forward to putting the pen down. Writing about each and every trip as soon as I got home was all very well after a red-letter day when I was all hyped up but very demanding, to say the least, after a series of blanks or miserable weather conditions when little had materialized.

Prior to contacting publishers I asked my good friend Nick Fletcher (then of the

Angler's Mail) to read the manuscript. He immediately gave it the thumbs-up, but publishers were not so enthusiastic and after negative reactions from a couple I was on the point of breaking it down into separate chapters, thus enabling Brian Harris to give it a monthly spot in *Angling* magazine, when A & C Black, to whom I had also sent the manuscript, confirmed that they would indeed like to publish my diary. By its very nature of being a diary it quickly became out of date and has been out of print now for several years. So much has changed in our fishing within the past twenty-five years that I am compelled to make comparisons between what happens today and how it all was then.

Remember 1976 and that heatwave? It was a time without sophisticated electronic bite alarms and boilies, thermal one-pieces and two-man bivvies. There were no carbon, boron or kevlar wrapped rods on the market, although I did actually test fish with one of the first prototype carbon trotting rods ever produced that year. But we did have one precious asset which for the most part is not there today: roach in our rivers. Personally I would much prefer to go back to those days of less gadgetry when you could trot a swim which not only looked like a roach swim, but actually had roach in it. But that's life, ain't it?

My diary book started in January 1976 with what can only be described as a mountainous glut of incredibly large roach, because the clear-flowing upper reaches of Norfolk and Suffolk rivers were as prolific with quality roach then as they are barren today. For instance, my diary entries for 4 January 1976 – despite a severe overnight frost and snow showers – included two big roach of 2lb 9oz and 2lb 10½oz from the River Wensum at Taverham in the 'rushes' stretch. Both came long trotting too. On 5 January I caught one roach of 2lb 2½oz plus a string of others over the pound. On 7 January I achieved a huge bag including five over two pounds, the best being 2lb 13oz. The next day I got a roach of 2lb 3oz followed, on 11 January, by a 2lb 1oz and a 2lb 7oz. Then I caught a 2lb 4oz on 12 January. Many of these beautiful roach actually came in very short sessions fitted in before I had to set off to open the shop and whilst long trotting maggots. It was fairy-tale fishing; it was just too good – unreal almost.

Rod sales over the tackle shop counter were not of designer long-range carp poles but 13ft trotting rods capable of picking up twenty to thirty yards of line and setting the hook at that distance. There were no production carbon

BELOW This is one of the many fine roach catches that came my way from long trotting the River Wensum during the 1970s which included specimens to 2½lb.

rods then, remember. All the winter talk was of big-river roach when anglers got together. With friends like Terry Houseago, Jimmy Sapey, Jimmy Henry and John Bailey I concentrated on the Wensum from Bintry Mill all the way downstream to Taverham. It was a wonderful period, with the River Wensum rightly hailed as the finest roach river in Britain – a crown it held for over a decade.

In the 1975–76 season I caught no fewer than forty-nine river roach over the magical weight of two pounds from four different rivers. You can only guess how many there must have been below two pounds to produce the whoppers. I simply lost count and even became blasé, I regret to say. The roach fishing was that unbelievably good. And yet even then I made the occasional reference in my diary book about the future of the upper rivers, particularly the Wensum. I was obviously worried because it was easier to catch ten roach over the pound than five of just six ounces. Without a healthy pyramid containing myriad lesser fish to follow on from the shoals of specimen roach, I could see no way the river could continue rich in roach once the biggies died off. And that is exactly what has happened.

It was during the mid 1970s when the late Doug Allen, who was to be my regular weekly companion for over ten years, first came into the shop. Doug, who had been a fighter pilot during the Second World War and was exactly twenty years my senior, was known locally for catching some big pike from several Bure-fed Broads to which he had access. But he had never landed a roach over two pounds. So we got together: my wish was a pike over twenty pounds, his a two-pound roach. With each other's help we both achieved these life-long ambitions. Amazingly my first ever twenty-pound pike was one of a brace taken on the same day whilst fishing with Doug on a shallow, strictly private Broad. I had waited for so long to see a twenty-pounder come sliding over my waiting net and then I went and caught two of 22lb and 23lb respectively during the very same session. But that's fishing!

Doug and I shared so many catches of big pike together. We travelled up to Loch Lomond in Scotland for pike and to the River Isla for grayling, a species we both loved. We caught pike to twenty-five pounds from the River Waveney at Beccles, plus dozens of specimens to over 30 pounds from all over Broadland, but allow me to recall one particularly memorable occasion on a Bure-fed Broad.

We had in fact been lucky and picked a cracking day with big pike potential. Dawn greeted us with a good south-westerly blowing – super weather for fishing deadbaits – and with the sky nicely overcast we looked to be in for a treat. What's more the track running round the outside of the spinney where the boathouse is hidden was fairly hard, which meant that I could drive my Mini Traveller to within a few yards of the boat instead of lugging all the gear on a long walk across newly ploughed fields from the lodge house.

The Broad was well coloured from the heavy winds, with a visibility of just a foot or so, and literally within minutes of putting down the mud weights in the centre of a four-foot deep bay, the action began. Before I could get the second bait out the first float-fished static herring had been snapped up and line was fairly hissing from the old

'300'. It's a lovely feeling watching a sliding float sneaking upwind across the waves and even better when the rod goes over on the strike and stays there! A long, lean fish boiled on the surface twenty yards out, and to be honest, it stayed on the surface while I reeled it in. I thought that any second it would see me, the boat, the net or all three and then make a last-ditch dive around the anchor rope. But it didn't, it simply lay on the surface throughout the twenty or so seconds from striking to netting. It was a really thin fish of 18¼lb but nicely spotted and in super trim despite its lack of lustre.

Still some pike don't fight and at that time I was eager for another after returning it. I was not disappointed. The second fish snapped up the herring on my second rod almost as quickly as the first but it felt decidedly heavier and was really fighting. There was nothing spectacular though, just a few runs powerful enough for me to hear the magic of a slipping clutch (yes, I've always been a traditionalist at heart) plus a heavy boil, head-shake and dive close in after which the fish went straight into the net. A long beautifully marked pike pulled the dial scales round to 24lb 2oz – at that time a personal best. Talk about being over the moon – over forty pounds of fish in just two casts, and the day had only just begun . . .

Then Doug started to get in amongst them and hit into pike on four consecutive casts – all on freelined herring. They ranged between 9lb and 16½lb and put up far more of a show than either of mine. It was really a mad spell and, like all mad spells, it was over far too quickly.

I can remember the 16½lb pike well due to a ghastly gaff wound (the odd elderly angler still used a gaff in those days) under its chin through which protruded its tongue. In fact from more or less the same spot around a year later Doug caught exactly the same pike again, which we affectionately called Stumpy, now weighing nearly eighteen pounds. A year later it turned up again almost touching twenty pounds, again to Doug's rod. Then for two years it didn't show, until one freezing cold day at the end of February.

Doug had just landed a superbly conditioned specimen of exactly 24lb. In fact he was still unhooking it when one of my static deadbaits was away and I struck into what felt like a heavy fish. It was too; it was Stumpy now also weighing exactly 24lb. What a brace!

But back to that memorable occasion and what seemed a perfect day where we sat for the rest of the session with just one small fish apiece late on into the afternoon. What a session to remember! It was the kind of day when we were actually glad to put down the rods and enjoy packing away the gear and cleaning out the boat because Lady Luck had been so very kind. Even the drive home was to be savoured, with much talk about the day's events. And to top it all, to give us that extra feeling of inner warmth, within seconds of bundling all the gear into the back of the Traveller, after a completely dry day, rain started to lash heavily against the windscreen. We had missed a storm literally by minutes. 'Thank goodness the rain held until now, otherwise the track might have softened up and proved difficult,' said Doug. What an understatement! On went the headlights and wipers and away we went along the

LEFT My winter pike
fishing partner for
over a decade, the
late Doug Allen,
and I with a fine
brace of 24-
pounders caught
from a River Bure-
fed Broad near
Wroxham.

track towards the lodge, the rain absolutely bucketing down.

At the first bend where a huge pile of cut pines trespassed on to the track, I kept well over on the other side close to the field not realizing the depth of recent tractor ruts. Doug's prophetic, 'Keep left or we'll get stuck' came too late. I felt the Mini's sump give a thump as the front wheels dangled into a pair of deep ruts. 'Never mind, we'll bump it out,' says Doug. So out into the storm we went, not anticipating the gravity of our plight and became drenched within minutes. Our waterproofs had, of course, been taken off and packed away for the drive home and I had even swapped my Wellington boots for carpet slippers. What a muddy mess they soon became and naturally the Mini just wouldn't budge. Our 'perfect day' was changing rapidly.

Unfortunately the car battery wasn't up to much and had been playing up for weeks so my turning the engine off for five minutes, but leaving the headlights on while we surveyed the situation, hardly did it any good. In short it was knackered, with the inevitable result of refusing to turn the engine over. We would, however, be able to bump start her easily if only we could lever the front end out of the ruts and back on to the track, so I didn't worry unduly at this stage.

It was by now pitch dark, getting a bit chilly, raining at a steady inch an hour, backed up by at least a force eight gale, and so without a torch we set about finding a couple of suitable logs to move the Mini over. The pile of cut pine logs was like a gift from heaven and we soon found a couple of thick ones to lie along one side of the car with another to act as a lever. 'We'll soon have it out,' said Doug with authority, choosing to do the levering while I strained to lift the front end and bounce

the sump over the rut 'One, two, three lift!' For a second the front end rose a little and began to move over but suddenly it slumped back again to the sound of a muffled crunch from somewhere inside the car. Doug opened the driver's door and there sticking up through a jagged gaping hole in the floor was the end of a six-inch pine log. That was enough for me. I suggested we trudge along to the lodge and use Mrs Dodd's phone to ring the farm for a tractor. I was about to find out the hard way that secluded private estate waters are all right unless you become stuck miles from nowhere because it just did not occur to me that Mrs Dodds might not be on the phone.

'My husband does have an old bike though,' says Mrs Dodds, 'but you'll have to be careful with the chain, it sometimes comes off.' Doug looked at me, I looked at him and he said, 'You're the youngest, John.' So off into the rain along the track went Wilson. There were no lights on the bike – a boneshaker from the 1930s – so how on earth I navigated between the potholes and missed the dykes on both sides of the lane on the mile-long pedal to the farm, I'll never know. But make it somehow I did and found Henry, the tractor driver who, bless him, bolted down his supper to come and drag us out. At the first attempt off came the front bumper complete with number plate. Henry apologized, mumbled something about rusted brackets and reshackled the towing chain somewhere around the rear end while I threw the bits into the car. This time the chain slipped and, in addition to one half of the twin rear bumper, most of the exhaust system was wrenched away. It had actually cracked off at the manifold. Round to the front end went the chain now that my wrecked heap was out of the ruts and like a lame dog it was dragged unceremoniously along the track, now an absolute quagmire of mud, back to the lodge. Miraculously it started first pull and as the headlights were still intact, Doug and I continued the drive home to our worried wives, three hours later than expected.

It was around this time, during 1977, that I moved my John's Tackle Den business from Bill Cooper's old shop, in which turnover had become impossible to increase due to its diminutive size. I was also finding my day-to-day existence somewhat claustrophobic. I was becoming more and more frustrated by potential customers peering in through the window and walking away because they thought I was too busy, when actually the shop was full of local anglers hanging around and swapping stories whilst buying tackle. This is a problem faced by small tackle shops the world over. Location was in fact solved overnight by Colin, who ran the gent's outfitters next door, telling me of his imminent bankruptcy and saying that if I wanted his shop I should ring the landlord. I had previously mentioned my liking for his unit should he ever decide to call it a day.

This was a shop unit with three times the floor space I had been used to with much larger store rooms and a huge attic. There was a back yard large enough for me to construct a cold house for the maggots, and it was exactly what I needed. So I visited the landlord and secured a lease. The trouble was, once Colin had departed several weeks later, I was left with the daunting task of completely fitting out the new shop on my own. This I decided to do over a period of six weeks during the close season in the evenings, with a view, once complete, to swapping everything from one shop to another, literally overnight. Thank goodness it was next door.

Frankly I could never have completed on time had I not been helped by my friend Nigel Thomas, a local copper who, due to his shift work, gave me a few hours' hard work every evening. And if I say so myself, for a couple of non-professionals the new John's Tackle Den didn't look at all bad when we had finished.

Moving shops to some degree prepared me for what now lay ahead on the home front, because after spending five years in our first bungalow with children, Lee and Lisa, now six and four years old, plus a large German Shepherd called Guy, it too seemed awfully small. So Barbara and I started looking for a larger property in Taverham. We found a pre-war bungalow, albeit needing much work, with a third of an acre of garden, and it was quite close to the local schools and shops. So we put our bungalow up for sale and quickly clinched the deal, although had I known the extent of the work I had let myself in for that summer, I might have thought twice.

Plans were passed for a roof conversion to construct two large bedrooms with dormer windows so Lee and Lisa could each have their own room, and downstairs I decided to knock through from the tiny drawing room into the kitchen. Being a retired builder, Dad came up to help for a few weeks during which time we sorted out most of the structural work and even built a brick wall separating the garden from the long drive.

Then about one year afterwards I set about building the biggest garden pond Barbara would allow. From as early as I can remember I always wanted a large pond:

from my childhood in north London, when a fifty-gallon galvanized water tank was all the veranda to our tiny flat would allow, to the previous bungalow where I had built a small pond.

Our predecessors in our new home had kept over thirty greyhounds with the garden divided up into pens and runs and bordered at the rear by brick kennels. My first job throughout the winter was to clear and level the entire plot. I then planted a few fruit trees and shrubs for screening, before setting about the most enjoyable part of all, actually sitting down one evening with a pencil and paper to design the sort of pond I really wanted. Little did I know then that within five years we would be moving again and I would own my own lake, and have a second excavated to my own design.

Anyway, within a year the huge garden pond – complete with wooden bridge across – was finished, nicely stocked with tubs of plants from the wild and an assortment of both natural and ornamental fish, from golden tench to double-figure carp. I then became particularly interested in biological pond filters and in carp culture, and dug two more ponds for growing on the fry of various species. This incidentally led to my writing a series of articles for *Practical Fishkeeping* based on my experiences. I even went into selling a few home-bred carp and goldfish, having converted the previous occupant's old kennels at the end of the garden into a huge fish house complete with filtration units. Barbara must have had the patience of Job . . . though I was always pushing it too far.

I then became fascinated by what everyone refers to these days as ghost carp. At that time these beautiful variants were offered for sale in *Practical Fishkeeping* as metallic carp (a name I still prefer to use) by a Mr Villis (Latvian for Bill) Michaels of Newhay Fisheries in Selby, Yorkshire, who crossed a male Japanese white ogon koi carp with a German Dinkle spula naturally coloured table carp. This produced stunningly coloured little carp etched in various densities of silver and white, of which I purchased 400. They were barely four inches long and the entire batch fitted into one large poly bag. (Bill, incidentally, who was born in Eastern Europe where the carp culture is a way of life, was one of the first importers of Japanese koi into the UK.)

I also purchased a dozen or so of his original unusually coloured grown-on metallics, all of around one and a half pounds a piece which, together with a few of the four-inch metallics, all went into my garden pond. The remainder I sold on to some local clubs and these same carp still live in their waters, having grown to weights well in excess of twenty pounds over the years. Due to their durability these

(metallic or ghost) carp really are a splendid strain for stocking as you will discover when I later discuss the creation of my own lake. I have now been monitoring the development of some of these individually recognizable metallic carp in both pond and lake using photography for identification purposes for close on twenty-five years. But more of this later.

Referring back again to my 1976 roach-rich diary book for a moment, it is painful for me to state that today ninety-five per cent of the River Wensum is devoid of roach. For myself and all other roach lovers it is a crying shame. I actually came to live in Norfolk because I wanted to be near flowing rivers where I could long trot for quality roach, for I am and always will be a roach angler before I am anything else.

ABOVE The finished result: my garden pond stocked and planted with both ornamental and wild fish and marginals, complete with a double-figure carp rolling in the middle.

As far as I can fathom, the only common denominator that exists between the rivers that have declined is the escalating use of farming fertilizers, phosphates, nitrates, fungicides, pesticides and insecticides. I am not alone in believing that intensive farming methods and the subsequent increase in chemicals leaching into our river systems have an awful lot to answer for. I am sure that things like unsympathetic weed cutting, winter run-off, better drainage, water abstraction and even the endemic roach diseases are also major contributing factors to there being fewer roach.

Throughout much of the Upper Waveney, for instance, the concentrations of ammonia leaching into the river from slurry created by intensive pig farming units is one of the identified causes of pollution and subsequent fish losses. With the Wensum, however, the loss of roach stocks is perhaps more complex and puzzling. It could be attributed to any number of invisible toxins and pollutants in what is generally a clear-flowing river, even if it is somewhat over-weedy and choked with dark green blanket weed during the warmer months. I personally think that the levels of toxins created from chemicals leaching into the rivers from the huge amount of land that is given over to intensive farming are what affects fry survival and the ultimate existence of roach in actual shoal numbers. Such levels could affect the young fishes' respiratory systems and/or the food they eat. Minute algae, for instance, which are needed for fry growth in their early stages, may well be eradicated by these chemicals and/or they may even affect the crustacean foods like daphnia, assellus and shrimps. I truly believe that within the next few decades, just as lung cancer was eventually associated with smoking (and it took some time), a correlation between farming chemicals and the inability of silver shoal species to maintain their numbers will come to light.

It is a peculiar thing however that while roach are in decline at present the chub is having a field day. They have colonized much of the Upper Wensum as they have also done in most other Anglian rivers and streams, the Suffolk Stour being a prime example. And while they are not the reason for the roach decline, as many would have it, their presence will certainly hamper roach trying to re-establish themselves, because they occupy all the best roach-holding areas.

I cannot therefore really foresee any immediate improvement in my local upper rivers in so far as the smaller shoal fish like roach and dace are concerned. But abstraction and farming are not totally to blame. What about the cormorant phenomenon? This incredibly voracious, predatory seabird has destroyed an endless list of inland stillwater and river fisheries throughout the British Isles. It achieves this by consuming vast quantities of dace, roach, perch, young bream and chub – not to mention both salmon and sea trout parr which the country's game rivers can ill afford to lose, plus of course stocked rainbow and brown trout which are introduced into all our man-made reservoir trout fisheries at perfect swallowing size.

Take Rutland Water for instance, the pride of Anglian Water reservoir game fisheries and the largest man-made lake in Britain. There are no fewer than 200-plus pairs of breeding cormorants living in the nature reserve and cocking two fingers to all. Goodness knows how much money in swallowed trout they have cost the fishery's management and of course ultimately the consumer, who is supplied and charged through his tap by Anglian Water. So inevitably their presence affects every man on the street – not just anglers.

At the bottom of my garden is a lake – someone else's fortunately – which over the past few years has been totally depleted of its once unbelievably prolific roach and rudd stocks. This is a well-matured, clear-water gravel pit covering eight acres. Every morning I have witnessed through binoculars ten cormorants flying from their roost in the top of a tall birch tree, which is a hundred yards from the house, to gorge on stocks. If I had not witnessed it I would never have believed it. But like many a frustrated fishery owner, I have observed what the 'black death' is capable of achieving at first hand. And when you consider what an adult cormorant can put away, even at the conservative figure of one pound of fish per day, you don't need to be a genius to work out that in a year just ten cormorants can remove getting on for two tons of fish.

Two tons of roach or rudd or trout! That's an investment of several thousand pounds at least. Small wonder then that so many clear-water club fisheries are not worth a cast and that all the members' hard work over many, many years has been for nothing. But worse still, because both his job and income have been hit, is the plight of the fishery owner who has had to close down due to cormorant activity. I wish I knew where it was all going to end. I wish that someone up there in the godly realms of government departments such as the Ministry of Agriculture and Fisheries would wake up to the fact that we have all but raped the North Sea through overfishing, which of course is the reason why cormorants have been driven to find easy pickings in our clear-watered rivers, gravel pits, lakes and reservoirs. As pigeons, rats, crows, squirrels and rabbits are put on the vermin list in order to conserve our farming industry, isn't it about time we put cormorants on the same list so they can be legally shot to reduce their numbers dramatically? I'll bet if the cormorant turned vegetarian and took to raping ploughed and seeded fields, attitudes in Westminster would change overnight. At present only a handful of game fisheries (what about coarse fisheries?) are granted licences to shoot cormorants. And taking the country as a whole it does nothing. Because as a sport we are so fragmented, poor old freshwater fishing in Great Britain has to suffer continually. I just wonder for how much longer.

The trouble is, in the meantime freshwater fishery owners all over the UK have to sit back and watch their life's work destroyed. Also there are other far-reaching consequences. The RSPB is totally against the culling of cormorants, though it happily sanctions the culling of the North American ruddy duck in Britain, which dares to breed with the Spanish white-headed duck. I wonder if they have considered the plight of grebes, kingfishers, herons and the like which, due to a serious lack of small silver shoal fishes to eat, could find their natural food larder (thanks to the cormorant) unnaturally bare in the future. Are we really going to wait until indigenous water birds suffer near starvation as a direct result of cormorant predation upon their daily diet?

But there is an even more sinister consequence yet, one I have unfortunately witnessed in recent years, not fifty yards from the house at the bottom of my garden. In the spring, with little left in the way of silver shoal species to eat, what do you think the lake's pike population prey upon? Yes, that's right, a much larger proportion of young ducklings, goslings and coot or moorhen chicks than they would normally take. In fact I have witnessed more young waterfowl disappear in ferocious swirls during the past five years than in my entire life before. The pike patrol purposefully along the margins for new clutches of youngsters fresh from their nests. And they have a field day.

Now I have said this many times before and I will say it again. Although I would sooner be trotting for roach than any other form of fishing, I would sooner be catching carp from an attractive well-stocked lake than catching absolutely nothing in a river. I do have a few personal reservations about modern carp fishing, however. I dislike the pressure of round-the-clock fishing on many waters and the subsequent harm it can do in terms of the repercussions for the state of bankside foliage and acute pressure on fish with lines permanently in the water. And I feel sorry for youngsters who come straight from snooker table or table tennis bang into the cult of modern carping and who, because they see everyone else doing it, misguidedly think that sitting inside a bivvy all day with a pair of matched bolt rigs out near the horizon is what carp fishing is all about. Because it ain't. I have on all too many occasions seen newcomers become disillusioned with our sport and drift on to another. Just look through the tackle ads and you'll see what I mean. Look at all the complete designer carp-fishing outfits there are for sale. I would love to see more carp anglers become all-rounders and learn the craft of catching other species on numerous methods and different baits. Then they could return to carp having served an apprenticeship. They would be much better for it and go on to enjoy catching carp when the situation arises, using a variety of techniques, instead of just one. Unhappily for many anglers today, when the bolts and boilies fail to score they simply have nowhere to go.

Although the pressure syndrome which affects carp fishing is comparatively quite new, it has of course crept into the pursuit of other species, tench and barbel in particular. Twenty years ago I used to think I was uptight and fishing heavily when I put in two or three early morning pre-work sessions during the summer weeks, or maybe an all-nighter plus one early morning – and I still opened my shop six days a week. But compared to the sort of hours some anglers are now prepared to put in, these efforts would hardly seem worth it. Each week we read reports of tench, bream and carp anglers finally achieving success after ten, twenty and even thirty consecutive biteless all-night sessions. Even the thought of someone actually spending anything up to a week in a river swim, as some do nowadays after species like barbel, would have been mind boggling just ten years back.

Freshwater fishing certainly has entered new realms as far as catching big fish is concerned and I am not altogether sure it is a good thing. Once upon a time you could relate to another man's achievements because everyone had more or less about the same amount of leisure time to put into their sport or pastime. Which is not the case now, in these obsessive times. There is so much in today's fishing that simply does not really mean anything; the farcical record fish lists for one. But that's life. I shall now continue with the happenings throughout the 1970s of yours truly.

Something I haven't yet really covered concerning the 1970s is the way in which anglers bent on catching larger and larger specimens got together to pool their knowledge and formed specimen and specialist angling groups. In my area we formed the (now long-since disbanded) Broadland Specimen Group and were, amongst other things, perhaps best known for developing long-range feeder fishing techniques to capture the then specimen tench from Norfolk's silt-rich shallow estate lakes. We caught our fair share of big Broadland pike too, and one of our members, Pete Stacey, was for several years active in the big carp syndicate at famous Redmire Pool. All this is of course by the bye now because things have moved on beyond all expectations.

Nevertheless, such groups played an important and pioneering part in formulating fishing techniques within the British Isles as we have come to accept today. In those early times big fish were thin on the ground and consequently hard earned by those willing to devote long hours by the waterside developing baits and specialized terminal rigs, some of which have now been accepted as standard.

One of the most interesting modern phenomena to have occurred during the last quarter century is the way in which tench have on average grown to much larger sizes

LEFT Back in the mid-1970s tench were considered specimens from 5lb upwards. I took this bag on long-range feeder tactics while ledgering a shallow Norfolk estate lake. Note the red, fast taper, hollow glass rods – carbon fibre was not yet available.

all over the country. You might put this down to the sheer numbers of HNV baits tench now consume and, in certain waters, no doubt this is fact. Yet monsters over twelve pounds and countless doubles have come from undoctored waters, like the reservoirs at Tring in which the bream and tench grow to huge proportions on zooplanktons and bloodworms alone. The tench growth phenomenon is certainly one hell of a modern mystery, because back in the mid-70s when those of us in the Broadland Specimen Group were taking huge numbers of six pounders plus the odd seven from the Marsh Lake in North Norfolk, our catches were highly rated countrywide. But today seven- , eight- and even nine-pounders are regular catches in a whole string of fisheries up and down the country. These weights seem even more incredible when you consider the tench record stood for many years at 8½lb and prior to that in the early 1950s at just 7lb. Now it's over fourteen pounds. Could it be that gravel pits dug during the Second World War, which produce many of the largest tench today, have only reached their peak in food potential during the 1980s and 90s? Have modern techniques and baits made more of an impact than many of us believe? Are tench simply holding more spawn when they get caught because our summers start later and is it simply an effect of global warming? Well, you can put all these arguments into the computer and every time out will come the same answer: one big mystery.

What about the way in which the bream record keeps leaping ahead after sticking at 13½lb for so many years? This too looks set to be another peculiar phenomenon, though as I write this a twenty-pound bream just does not seem to be possible. But I wonder! It's already happening with the barbel record which hovered at just over fourteen pounds for the best part of a century. Yet in the last five years of the 1990s, sixteen-pound-plus barbel have been caught from several different rivers.

I should also perhaps mention how nowadays we seem to recognize so many of the individual big fish we catch. This was something totally alien to many anglers in the 1970s when more, albeit smaller, specimens were about. We recognize repeat captures not only of carp and pike, but of tench, chub, bream and barbel – even big roach. It just goes to show how few large fish there are actually about, how often we put pressure on them, and how much we should value their existence for continued sport.

The 1970s were certainly an exciting time for everyone on the cutting edge of the big fish scene. As a keen photographer I was starting to demand more impressive results for my efforts which aroused my interest in medium-format cameras. Nowadays of course film emulsions are so good, with the entire photography and printing industry geared to producing unbelievably sharp colour plates from 35mm transparencies, that there is little need for the expense of larger formats. Back in the 70s, however, magazine and newspaper editors were not only more impressed with, but far more likely to accept and use, the larger 2¼-inch (6 x 6cm) format transparency for their colour work than the significantly smaller 35mm, particularly for front covers. It was a lucrative field which only a handful of angling writers was then into, probably due to the high initial cost of a quality medium-format camera.

Until now I had been relying on my old 35mm Minolta SR7 plus a couple of lenses purchased whilst on board SS *Oronsay*. So I decided to go up the ladder carefully by first buying a Yashica 630, twin-lens reflex 2¼-inch square camera. This almost paid for itself with my first front cover on *Angling* magazine. However being of the upright Rolleiflex style with two lenses (hence the term 'twin lens'), one for focusing and one for taking the actual photograph, it was rather old fashioned and completely useless for close-up photography, though I loved the size of the transparency and the fact that the square format could be cropped to produce either a landscape or portrait picture.

While ledgering for tench in the Marsh Lake at Wolterton Hall (now private) in north Norfolk with fellow writer, Kevin Clifford, I had a good look at his Bronica S2A 2¼-inch square single-lens reflex camera. It produced excellent results and I immediately decided to buy one. When I got home in the late morning after the tench fishing, I scanned the adverts in *Amateur Photographer* only to find that someone in Bristol was selling a complete second-hand Bronica S2A outfit with both wide and telephoto lenses in addition to the standard. Luckily he was in when I rang a few minutes later and we agreed on a price of £420, which then was probably more than my Mini Traveller was worth. Barbara thought I was mad. Nevertheless we arranged to meet at Liverpool Street station a few hours later to clinch the deal. When our two trains arrived, to the amazement of fellow passengers, this chap sat counting out my fivers while I carefully inspected the large aluminium photo case full of Bronica goodies. Obviously everyone thought some sort of shady deal was being

transacted. It was in fact one of the best investments I ever made because it started me on the road to more 'thinking' photography.

Unfortunately the S2A also became rather limiting in that exposure still had to be calculated by a hand-held meter (an old Weston Master) and that due to the large film transportation handle the camera had to be taken down from the viewing eye in order to wind on. This obviously precluded any action photography. And so after a few years I sold the S2A (for £100 more than I paid for it incidentally) and bought a Bronica ETRSi 645 which, though slightly reduced in format to a 6 x 4.5cm transparency, produces fifteen frames on a 120 roll film to the 6 x 6's twelve shots. But more importantly the 645 is coupled to a lever wind handle and has an automatic exposure system. It can therefore be used in the same way as any 35mm camera and produces stunning transparencies. It is not light, however.

Today I have two ETRSi Bronicas plus several lenses but sadly have to admit that I use them only periodically. I guess that as so much of my fishing necessitates considering the actual weight of my camera equipment, whether making long-haul flights or simply walking for miles along the Wensum stalking chub, I stick to the lightness of a 35mm camera. I have almost as many different-size camera bags as I have cameras, in order that I can take along exactly what is required by the excursion in hand.

I am not a great lover of automatic everything and totally computerized camera systems. Well, I've got to exercise my brain on something! For quite a few years now I have relied on a pair of Nikon 301 cameras which have a built-in motor drive and an excellent auto-exposure system. The additional lenses I use go down to 24mm at the wide end – so essential for boat fishing – and up to 300mm telephoto for wildlife shots. But unquestionably my most useful Nikon – and I also have two of these – is the 35mm auto-focus/all-weather compact. These have now long since gone out of production but if you should ever come across one second-hand in good order, snap it up straight away.

Many of the thousands of colour transparencies used in my books and articles during the past twenty years have been taken with this wonderful back-up camera. It has a great fill-in flash and can take sub-surface shots down to fourteen feet. Whilst capturing mahseer action shots in India, for instance, I simply sling both Nikon compacts around my neck, get just downstream from both the angler and the fish about to be landed and jump in. Similarly whilst boat fishing either in heavy rain or with sea spray coming over the side, this Nikon compact is invaluable. There is never any worry of malfunction or damage should it become swamped with saltwater or even dropped in the mud. A rinse over with fresh water and that's that. What more can a man ask of any tool, especially a camera?

During the summer of 1978 I was pointed in yet another direction by an invitation from Mike Fuller of the, now defunct, local BBC Radio 4 station in Norwich to accompany him on a series of 'roam-about' fishing programmes. Mike asked me to choose topics for six ten-minute weekly programmes to run consecutively and I came up with a bait-gathering session for the first. The idea was then to lead in on the second programme by using the crayfish, grubs and so on that we had collected from a small stream in the first programme (the evening before) while in search of early morning chub along my local stretch of the Upper Wensum. For the other programmes that followed, I chose roach, carp, lake trouting and pike, and a bit of summer plugging to finish which would, I thought, go down quite nicely with lots of jacks thrashing about – but how wrong can you be?

Anyway, throughout the series the format was to be both informative and light-hearted. This is exactly how it went because Mike and I quickly became friends and built up a definite rapport. Now over twenty years later we have also taken similar routes, in that Mike is now a television producer based in Hampshire. But back to those radio days. Quite simply Mike asked the questions while I tried to produce the goods. While I suppose anything can be botched in the studio or end up on the cutting-room floor, once involved in the programmes it became imperative to both of us that the true 'feeling' of fishing and one's thoughts in relation to any number of things which may or may not have occurred as a result of being by the waterside, really came over. And for my part there were the personal rewards to be gained from doing the series, quite apart from the laughter and actually putting some good fish on the bank.

Through thinking deeply about what I was going to say into the microphone (and this applies equally to my *Go Fishing* programmes nowadays) so that listeners could relate to what was happening, I found that I became more acutely and consciously aware of all the beautiful things which surround my fishing – things which must still be there even when I blank. Wild flowers, for instance: their perfume, their colours, their habitat, their abundance. Or grasses, reedmace, sedges, birds, amphibians, flies, caterpillars – the list goes on and on, dictated only by how much you really want to see. And while I was aware of such things before I started the series, and always have been when actually mentioning everything by name, their importance now to me seemed to be amplified. Consequently the enjoyment of that particular plant, insect or fish became greater.

Other curious but certainly beneficial side-effects sometimes came about when I stayed longer in a swim than I would normally, or made more casts than seemed necessary. When attacking a favourite location during the early morning chubbing programme a huge weed raft gathered over trailing willow branches harbouring at last twenty chub. Mike repeatedly recorded all the subsequent noises such as the casting sounds – bale arm clonk, the 'plop' and the reeling in. All good audible stuff but no chub! I told him that as a chub hadn't hit the crayfish on either the first or second cast, the chances of catching one now on the seventh or eighth time of lobbing it out and going through the motions in water as clear as gin were just about wham! Yes, there was a chub about to break all the rules – a long, lean fish of 4lb 9oz which should have weighed more (that's the trouble with summer chub). It hit the bait at a time when, had Mike not been there shooting tape, I should have been at least three more swims along the bank. Just goes to show doesn't it? Patience, Wilson, patience!

For the roach programme Mike said, 'What about a blank, John, so we can concentrate purely on dialogue about the Wensum and roach chat in general?' I agreed and deliberately walked a remote part of the river I had never seen before, let alone fished, and found a good-looking swim which three or four years before might well have produced several big roach. But the roach fishing on the Wensum had started to deteriorate and many of the big ones which made headlines in the mid-70s had naturally died off. It was really an all-or-nothing session and we settled in the thick rushes at the upstream end of the swim half an hour before dark to quivertip breadflake downstream on 3lb line and size 8 hook after putting in a couple of handfuls of mashed bread.

Two hours later I returned a chub of 4lb 1oz and a roach of 1lb 12oz, having missed two other bites while Mike had enough tape to treble the programme's time limit – even if he did have the recorder switched off when the chub took! By now we were really feeling cocky as a two-man radio team, and programme number four seemed another dead cert, especially as I had arranged to fish a wildie pond where fully-scaled commons between one and two pounds normally did their level best to crawl up the rod, even in the worst of conditions.

RIGHT In 1978 Mike Fuller (*left*) and I teamed up to make a series of fishing programmes for the then local BBC Radio 4 station in Norwich. It proved great fun and, though unbeknown to me at that time, a valuable experience for me as a television presenter.

We baited up with trout pellet paste, put up three rods on the bite alarms and sat back waiting for darkness. An hour after dark, however, I feared the worst. We had but one 12oz wildie to show for our efforts when runs should have been coming every couple of minutes. And that fish was to Mike's rod – the only run of the evening. I just could not understand it. Perhaps a heatwave was on its way, or the air pressure was too low, or pea silage had fouled the pond . . . I had no explanation for Mike who, due to my ramblings on how easy it was going to be on the way there, had obviously built himself up into a fever pitch about carp fishing. It's funny how within only a few trips an almost complete novice can become addicted to the fervour of fishing.

Anyway we did have enough tape about the history of the pond, how the carp got there and so on. All interesting stuff plus the bite alarms bleeping away to the one and only run. So really we were reasonably happy with the programme material and ready to call it a night at eleven o'clock when a set of headlights appeared at one corner of the field and over the bumps came Stephen Burroughs, owner of the water, in his farm truck. Well at least we should now find out what Stephen had been catching recently and why sport was now so bad. Perhaps he'd gone barmy on the protein baits and 'pellet' was blown.

'Hi Stephen,' says I, introducing Mike. 'It's been a useless night.' 'I'm not surprised,' said Stephen, pointing to the ground where several thin pieces of string were disappearing into the pond which I had failed to notice on arrival in the half light. 'I would have told you earlier on,' he continued, 'when you rang, had I not been out. We put some fish traps in there this afternoon to get rid of some of those bloody little crucians and wildies.' He picked up the nearest string and pulled slowly, while twenty feet out in the pond (exactly where our baits had lain all evening) a huge 8ft by 4ft fish trap slowly rose to the surface like the back of a whale. 'I've got four of these out there,' he said. 'It's a wonder you didn't get caught up.' 'Wasn't it,' I said.

I made sure I picked a 'dead cert' venue for the trouting programme. Curiously, in terms of sheer sport and action it proved the most spectacular. We visited a new gravel pit fishery in west Norfolk where rainbows fight like stink, and I quickly took a 2¼ pounder and then a larger fish within minutes of each other, but then I went through a succession of lost fish including one of at least four pounds as darkness loomed over the valley. Then, quite suddenly, as the surface went silver, the margins all along our bank started to erupt with rising trout. It was a beautiful sight, and I took another two nice fish on successive casts both on a Corixa.

There were some beautiful pieces on this programme of my giggling away while trying to subdue a thrashing rainbow before Mike's last reel of tape ran out. And unfortunately the fact that rainbows fight for several minutes (although it doesn't seem as long when you are enjoying the fight) restricted the use of further dialogue in the short space of the ten minutes allocated to each programme. The result was that this particular programme, although entertaining, never really flowed and unfortunately sounded clipped or edited.

When we set off on our last programme I was not just a little sad because, as I stated earlier, I had re-taught and re-explored for myself a few of the basic moods of fishing. It was like catching that first goggle-eyed perch on a penny hook as a six-year-old all over again. I had indeed explored old values, forgotten feelings, and my only regret was that I would fall again into the modern trend of only caring about the end result and only wanting to catch the biggest fish when the programmes were completed. I am still very much aware of this thought, thank goodness, all these years later.

Plugging for pike on the Upper Wensum close to home is great fun. It's really easy in the summer; the jacks will even grab flake and crust as it's wound upstream against the current, and worms, when twitched, are fatal. But for some reason, known only to Wensum pike, on that particular day my Shakespeare 'Big S' plug might not have existed. I even found myself apologizing to Mike for the lack of interest and, for fear of blanking on the very last outing, we moved twice to new parts of the river – each time to no avail. I blamed the wind, the sun and the fact that we could only make the session at midday. 'We should have arranged an evening stint,' I said. Then I made a snap decision an hour before the pubs opened and started the car yet again, making for another part of the river.

On the second bend downstream, we struck gold. 'I'm in,' I yelled into the microphone, as what felt like a reasonable fish chugged away close to the bottom. There was no tail-walking or surface fighting, which seemed curious, but I didn't care. It was a summer pike on a plug and that's what we had set out to catch. As the fish neared the net Mike remarked that it didn't look much like a pike – and he was right. Those old rubber lips I knew so well. It was a four-pound chub and what a surprise! It seemed that throughout the series I just couldn't get away from them.

Half a mile downstream the 'Big S' attracted a peculiar swirl as soon as I twitched it. I missed this take but two casts after the culprit made its mistake. Yes, you've guessed it – another chub. This second chub went 2½lb and would have had great difficulty in swallowing the 'Big S' but grabbed it anyway. It was a terrific end to a particularly interesting sextet of fishing stints, shared with Mike Fuller, who had and still has that rare ability to ask just the right questions, the answers to which as I said earlier on can, if you think about it enough, portray the real 'stomach' of fishing.

Writing about chub reminds me of oh so many sessions I spent in search of that 'then' elusive six pounder during the late 1970s. I've since taken more six pounders, including two over seven pounds in recent years, but these were unwanted close season captures (so I don't count them) caught whilst trying to extract a particular carp from a friend's ornamental lake. And besides, as already mentioned, many species today, including chub, are growing much larger. So a six pounder now means much less than it did to me over twenty years ago when they were less attainable. You make your own challenges!

At that time I decided to devote an entire year to catching a whopping great chub and walked many miles of the Upper River Wissey in north-west Norfolk during the summer months simply fish spotting. In so doing I came across the moat circling nearby Oxborough Hall, which at that time looked to be stuffed full of monster chub running into double figures. But it was too good to be true and close inspection revealed they were in fact grass carp experimentally stocked by Anglian Water. But the two species do seem so very similar and for a few moments I thought I'd located chub heaven.

I also spotted along miles of my favourite Upper Waveney, and naturally along the Upper Wensum close to home where I had accounted for some superb winter chub to within just an ounce of six pounds. Then I eventually struck gold one mild February evening as dusk fell by catching a monster Wensum fish of 6lb 7oz on floating crust, not from the river but from a tiny overgrown adjacent gravel pit into which it had apparently been introduced from the Wensum a few years previous. It measured exactly 24 inches in length and coughed up the remains of a large toad into my hands as I removed the size 4 hook. So much for fish not wanting – as folklore has it – to eat toads or toadspawn because of the bitterness!

Something I also found out that winter when several weeks of ice covering my pond had thawed out, was where frogs get to all winter through. I knew toads hibernated on land, as do newts, beneath old logs and other objects. But I must admit I had not consciously pondered on the whereabouts of frogs; at least not until I pulled some of the larger tubs of marginal plants from the pond (which had been under ice for three weeks) to trim around the edges. The disturbance caused numerous large frogs, all now nutty brown in colour (from the peat-based compost they had been lying in) to jump from the tubs. So that was it, quite simply frogs hibernate under water, absorbing oxygen through their skin.

It was during the following summer that I made the mistake of promising my mate, Doug, a few wildies for an ornamental pond. Doug was an ice-cream salesman and parked his van just inside the gates at Kilverstone Wildlife Park (now closed unfortunately) owned by Lord and Lady Fisher, who at that time thrilled visitors with their miniature horses. Doug even sponsored one of the monkeys at the park. Anyway I obtained a dozen or so wildies averaging around a pound a piece for Doug to put into Lord Fisher's ornamental lily pond around which visitors sat and ate their lunch. Lord Fisher had cleaned out and refilled the pond with clear water after trimming back the lilies. I left the wildies in my huge livebait tank in the garage complete with net and a transportation tub and told Doug to collect them sometime in the morning while Barbara was in. This he did and rang me in the tackle shop to thank me. 'I didn't know they were going to be *that* big,' says Doug, 'but thanks ever so much. Lord Fisher will be pleased.'

Now this had me rather puzzled but the matter was soon to be clarified. Within the next half hour another friend (who shall have to remain nameless) rang and told me that he had finally managed to get hold of a couple of nice grass carp, scale perfect and around three and five pounds a piece. He had put them in the tank. Oh no! Doug had taken the grass carp! Now at this time grass carp were not supposed to be for stocking Wilson's pond, being a totally experimental alien species (that's why I can't

say where they came from) and I couldn't risk them being seen in Lord Fisher's goldfish pond and their presence being traced back to me. I just hoped Doug hadn't put them in yet. But he had, and a heated row broke out over the phone. So in the middle of a hot summer's day when visitors were flocking through the turnstiles at the park Doug had to roll up his trousers and wade through the large ornamental pond with his pan landing net trying to retrieve my two grass carp.

Unfortunately this failed and it cost Doug half a day's lost ice cream sales. It took all afternoon to have the pond pumped out sufficiently low to recapture the aliens. This was an escapade we often laughed about over the following years whilst fishing the Broads together. (What I hadn't the heart to tell Doug a few weeks later was that I arrived home one evening to find the largest grass carp – which he'd so carefully retrieved – lying on the paved garden path beside the pond, as stiff as a board. It had jumped completely out of the pond and asphyxiated itself.)

Looking back I guess the latter part of the 1970s was a rather busy time for me. I updated and revised the second edition of my book *Where to Fish in Norfolk and Suffolk*, wrote chapters in other books entitled 'The Big Fish Scene' and 'Zander', and started writing for Marshall Cavendish Partworks. Edited by Len Cacutt (first editor of the *Angler's Mail* incidentally) this started with the *Fisherman's Handbook* and then the *Handbook Advanced Guide* published weekly as a continuation of the original handbook. This was followed by the *Fisherman's Weekly* magazine, and later in 1982 with four volumes of the *New Fisherman's Handbook*. Considering the sheer number of my colour transparencies consumed by these weekly all-colour publications, my earlier investment in professional camera equipment had more than paid off. Moreover the need for 'how-to' angling literature amongst Britain's army of up-and-coming anglers had well and truly been established by Marshall Cavendish, then the partworks experts, which was something the general angling press at that time simply could not grasp. In addition to this I was of course also contributing my regular monthly articles to *Angling* magazine and periodically writing features for *Angler's Mail*, plus working six days a week in the shop, fishing either before or after work and on Sunday mornings when family life permitted.

There are so many hours in a day and workaholics never count them. I have purposely never drawn a line beyond which I am not prepared to work, fearing that if I do I will also be drawing an indelible line marking where my standard of life can advance no further. However, my preoccupation with everything to do with fishing (which happens to encompass both work and hobbies) must have put enormous strain upon my family at that time. It's a real catch twenty-two.

Television Calls

The 1980s started pretty much how the previous decade had ended, extremely busy. I added the German magazine *Fisch und Fang* and the Swedish *Fiske Journalen*, plus *Practical Fishkeeping*, to the list of publications for which I contributed monthly material. I also produced chapters for the *Angler's Mail Guide to Basic Coarse Fishing* and the *Angler's Mail Annual* – both IPC magazine publications. It was in fact most gratifying to have the editors of all these and previously mentioned magazines and partworks contacting me not only for copy but for my comprehensive library of colour transparencies. This library has now grown to immense proportions; I have around 200,000 transparencies, most of which are catalogued. There are, for instance, several thousand on fishing in India alone.

But as busy as I was in the shop, trying to steal enough hours before work in order to catch big roach, barbel or chub which I would then write about, finding time for scuba diving with Sid, being father and husband, and keeping the garden and pond in order, there was even more work and responsibility coming my way.

I was on the point of digging yet another pond in the garden, which had been extended by purchasing from the lady next door the last third of her plot, when I heard that just the place I had been looking for was coming on to the market. Like many a fisherman, the thought of actually owning my own fishery, undisturbed by the actions of others, had always appealed. I guess the constructing of so many ponds was simply building the stepping-stones in that direction. Now the opportunity had finally presented itself.

This place was part of a large estate in Lenwade, some eleven miles west of Norwich, owned by a friend, Richard Barry, who after having it on the market for over a year without a single enquiry, decided to split the sixty-acre sporting estate into five lots. Lot two was the one I could just about afford. It comprised a spacious three-bedroomed bungalow with six acres of surrounding woodland including a three-quarter-acre gravel pit. Ah, seclusion at last!

Barbara and I went and viewed the bungalow immediately and the next day rang with an offer that was accepted. But over the months ahead there were those terrible times when everyone feels so uncertain and we were kept on tenterhooks right up to the moment of signing contracts by both the couple purchasing our house and the second buyer responsible for purchasing the remainder of Richard's estate. Naturally

OPPOSITE This 35lb 15oz catch of bream and a single chub from the tidal reaches of Hampshire's famous Royalty stretch of the River Avon decided the three-match outcome between Dick Clegg and me in the winter of 1989.

RIGHT Before we had a lake excavated from our birch scrub woodlands, Lee and Lisa, aged 13 and 11 years old, had a great time scrambling on their motor bikes.

he wanted to sell all the lots at the same time, so had the larger buyer pulled out, our sale would have been held up. Fortunately it was not and in October 1982 the Wilsons moved lock, stock and barrel, including the cat, two German Shepherds, a Labrador, Cheeko our African Grey parrot (who is garbling away as I write this), Lisa's rabbits, Lee's snakes, plus tank upon tank of golden tench, orfe and carp various, plus Barbara's mother Nora into our new lakeside home.

Having moved Lee and Lisa, now twelve and ten years old, from the environment where they grew up and away from their friends, we had to drive them around a bit, but I'm sure this was compensated for by their new quality of life. They had six acres of woodland where they could do as they liked. In fact within months of moving in I bought both of them motorbikes and they were soon zooming up and down through the woods loving every minute.

Extraction had last taken place in the woods – which are bordered by an eight-acre lake (privately owned) along our north-east boundary – during the Second World War and most of the gravel and sand was taken away by Atlas Aggregates for the nearby airfields at Weston Longville. It left our three-quarter-acre pit with depths to fourteen feet now nicely mature in its own right with a stock of rudd, roach, gudgeon and small tench. To this I added all the various carp, golden tench and orfe from my garden ponds.

Over the following months I arranged to have our lake netted and most of the prolific rudd and roach stock removed. These I swapped for some common carp, and I also purchased a quantity of both mirrors and commons in the six- to twelve-pound range, together with a handful of grass carp (now allowable). During the winter of 1982/83 I also introduced a few chub averaging 3–4lb from the nearby River Wensum in the hope that they would help to keep down the stock of rudd and gudgeon. Under two years later, incidentally, one of those chub was caught. It weighed 5lb 5oz.

Several customers and friends who used the shop suggested they would be interested in joining a syndicate should I form one to fish my newly acquired lake. So we had a working party to clear a path through the steep bramble-covered banking which restricted access to much of the perimeter, creating a dozen fishable swims. We didn't go all the way round, but left a jungle area where no one could fish – always a wise decision on any fishery, this.

During the summer of 1983 I planted white and red ornamental lilies and the common yellow lily with its cabbage-like sub-surface leaves. In addition I introduced a good margin coverer, the dwarf pond lily, which has tiny round pads and buttercup yellow flowers. As much of the little lake shelves immediately down from one foot in the margins to eight, ten and twelve feet, this little plant is ideal for a marginal covering; however it does tend to go rampant in lakes which are shallow all over.

In June that year I contacted Atlas Aggregates asking them to consider future gravel extraction from the wooded valley running parallel to the little lake. I could easily visualize how beautiful the area would be with a lake running throughout its entire length. From digging down deep to plant shrubs, it became apparent to me that the whole area had not been dug and back-filled and all the gravel removed, as I was led to believe by everyone who was familiar with the property. The top six to ten feet of good-quality gravel had simply been skimmed off and the whole area left to grow up in birch shrub. There was more gravel underneath several feet of sand.

As Atlas already owned the mineral rights to an acre of the land anyway (due to a transaction years ago with the previous owner) I was more than hopeful that something could be worked out. The company was in fact excavating a pit just half a mile away at that time, so it would be ideal simply to move the machinery along when they had finished that job, providing there were enough gravel deposits. So we left it that a test digging would be completed in the months ahead and things would go from there.

In the autumn of 1984 Atlas Aggregates sent in their local site manager, Bernard Housden (who by coincidence lived just a few hundred yards down the road), to test dig for gravel potential. After hacking down a few tall, thin birch saplings to make a path for the JCB with an enormous telescopic bucket, Bernard made five test digs over the low level of the valley down to a depth of eighteen feet. The water table was around six feet deep and water could be seen gushing in to fill the hole as the sand and gravel were removed and stacked in enormous piles beside each gaping hole. Things looked good right from the start. There was enough sharp sand, building sand and gravel (called stone in the trade) to make reworking the site worthwhile. And whilst a polybag of gravel from each pile was taken away for full analysis Bernard assured me that it was now just a formality and that they would probably start excavating in the new year.

To a very large extent the future of totally controlled good-quality coarse fishing in the UK relies on continual excavations of sand and gravel. As both minerals are in constant demand for the construction of everything from motorways to houses, the scope to create new fisheries from exhausted pits is enormous. Some pits, of course, remain dry and these are invariably back-filled by the local council and top soiled for agriculture. But as most sand and gravel deposits were laid down along river valleys during the last ice age, most new excavations soon fill up from the local water table. Thus new recreation areas suitable for sailing, windsurfing, and angling are continually being made available. What's more, anglers need not wait up to twenty years for these new waters to mature, which has often been the case in the past. Even during digging, provided anglers are consulted, there lies the opportunity of creating numerous features, such as islands, with the option of immediate tree planting to attract wildlife and to make the finished result visually a more beautiful place to behold. Provided various marginal plants, shrubs and trees of the correct types are introduced straight away, a quick transformation from a barren flooded pit to a beautiful, well-stocked lake can result in a handful of years – as indeed I was soon to discover.

All that was left now was to arrange a deal which suited both parties and we settled on a simple arrangement. My gravel – plus all the soil and unwanted poor-quality sand – was to be removed from the site, in exchange for a lake as large as possible dug and landscaped exactly to my design. No money changed hands; there was no contract, simply a handshake. How I wish all business could be done like that. And Atlas Aggregates' local manager Peter Charlton and I have been firm friends ever since.

The chance of creating my very own water, with total control of the future fishing potential, had arrived and during the autumn of 1984 I started to plan the fishery. This was not easy because until excavation starts no one really knows what depths are possible. Nevertheless I played around with lots of ideas. Should I have one large lake by joining the new one with the existing lake or should I have two separate lakes? I settled for one. The nice thing as far as I was concerned was that I could design on

BELOW By January 1985 before heavy snows fell, with help from all the family, most of the birch trees covering the proposed lake site had been cut down with bow saws.

paper more or less how I wanted the shape of the new lake to be. I didn't have to put up with the veritable hole in the ground with monotonous bankside contours and awkward spots to fish from, as many ex-gravel workings turn out. I wanted a lake with an interesting, inviting bankside, deviating every few yards from peninsulas to little bays and inlets occasionally, offering a variety of swims where anglers would not be aware of the guy in the next swim. With the help of Barbara, Lee and

Lisa I started to clear the valley floor of the tall birches. Poor Lee, I'll wager few fourteen-year-olds get a bow-saw for their birthday!

October onwards saw us using it on birch trees. We stacked the cut trunks for future swim-making where step downs would be required due to the steep sides which would surround the new lake. I enjoyed the exercise of bow-sawing immensely and Sunday after Sunday for week upon week, whatever the weather, we gradually cleared the area. We had a great bonfire to dispose of all the brushwood on 5 November with more than thirty friends round. One couple said they thought the entire woods had gone up, as they could see thirty-foot columns of flames from the main road prior to driving down the narrow track to our bungalow. Had me worried for a while, too!

By January much of the valley had been cleared and Bernard helped by chain-sawing down some of the larger trees. Heavy snowfalls then covered everything and for a few weeks nothing could be done. But at the beginning of February 1985 a Massey Ferguson front loader with tyres six feet high and a 2½-ton capacity shovel arrived. This made short work of widening our drive to take the huge lorries required for gravel transportation, because no processing was to be done on site. All minerals were to be transported to Atlas Aggregates plants either at Swanton Morley or Costessey, both five miles away.

Huge piles of soil, sand and gravel were heaped opposite the house and quite suddenly the property took on the look of a working gravel pit. It is truly amazing what one piece of heavy machinery can do in just an eight-hour day! I assured

LEFT It didn't take long for the heavy machinery to turn scrub woodland into a working gravel pit, taking off top soil and sand to just above the water table where the richest gravel deposits started.

Barbara, however, that within a couple of years the beauty of our secluded setting would return – all the better. She didn't believe me! The kids of course loved the huge piles and steep levels of aggregate and sand all over the woods and zoomed through on their motorbikes. They never really wanted the digging to end.

After three weeks of clearing by the Massey Ferguson, the dragline arrived by special loader. Bernard also brought in the site caravan, portable loo and even an old boy from the village complete with dog, whom they had inherited from their previous site. Gravel was spread over the drive all the way from the main road, as the first batch of lorries taking away minerals badly cut up the track. Bernard also had our drive levelled and shingled in front of the house – a most useful by-product of the digging.

Although the Massey Ferguson had totally changed the look of our land by removing in places up to six or seven feet of poor-quality sand down to gravel level – which started more or less at the water table – what the dragline was able to achieve in just one day was unbelievable. I came home from the shop, stopped the car and just gawped at this enormous, lovely hole with sheer sandy sides. The water may have been brown and frothy but I didn't care – it was the start of our lake.

Planning permission had to be obtained from the local county council before gravel extraction and the formation of a wet pit as a fishery could be carried out. Fortunately most councils are sympathetic towards the construction of anything to do with leisure, nature reserves and fisheries, provided heavy vehicle access and subsequent transportation of minerals for months – possibly years – on end does not inconvenience the owners of adjoining properties. I had no trouble in securing planning permission due to the fact that Atlas Aggregates already owned mineral extraction rights to some of my land, coupled with the plan that the new lake was to be joined to an existing one.

After a couple of days digging, Bernard, the site manager, decided that as most of this new lake would not be much deeper than between four and six feet, due to the gravel seams running quite shallow above a heavy belt of blue clay, he would not bother with the pumps during extraction. Now as far as gravel companies are concerned, to pump out the water as it pours in when minerals are taken out means far more precise digging in comparatively dry conditions. The gravel then

BELOW Dragline operator, Barry, skilfully scoops out a steep pathway from the lane in front of the house down to the lake level, while behind him Albert fills up a 20-ton lorry using the massive 2½-ton capacity shovel on his Massey Ferguson front loader.

doesn't have to be stacked to dry out before being loaded on to twenty-ton lorries and taken to the processing plant. It can be dug and carted away immediately, which saves time and allows more space on site. However my pit was easier to dig wet. It was allowed to fill up from the water table and reach its own natural level while the dragline removed the sand and gravel.

This resulted in a rather uneven bottom due to the scooping action of the dragline shoe, which I was not bothered about. But more important, by being dug wet, it meant that I could immediately start organizing planting of the margins and building swims – something impossible to achieve when a pit is dug dry, because there is simply no way of guessing where the eventual water line will be to the nearest foot all the way around the perimeter. Within a week of the dragline arriving and starting to dig along the south-eastern boundary during March I was able to start planting. That I appeared to be planting as quickly as he was digging actually became an ongoing joke with Barry, the dragline operator, who I swear could have iced a cake with his machine despite its massive 1½-ton capacity shoe, such was his skill in operating. I would ask for a flat, level bank in a particular spot with perhaps two feet of marginal shelf, followed by the drop-off, and, lo and behold, it would be done by the time I arrived home from work.

I really enjoyed our early morning planning talks. We were literally creating the lake features based on paper drawings on a day-to-day basis. Due to the low water table, the only feature no one could do anything about was the incredibly steep sides of the new lake, in places some fifteen feet above water level. But as they shelved down from the woodland all the way round, I could easily picture what a beautiful valley it would eventually become. 'Vision' is, I believe, the word I used to convince Barbara that one day the upheaval would all be worthwhile.

For angling access I had to build numerous step-down pathways. These I constructed from the birch logs during the early mornings, evenings and on Sundays throughout the spring. They blended in wonderfully with the hundreds of birch trees left on the higher level but were back-breaking to install. Each step required two holes, each two feet deep, to accommodate the support logs which were chocked in with large flints and then topped up with sand. Rather than nail the horizontal (stepping) logs in I simply picked one or two fairly smooth thick ones and held them in position by back-filling. This was so that they could be replaced easily, which was just as well really because birch rots too easily, and I had to replace most of the logs with oak within the first year. That was a lesson well learnt. So if you are planning any home construction work, never put birch in the ground.

Starting the excavation at the south-eastern boundary close to the house allowed me systematically to plan and construct log pathways down the steep banking once it had been top-soiled. I was also able to plant both shrubs and marginals as work progressed north-westwards along the site towards the old lake where the two would eventually be joined a few months later. But before Barry's dragline left the house end I had a small pond dug some twenty-five feet across and four feet deep, with just a narrow pathway between it and the lake. It has turned out to be very useful, and is now a lovely wild pond, used by newts, frogs and toads as well as dragonflies.

Obtaining shrubs and plants to cover the banks of a newly-dug lake could well cost a fortune at a garden centre. By asking around, however, it was surprising what turned up. For instance, my friend Chris Newell, over the other side of Norfolk at Downham Market, happened to be clearing an island on a fishery he runs. It contained some ancient dogwood, that lovely shrub whose bark turns bright red and glistens in the winter sun. The tops of the original shrubs had dropped down into the water and actually rooted on the bottom, which provided me with hundreds of ready-to-plant stems once they had been cleared. It was a job I was only too pleased to lend a hand with.

In addition, the estate game-keeper donated dozens of young rhododendrons which had self propagated in the rich peaty soil. In one day by the late afternoon Barbara and I had planted out a good sixty yards of steep banking with dogwood, hoping the spreading rootstock would help stabilize the slope.

A few weeks later fishing buddy, Steve Allen, mentioned that a close season working party was on at a lake near Norwich and that lots of yellow iris beds were due to be cut back. After an enjoyable evening's work I was eighteen bin liners full of iris tubers to the good, with a promise of more should I require them. I was very worried about the car's suspension on the way home though! By offering to clean up a friend's little carp pit which was overgrown, I obtained mountains of common reed, reed mace and common sedge, plus a bucketful of frog spawn which went in the wild pond.

From an overgrown water meadow beside my local River Wensum, the farmer was only too pleased for me to thin out numerous roots of reed grass and reed sweet grass (often called sweet rush). The word soon got around that Wilson was after plants and all sorts of offers came pouring in. I cleared out friends' overgrown garden ponds, farmers' drainage dykes and ditches and tidied up swims around a small club lake. Eventually so much was on offer I had to start declining. I was collecting in the evening and planting it all in the morning before work, day after day.

It is really puzzling just where a whole estate car full of marginal plants disappears to in a natural setting. You will know exactly what I mean if you have popped along to your local nursery or garden centre and spent £50 or even £100 on shrubs which, when planted, are hardly noticeable. Planting a lake is exactly the same, on a larger scale. The plants seem to go absolutely nowhere. However I stuck to my goal of planting every foot of the lake's perimeter with exactly the variety I wanted, so that undesirable plants could not take hold. For instance, only in one spot where the marginal shelf drops immediately down to over eight feet did I plant reed mace. In a new lake which has depths under four feet, should this marginal – often wrongly called bullrush because it sports cigar-like seed heads – start self seeding, soon large areas of the margins could be ruined. The good thing about marginal plants is that you can choose exactly the right one for a specific area and for a particular reason. For

tall close-in cover where the shelf dropped quickly away I installed either common reed or reed grass, a similar though slightly shorter reed type, whereas in the shallow areas I opted for the visual beauty of yellow iris which will not spread outwards into the lake and can easily be cut back by paring the tubers with a spade. It has no creeping rootstock and provides a wonderful splash of brilliant yellow flowers throughout June.

Water gardening is the same, be it a tiny pond or a lake. You can spend the first couple of years waiting impatiently for everything to double its rootstock and grow large, and then the rest of your days are spent cutting it back trying to keep the vegetation under control, as I have now been doing for the past decade. As Barry and Albert, who worked the Massey Ferguson front loader, moved quickly along the site piling up great mounds of gravel which were taken away with equal speed by a succession of lorries, I decided where the first island should go. I decided it should be straight in front of the house so Barbara could have her favourite rhododendrons hanging out over the water within view of the kitchen. I had to make a few concessions, didn't I!

Bernard, the manager, said that during the thirty years he had been digging pits in Norfolk no one had ever asked for an island to be made, and he reminded me that I would have less water for the fish. I then explained that in my comparatively small lake the last thing I wanted was anglers casting over each other's lines and going after

ABOVE The lake, now almost half excavated, takes shape. On the right I had a small growing-on pond dug (now a wildlife haven for newts, frogs and toads) prior to the first island being made. Note how the bank in the foreground has already been planted with yellow iris and various shrubs.

the same fish, as is the problem these days on many popular heavily fished waters. And if there was a narrow, tall island in the way running lengthways down the lake they would not even be able to see each other.

So an island it was (the first of three) made by utilizing a great deal of poor-quality sand plus blue clay, which otherwise would have been disposed of, with a good layer of top soil to finish. I then planted it out over a weekend, totally with evergreens including rhododendrons, cotoneaster, pyracanthas, laurels, leylandii, plus a blue cedar and my favourite conifer, the beautiful *Cedrus deodara*. I then asked Barry to leave a gap of around fifteen yards before starting on the second island, which I wanted quite flat with gently sloping banks to accommodate water birds. On this second island I planted five Lombardy poplars, a few dogwood roots, some mixed dwarf conifers, and evergreen shrubs including elaeagnus and stranvaesia which both sport berries during the winter. Also planted, using Barry's dragline, were two large tree roots – one crack willow and one alder – both lifted from where the old lake would eventually join the new.

Originally I had planned on having no deciduous trees anywhere near the waterline of the new lake due to its overall shallow contours. I feared that eventually it would silt up as a direct result of leaf fall. So most shrubs and trees are evergreens. But with the poplars, willow and alder I cheated a little. Along the margins of the island I enjoyed mixing cultivated varieties with plants from the wild, amongst them being the purple flowers of water mint and golden yellow of marsh marigold, the deep blue of hybrid irises and the pinky white flowers of bogbean, sea club rush and water forget-me-not, plus various sedges and variegated irises. Between the shrubs on the islands I mixed the orange tones of montbretia and day lilies with the yellow of St John's wort. But this is not meant to be a garden catalogue so I won't list them all. I can't remember half the names anyway! Suffice to say that throughout the calendar year there is always something in leaf, in bloom or in berry, because although the lake is now first and foremost an angling water, it still remains my front garden.

I enjoyed rowing out to the islands in a little dinghy every evening to plant out. It was exciting just being there on this totally new piece of water, always muddy from the disturbed clay bottom, but which over the weekends soon turned almost crystal clear. Like all newly dug gravel pits it had that lovely blue-green clarity that only lasts a few weeks until Mother Nature has stocked her larder. Actually, long before the excavations were finished and the two lakes joined, the fly life cycle was turning over very quickly, with shrimps colonizing the bottom stratum . . . so I thought I'd try a bit of an experiment.

One morning Barry suddenly stopped the dragline's diesel motor and came rushing over to where I was walking the dogs. 'Hey, I've just seen a goldfish,' he said. 'Yes,' I replied, 'I put in 5,000 yesterday evening.' The look on his face was absolutely magic; a mixture of total disbelief and simple sufferance. After all, who'd be nutty enough to introduce fish into a small lake while it was still being worked? As it turned out the goldfish were a sound investment and trebled their size in twelve months, helped

LEFT With the new lake now nearing completion, Barry used his dragline to contour the second island, as the machinery moves closer towards the trees surrounding the ¾ acre existing lake.

along by a regular supply of floating trout pellets. As the lake was not going to be fished for a year or two until the banks and margins had matured, the goldfish, along with some carp, allowed me both to enjoy and monitor the new lake which by June – after just four months of excavating – was almost complete. Then on the last knockings Barry struck a large area of blue clay at waterline level which Bernard was keen to make into a car park. But the deal was the removal of gravel, sand *and* blue clay, and so a special machine was brought in for moving the clay across to the opposite side of the site where it could be hidden in a large natural depression in the woods. Although the area was little larger than a tennis court, and resulted in just two feet of water, I felt that a pretty bay full of lilies was more desirable than extra car parking. As it turned out this area is used by the carp at spawning time and the warm shallow water plays host to huge shoals of roach and rudd fry throughout the summer months. The beauty of numerous varieties of water lilies is yet another bonus.

At the beginning of June I donned a wet suit and visited my local club lake where I usually have the job of thinning out the massive beds of common yellow lilies which grow much too thickly if not kept in check. This particular year they were not thrown on the bank to rot but put to very good use. Using a well-sharpened bagging hook I hacked from the thick bottom silt over 200 large crowns, each with flower buds and pads intact and with massive tubers as thick as my arm. After distributing half between committee members of three local clubs for planting in their lakes, I just about managed to cram the rest into the car. Even curled gently in dustbin liners the odd stalk snapped off, but three hours later they were all replanted in the new lake at various spots around the islands and along the margins in depths of three to four feet as cover prior to the shelf dropping away. Not one was planted in open water, only along the bankside shallows. Patches of lilies out in the open can create problems when playing fish, which get snagged in them. I wanted to avoid this especially and the resulting parrot-mouthed carp which result from being hauled through lily roots. There was no possibility of planting each tuber in its own container with loam as I would have preferred; there were far too many. I simply pushed a spade into the bottom strata, mostly blue clay topped with sediment, and wiggled it back and forth to open a large wedge-shape crevice. Each tuber was then trodden into the wedge with the stalks pointing upwards, as the spade was wiggled out. This proved most satisfactory as only two of the very buoyant roots popped up to the surface and needed to be replanted. After eight hours in the water working in a wet suit I awoke the following morning with aches and pains from muscles I never knew I had – but it was worth it.

One week later I installed another batch of lilies, this time a large white hybrid from a lake in the village owned by a good neighbour. He helped me to fill over twenty bin liners, in addition to accepting the temporary destruction of his beautiful beds. These went into slightly shallower margins than the common yellow variety, in depths between eighteen and thirty-six inches, and were planted in the same way. I have subsequently added many more varieties of beautiful lilies including reds and pinks. In total I have over twenty different varieties and what a wonderful splash of colourful cover they provide throughout the summer months. Ironically the one

RIGHT Lee and I start the laborious 'hands on' task of planting hundreds of lily roots along the lake's marginal shelves, something best achieved by wearing wet suits and getting stuck in.

variety I have not been able to obtain is the original white water lily *Nymphaea alba*. I am quite aware that many water garden centres call all their white lilies by this name but they are usually, in fact, hybrids.

Back in the late 1800s a Frenchman called Joseph Latour Marliac used *Nymphaea alba* (then very common) to crossbreed so many of the beautiful hybrids which today bear his name and grace ponds all over the country. *Marlicia albida*, *Marlicia carnea*, *Marlicia chromatella* are the names of just three of over seventy varieties created by Marliac. Strangely the world's most gifted lily hybridizer took all his secrets to the grave when he died in 1911 and as yet no one has come anywhere near to achieving similar success. Today because Marliac's robust, large-flowered hybrid lilies exist in just about every pond, pit and lake throughout the country, the true, original *Nymphaea alba* cannot be found. Even my local Norfolk Broads, once crammed with original white water lilies up to the 1920s and 30s, contain them no longer. Incidentally, whilst fishing the River Shannon at Meelick a few years later, I came across some white lilies that could well have been the true wild *Nymphaea alba* – but I didn't fancy diving down eight feet to obtain a root. Perhaps it's simply down to the general change in water quality which has effectively made this particular species extinct (just like the burbot). But enough of lilies. At least that's how I felt throughout June and July 1985 having physically removed from source and replanted over 300 large roots!

Once the new lake had achieved its final shape, joining it with the existing one meant a tricky job for Barry. He had to swing the dragline shoe between some mature alders literally only three or four yards apart and scoop out a five-foot deep channel that would be spanned by a bridge. Back into the wet suit again, and beneath where the bridge was to go I installed a sheet of one-inch steel mesh, reaching from above the surface right down to the bottom. This was to stop the carp in the old lake from swimming through while the new one matured, and was removed a year later when I allowed fishing in both lakes. Ironically, while the mesh stopped most of the carp from passing through, what I had not bargained for was the goldfish – remember the 5,000 I had put in the new lake to grow on? – swimming through in droves. The syndicate members made a few humorous if somewhat cynical comments about how suddenly, from nowhere, just when the carp were on top taking floaters, up would come swarms of goldfish and devour everything. Fortunately everyone seemed to take their presence in good part, with the promise that the orange devils would be netted out at the end of the season. Barry put the finishing touches to the new lake by gently sloping the bank from the lane down to the water's edge, following up with some top soil. Work for both the dragline and the Massey Ferguson front loader had ended. The following morning I was not woken by the noise of their diesel engines roaring into life and, if the truth be known, it was something I actually missed after close to five months of excavation work. I also missed nattering to Barry and Albert every morning about how the shape of the lake would progress that day and then arriving home in the evening to see it. As it had more or less come to the end of its working life and could no longer be safely towed, the old site caravan was donated by Bernard, the manager, as a club house for the new fishery. He left it exactly where it had stood for five months beneath a clump of silver birch now just three yards from the lake. Once painted matt leaf green, it blended in beautifully with the trees and provided refuge to the anglers during foul weather and a place for them to get their heads down during a cold night. This, incidentally, has long since been replaced by a cedarwood summerhouse.

Throughout the summer various shrubs and trees, both deciduous and evergreen, were planted near the pathways and step-downs to separate each swim so the anglers would feel content in their own little environment. Mostly the swims were neat and rather small, with an attractive birch log set horizontally, and two front supports at water level to minimize bank erosion. In a few swims which were low to the water the same objective was achieved by allowing the common fox sedge to form a thick mat-like bed. These have turned out to be great stalking spots.

In only a couple of swims did I leave enough room for a bivvy to be erected. I simply hate those huge patches of bare muddy bank – now unfortunately a common sight on most popular carp fisheries – where flowers and grasses once concealed the stealthy angler. I felt that with more than a generous stocking policy of carp in all weight ranges, scaleage, colour and shape, most of the syndicate members should be able to satisfy their fishing needs sufficiently from even short pre- or post-work sessions in addition to daytime plus the occasional all-night stint. What's more, I wanted anglers to be able to enjoy the sight of wild flowers, marginal plants and grasses without having to beat them down, and then feel the need to cast to the opposite bank because their cover had been destroyed.

The laborious work of collecting the seeds of numerous wild flowers, including some old favourites like foxgloves, Himalayan balsam and willowherb, has proved most worthwhile. Gorse and broom already existed in the sandy soil in abundance and have subsequently self seeded along the steep banks creating a profusion of yellow. In addition, just about everywhere along the margins and slopes – even along the high ridges between the birches – enormous clumps of soft rush (which looks not unlike a mini-bullrush, with onion-like dark green stems) have self seeded. I'm certain the seeds must have been lying dormant in the enormous ridge of top soil first stacked during wartime excavations. Then, forty years on, they sprouted when the ridge of top-soil was used for landscaping.

I felt that some willows and conifers would really help to achieve that 'valley look', from the marginal growth up the steep slopes to where mature birch stood on level ground along the top ridge. In August 1985 I got a job lot of over one hundred mixed conifers, mostly quick-growing leylandii with a few lawsons, from a local nursery and we planted these eighteen-inch trees mostly along the north-eastern slope which had received a good layer of top soil. Planting out this many young conifers was easier said than done. The sandy soil around the woods is absolutely riddled with rabbits, so after firmly treading in with a good peaty mixture and support cane, each sapling had to be protected – rabbits just love to chew the bark at ground level – by a two-foot diameter protective sleeve of chicken wire, two feet high. I really thought I had beaten the rabbits after this little lot, and so didn't bother with chicken wire around the evergreens on the islands. Rabbits would never swim out there, would they? No, but they have no trouble walking across the ice whenever the lake freezes over, the crafty little devils. Their tell-tale paw prints going straight across the lake are clearly visible after a layer of snow has settled on the ice. Nevertheless most of these conifers are now well in excess of twenty feet high and most beautiful, providing a distinct 'Canadian look'.

The last planting job around the new lake was installing some 300 willows along the high south-western ridge to help stabilize the banking. Dad and I set to and got most of them in and staked, complete with rabbit protectors, during the Christmas break. And the poor chap thought he had come up from London for a rest! We planted over twenty different varieties in all, which is nothing compared to the 200 listed in the Edgar Watts Ltd of Bungay, Suffolk, catalogue who specialize in willows, particularly cricket bat willows. I always imagined there were the standard types, like the weeping, crack, white and goat with those lovely fluffy catkins and which we lovingly call 'pussy willow'. But no, you can get willows with coloured barks, coloured catkins or leaves and special varieties with large fibrous rootstocks for consolidating steep banking, which was just what the doctor ordered for the job in hand. The two varieties of *Salix purpurea* and *Salix riminalis* were used along the steepest slopes. Every so often we popped in the odd evergreen between the willows;

LEFT With the excavation completed and the islands fully planted, I started tree planting along the steep slope adjacent to the lane, using fast-growing conifers. Note the roll of chicken wire for making rabbit protectors.

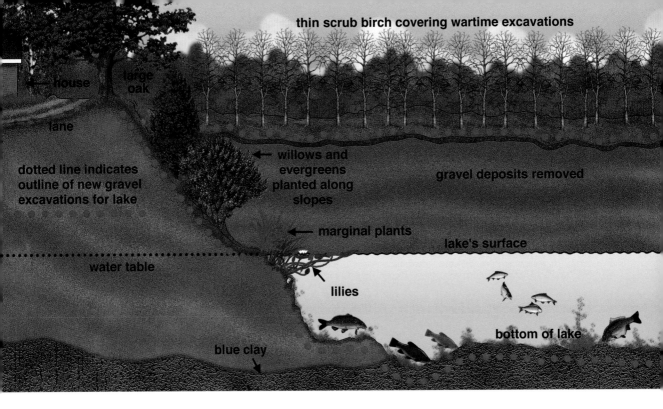

some Christmas trees, pines, cedars and leylandii. Evergreens dotted here and there look really nice in the winter, especially when there is a little snow on the ground.

Going back to June – the third to be precise – all the carp in the old lake spawned, with water temperature at 66 degrees Fahrenheit. I removed a mass of fertilized spawn, complete with the submerged willow roots it was stuck to, and introduced it to various spots around the new lake, and into the little pond which was by then nicely green with planktonic growth and ideal for fry survival. This resulted, one year later, in over a hundred three- to five-inch carp from the little growing-on pond and an unknown number in the new lake. Although it was not to be fished for at least a year (and that was providing things went well), I couldn't resist introducing a few more fish into the new lake. It's the same with a garden pond. Whoever waits for several weeks for the pond to become established like all the books tell you? You want to see fish in it straight away. I'm no exception, so in with the goldfish went 1,000 small metallic carp (koi/king carp crosses). The plan was to net out the majority of these the following spring, retaining a few to complement the stock of big metallics that had been in the old lake for three years and were then approaching double figures. Things worked very well when netting time came around.

To increase the food for planktonic growth still further, I purchased a hundredweight bag of triple super phosphate in granule form, and distributed it from the boat by hand all along the margins. It was just an hour's job, easy compared to the alternative and organic way of fertilizing by shovelling in a ton of well-rotted manure.

From the outset I deliberately did not plant any soft weeds, which would seem to go against the general picture most anglers have of the perfect fishery full of aquatic

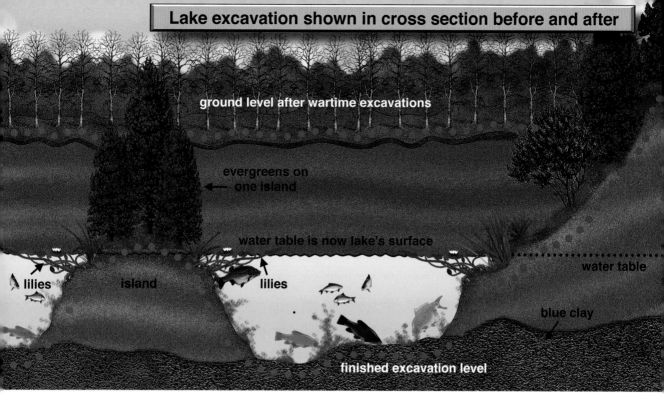

Lake excavation shown in cross section before and after

ground level after wartime excavations

evergreens on one island

water table is now lake's surface

water table

lilies

island

lilies

blue clay

finished excavation level

vegetation and thus full of food. With the high stocking density of carp I had envisaged for the lake, a soft weed environment would not have survived anyway. When their metabolic rate is high during the summer months, feeding fish churn up the sediment in the new lake by rooting for shrimps and those little red men, bloodworms. Contrary to popular belief, a fishery does not need to be clear and prolific in soft weeds to feed a large number of carp. Green-pea farm ponds with not a sprig of weed in sight are prime examples. Area for area and pound for pound they are the richest fish producers of all waters. Carp seem just as happy in coloured water which, from the angling point of view, is more desirable in a lake of limited proportions. Catching them on simple tackle close in to the margins is one of the benefits to be gained and of course the carp still have the protection and the insect food source afforded by extensive lily beds and thick growth of marginal plants.

Before it was even dug, my lake was to be carp-biased with all sorts of shapes, sizes, scale patterns and colours, even the odd koi, some big crucians and a sprinkling of grass carp – where incidentally they do very well without soft weeds to eat. To complement odd batches already introduced throughout the winter of 1985/86 I purchased selected carp when available in preparation for the season ahead when I planned to lift up the retaining grill beneath the bridge allowing the fish to move freely from one lake to another. In went a dozen or so nice commons and mirrors into double figures plus several dozen pretty, smaller fish in the two- to seven-pound range. I wanted neither bream nor tench which cannot live in small communities with carp, and opted for twenty or so adult eels up to four pounds and catfish. It makes sense really: being predatory, chub, catfish and eels do not compete on the

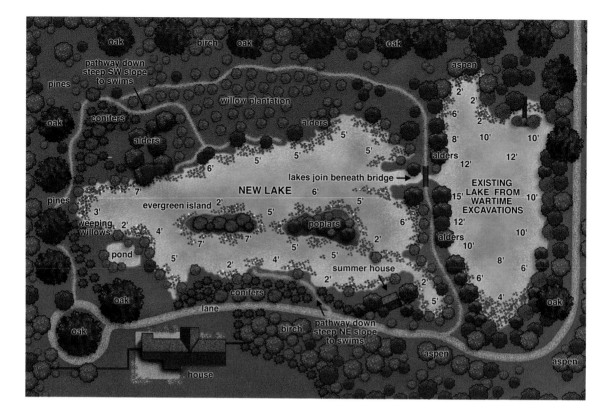

same level with the carp and all are caught on baits such as luncheon meat or mussels. Introducing predators which help to keep down the enormous population of gudgeon, small roach and rudd, which are continually breeding in the lakes, allows anglers the chance of catching three different hard-fighting species which grow to specimen proportions in addition to plenty of carp. This is better than catching half-starved tench or bream on carp tackle.

The Danubian wels catfish is not an easy fish to obtain a licence for stocking. In fact all river authorities treat the stocking of an alien fish with suspicion and indeed have good reason since the zander controversy starting back in the 1960s. However, providing the water where they are to be introduced is totally enclosed and complies with the conditions set out by the Ministry of Agriculture, Fisheries and Food, there is at least a chance of a licence being granted. Obviously only isolated lakes or pits far enough away from a river system without inlets or outlets, or low-lying banks which flood every so often, even get through the first round. There must be no chance whatsoever of the catfish accidentally going elsewhere and a map of the water concerned complete with its Ordnance Survey grid reference has to be supplied together with the application for a licence.

Before all this becomes possible however a batch of healthy young catfish from a disease-free stock bred in this country has to be found. Fortunately in the autumn of 1986 I was lucky to obtain thirty three- to four-inch cats, bred by a member of the

Catfish Conservation Group. Several of these baby cats were forfeited to the local Water Authority for examination, which in my case was Anglian Water in Huntingdon. They were cut open and inspected for various diseases, and duly certified as suitable. I was rewarded with an official document called an A30. This was then sent to the Ministry of Agriculture, Fisheries and Food and fortunately I was granted a licence for the catfish to be released. However simply releasing the young cats into a new and possibly hostile environment did not seem a particularly good idea, especially as the licence did not arrive until December.

A high survival rate was imperative and I didn't fancy having the little whiskers gobbled up by the large eels and chub already stocked or by one of the three herons which visit the lake every morning. So I decided to grow half of them on indoors in a large heated aquarium throughout the winter months and put the other half into the growing-on pond where they could take their chances in food stocks. There was an enormous supply of tiny carp, roach and gudgeon fry to see them through so it was up to them.

Much to Barbara's displeasure I set the tank up in the kitchen with one under-gravel filter grid, plus two internal power filters. As catfish are very sensitive to light and invariably seek seclusion in the darkest areas, several lengths of black plastic drainpipe were laid on the gravel. Within seconds of being introduced the baby cats took up residence in the pipes and unless being fed or the lights were turned out, that's where they preferred to be. It was great fun to observe their often comical reactions, especially when bumping into each other. It seemed to me they have very poor close-range vision, relying to a large extent on touch from the two long feelers. Such tiny eyes suggest they hunt more by feel, smell and vibrations than by sight.

The temperature of that tank was thermostatically controlled and after varying it to several different temperatures between 55 and 76 degrees Fahrenheit, around 70 to 72 degrees Fahrenheit seemed to suit them best. Their metabolic rate was drastically reduced when temperature was decreased to 60 degrees Fahrenheit or below, which would seem to fit in with in-the-wild experiences of most fishermen. As an experiment and to see how they would co-exist with another species of similar size, I netted out a four-inch home-grown metallic carp from the small pond and was pleased to see that in no way, at least on a size for size basis, could they compete against or dominate a king carp. In fact the carp probably had the lion's share of the granulated salmon fry crumbs which were introduced twice daily. The little cats took but a day to find this rich food source and would gorge till their bellies were full before retreating into their drainpipes.

When most of the tank's occupants had reached six to seven inches I supplemented their diet with inch-long gudgeon fry netted from the lake's edge after dark. The carp also took a fancy to gudgeon – as carp do to little fish in the wild – often taking the first three or four before the cats got a look in. As they grew their food size was increased to larger gudgeon, baby carp and roach fry. Once an average length of eight inches was reached I dispensed with the pellet food and went over to a

RIGHT Accompanied by my faithful German Shepherd 'Buzzy' (now passed on) I find good use for the remaining mature birch trees by tapping their sap for wine making. A recipe for this tangy wine appears towards the end of the 1990s chapter (see page 205) together with a photograph of how the lake has matured (see page 208–209).

completely fish diet, gudgeon of between two to three inches being the norm which were eagerly devoured by a quick, violent sucking motion from those ear-to-ear jaws – sometimes head first, sometimes tail first. Once a meal touched the front feelers, it was a goner. The carp too carried on munching a diet of live gudgeon.

In late May when water temperature in the lake reached around 60 degrees Fahrenheit, I released the cats, having first taken ten days to reduce tank water temperatures. The carp, now a beautifully coloured pond fish with plates of gold and silver enamel, was given to a mate for his garden pond. It weighed close on a pound. Since that first batch I have reared on and stocked a few dozen more wels catfish, some of which go to twenty pounds plus. Most however run much smaller and provide a thrilling tussle and the occasional surprise to those carp fishing.

My initial decision to base the fishing on a prolific head of carp of all shapes, sizes and colours with the additional back-up of eels, chub and cats has proved most popular with my syndicate anglers. It offers the chance of latching on to specimen fish of several different species, whilst at the same time enjoying old-time carping which doesn't necessitate sitting out all night to get a run. To achieve this calls for a delicate balance because, compared to most, the two lakes would seem to harbour more carp than is healthy. But as the lakes are literally my front garden allowing me to walk around regularly, there is no better opportunity for close monitoring things such as disease, overcrowding, oxygen starvation and so on.

I was of course still fishing as much as possible during the mid 1980s despite the extra labour of love involved in the creation of the new lake. I also updated my book *Where to Fish in Norfolk and Suffolk* during 1984/85. In fact life had taken yet another direction even before lake excavation was started with the opportunity of making some video pilots for television. I was introduced to Independent Television producer, Peter Akehurst, by a mutual friend, Jim Forte, who now lives in Canada, and we shot three pilots during the winter of 1984/85. The first was pike fishing on Rockland Broad, the second was roach fishing on Norfolk's River Tiffey and the last was on my local River Wensum after chub. These were sent out to television companies all over the country (fishing was scarcely represented on television in those days, remember) and luckily for us the tape eventually landed on the desk of Anglia's then head of production, Phil Garner, who decided (as he told me later) to provide us with a budget for a new series because he particularly liked the way I presented pike fishing on Rockland Broad.

(Peter Akehurst went on to direct the first four series of *Go Fishing*. The first two of these were produced in-house with Anglia TV crews and the second two independently for Anglia by Peter's own company, Wizard Productions. Then things turned rather sour between us and I suggested he find another presenter. Within a few months Anglia's programming commissioner, Colin Ewing, invited me to continue with *Go Fishing* independently as Peter had not come up with a replacement, and so I teamed up with one of the cameramen, Paul Martingel, as director and his producer friend Gelly Morgan, who was all set to produce *Go Fishing* series five through her own production company, Pretty Clever Pictures. However I told Paul that this would be the last series I made without being in total control. This resulted in the formation of Kazan River Productions – named after the most glorious fishing venue in Canada's

BELOW The proverbial three men in a boat. (*Left to right*) Dave Lindsay was not only soundman but wrote the music to over twenty *Go Fishing* programmes; Peter Akehurst who produced and directed the first four series of *Go Fishing*; and ace cameraman, Paul Martingel, who from series six through to eleven, became my partner in producing *Go Fishing* through Kazan River Productions.

ABOVE Well, someone's got to do it, haven't they! In this case it was a photo call publicity shoot organized by Anglia PR where I got to carry Page Three girl, the lovely Susan Mitzi, who squeezed into a mermaid outfit for the occasion on the Serpentine in London.

Northwest Territories – one year later. Paul and I then produced a further six series before he left Kazan to go his own way.)

The first six-part series of *Go Fishing*, using the first compact Betacam video system installed by Anglia Television (now superseded by Digi Beta), was shot during the summer of 1986 within the Anglia viewing region and screened in 1987. Fortunately it proved to be an instant success and was given rave reviews throughout the angling press. *Angling Times* in particular really warmed to the series and this led to my writing regularly for EMAP (now Emap Active) magazines which continues up to this day. (Under my company, Kazan, I also made specialist angling videos for Emap Active, but more of this later.)

Actually, it was during the first couple of years of being involved with *Go Fishing* that I met Sarah Mahaffy who founded Boxtree Limited, then an independent publisher of television- and media-related titles, now part of the Macmillan group, and Martin Founds of Anglers' World Holidays: two people who were greatly to influence the direction I took within television. I have now written seventeen titles under the Boxtree imprint and I shall be forever grateful to Sarah and her then co-director, David Inman, for their vision in wanting me to write that first all-important book, *Go Fishing*, which described the ins and outs of putting fishing across on television back in 1988. I had in fact already put a book together before I met Sarah because I could see the marketing potential. Unfortunately, neither Anglia TV nor *Angling Times* shared my view. Without Channel Four agreeing to take the series – which at that time they had not – nobody wanted to commit themselves and so I started chopping up what I'd written into articles for magazine use. But Sarah decided to take my book anyway. Within a few months her loyalty had been rewarded: Channel Four had decided to screen *Go Fishing* nationwide after all.

Anglers' World Holidays, the leading angling holiday operator in the UK, is owned by Martin Founds who provided me with a wealth of exciting locations for filming in *Go Fishing* three and four, and also series five, a twelve-part international series. Sadly, although probably best remembered by many viewers, series five along with series six (both international series) are not likely to be repeated due to the fact that as *Go Fishing* is now produced on budget money allocated for local programming, filming locations are restricted to within that same viewing area. Things have become even more complicated for my *Go Fishing* series in recent years in that having been bought out by Meridian Television, Anglia TV was then taken over by United News and Media. As a consequence Channel Four refused to screen *Go Fishing* third hand, so currently my programmes are filmed in both the Anglia and Meridian regions and subsequently shown only in those viewing areas. (Sadly anglers nationwide do not get the chance of watching them but the programmes are sold on to the satellite channel Discovery Home and Leisure.)

It was also around this time through their then marketing manager, my good friend Bruce Vaughan, that I became involved with Ryobi Masterline. I have now endorsed and designed tackle for them for the best part of fifteen years. Bruce went on to become co-owner of Wychwood, the well-known clothing and tackle manufacturer, and was replaced by Andy Orme, who then went on to form his rod manufacturing company, Seer Rods. Chris Liebbrant then took over as marketing manager and we enjoy an excellent working relationship to this day. Ryobi Masterline became Masterline International Ltd in 1999 and a range of specialist reels, rods and sundry items was designed by me and carries the Wilson logo.

But let's return to the days of researching and filming abroad in the late 1980s. I researched several Irish locations with Martin, mostly along the River Shannon where we caught mountains of bream and specimen rudd. We caught carp and trout in Austria; seatrout and the strikingly coloured golden ide in Sweden; roach and bream in Denmark; sharks and barracuda in The Gambia; plus barbel, mullet and carp from the Rio Ebro in Spain. In Canada we visited the bountiful province of Manitoba for channel catfish and carp in Winnipeg's Red River, steelhead trout and Dollyvarden in British Columbia, and huge lake trout, northern pike and grayling from the remote Northwest Territories. And what fabulous locations they were! It really opened my eyes to the fishing available elsewhere and I couldn't wait to share those experiences

LEFT Why I'm smiling in this crew shot I don't know. For four successive days I couldn't buy a pull in British Columbia's Copper River, despite the helicopter depositing us beside some fabulous steelhead pools. (*Left to right*) Henry Marcuzzi, Paul Martingel, yours truly, guide Jim Culp, Dave Lindsay and tour operator, Martin Founds.

RIGHT The *Go Fishing* crew about to leave Ferguson Lake Lodge for Nueltin in Northern Canada. (*Left to right*) Me, Martin Founds, Paul Martingel, Melissa Robertson, Keith Sharp and Henry Marcuzzi. Our transport: this ancient 1943 Norseman float plane. Was it hairy!

with my viewers. I particularly enjoyed our escapades in Canada's far north and chronicled a great deal of this in my *Go Fishing Year Book* which included much of the detail about putting the international series five together.

One of the stories included in the *Year Book* illustrates the unbelievably good sport Canada has to offer. It all started innocuously enough when our crew of six finally left Rankin Inlet on the edge of Hudson Bay (an old mining town full of rather merry Innuit Eskimos) having been fog bound for almost four days and was deposited at Ferguson Lake Lodge. This took three separate trips in the small Cessna float-plane with much grumbling from joint-smoking pilot Harvey, a Vietnam Vet. I can remember vividly on the first flight across those deserted wastelands, which comprised half land mass and half water, when with a map on his lap Harvey suddenly turned to me and said in all sincerity, 'Do you know where we are, John?' Having never seen the Northwest Territories before, let alone fished there, I obviously hadn't a clue. This didn't help Harvey who was simply matching the shapes of river junctions and lakes below us with those on his map, flying by compass being totally out of the question due to minerals in the rocks giving false magnetic readings. So it was sight flying or nothing (hence the reason for us waiting for the fog to disperse) and Harvey was looking for what appeared little more than a garden shed – Ferguson Lake Lodge – beside a huge lakeland and river complex. We were literally hundreds of miles from nowhere, the closest bit of civilization being some 400 miles away at Baker Lake. So it was Ferguson or bust. Making fishing programmes for television had suddenly taken on board a new facet – danger!

The jovial twenty-three-stone Keith Sharpe, who settled in the Northwest Territories to avoid alimony payments to his first wife back in Birmingham over twenty years previously, met us at the dock and organized his troop of nine (yes, nine!) children to stash all the gear into the cabins reserved for our stay. Keith had remarried to Alma, an Innuit, and was in the process of putting the Ferguson and Kazan River fishing for giant lake trout and huge arctic grayling on the map, deserted as it was and bisected by the 63rd parallel.

Once Harvey had brought the entire crew over from Rankin Inlet we settled down to a sumptuous dinner of caribou steaks. Then I made the mistake of asking Keith whether we had two boats for the next day's filming. 'Oh dear, no,' said Keith, 'but I do have a spare one left on an old outpost camp not far away.' (The eighteen-foot hull had in fact been left since last summer turned upside down with an assortment of supplies beneath.) Keith said we would have to make a short trip after dinner in the Cessna, followed by an overnight stop at his new camp situated close to where we would be filming on the Kazan River. We could even enjoy some spinning for lake trout *en route* 'to get my hand in' so to speak. I was certainly up for it, as was Martin Founds. Director Paul Martingel didn't fancy splitting the crew up but Keith assured him we would all meet up again the following morning. Keith then muttered something about an ice floe, but I was so excited I wasn't listening.

Thirty minutes later, Harvey skimmed the Cessna down alongside the small island and Keith, Martin and I prepared the aluminium boat for fishing. The thirty-horsepower Yamaha engine we'd brought along fired immediately and with darkness but two hours away the Cessna headed back to the lodge while we set off towards Keith's outpost camp at Yathked. That's where the mighty Kazan River merges with the Ferguson immediately above Kazan Falls, a maelstrom of white water so charismatic I named my production company after it. It contains mountains of two- to three-pound grayling and some of the world's largest lake trout which grow to sixty pounds and more.

Though we were about to experience the most terrifying time of our lives, for the first half hour the lake was completely clear and I had time to catch several sizeable lakers up to around fifteen pounds on large spoons cast from a small island. Then we could see what lay ahead, an enormous band of ice stretching seemingly over the entire horizon. Keith's prophetic words, 'I didn't think it would be this big', still failed to dampen our enthusiasm. Anyway we had no option but to press ahead in the direction of Yathked camp where we were to spend the night.

There was in fact more than a mile of pack ice between our boat and clear water on the other side due to the particularly late 'ice out' that year. In Canada's far north the ice melts by July but the rivers and lakes ice over again by September. It is an incredibly short summer which is why everything breeds so prolifically – the mosquitoes and black flies in particular. As dusk started to fall so the flies appeared from nowhere. With the plane now long gone back to Ferguson, it was a case of dragging the boat over the ice floes or perish from exposure. And while yours truly was wondering whether we go around or across it, Keith ran the bows of the eighteen-foot aluminium hull right up on to the ice, which he guaranteed was perfectly safe to walk on and a good one foot thick. So we all got out and started to pull. Despite the hull weighing over 600 pounds plus planks of timber, pots and pans and even a portable loo, which had been left with other sundry supplies beneath the boat all winter, the aluminium boat slid quite freely over the ice. It even looked for a while as though we would soon be in the warm at Keith's outpost camp. Little did we know!

After an hour of pulling and pushing, dark areas of thin ice became far more numerous and we needed to make long detours to stay on the firm, bright white parts. Midnight came quickly and went, though of course we could see easily because it never really gets totally dark that high up during the summer months. Did I say summer? It certainly didn't feel much like summer. Our hands were becoming painfully cold and we were starting to feel exhausted. We could see the clear water beyond the ice still a tantalizing way off; we had no alternative but to plod on into the unknown.

Whenever the ice could be felt cracking beneath our feet we immediately transferred most of our weight on to the boat by leaning across the gunnel. On the first occasion the ice actually gave way Martin got his feet soaked, which kind of served him right for only bringing trainers on a fishing jaunt. But he carried on without a murmur. With Keith at the front pulling and me and Martin pushing on each side, everything went well again for a while. Then quite suddenly the formidable hitherto reassuring figure of Keith Sharp, who was constantly giving orders from up front, disappeared through the ice with a crash that would have done a bull elephant proud. The boat lunged forward after him, while Martin and I jumped in and grabbed his collar. He managed to roll over into the boat at the first attempt, completely drenched in freezing water. It was a very close shave indeed because without Keith, Martin and I were goners, and without us so was he.

Not knowing if the next footstep would take us under the ice or keep us on it we became more and more anxious about our plight, especially when we saw the number of gaps now appearing between the ice floes. Keith even had a remedy for this problem however and showed us how to use the boat as a bridge, pushing it across from one chunk of ice to another, then pulling it on to firm ice once we had walked across. In areas large enough we actually pushed the boat in and used both paddles and engine for a few yards. Then Keith would run the boat up on to thicker ice and we could continue on our way. Throughout we were treated to a truly beautiful sunset, as the great shining globe sunk beneath the horizon fusing the icy background into a multitude of yellows, reds and purples.

At around two in the morning a horrible thing happened. I had always naïvely associated mosquitoes with stagnant water and the tropics, so I was surprised that here we were in the freezing cold being bitten by more mosquitoes than I had ever seen before, or since incidentally. Like all nightmares ours eventually came to an end when, totally exhausted and almost frozen to the bone, stinking of dried sweat and wondering whether we would actually make it, we finally broke through the last of the ice floes into clear water. What a relief it was; we hooted and whistled like three kids at a funfair. There was then just half an hour's journey to Keith's basic outpost camp at Yathked where we had to wake up Rob, a young American who guided for

Keith all summer, to sort us out some bedding. After a brew of strong tea and a warm up over the spirit stove we finally got our heads down shortly before four in the morning, completely knackered and not just a little lucky to be there at all.

What did we eventually catch? Well the lake trout fishing certainly lived up to Keith's promises with everyone in the crew catching lakers of twenty pounds plus on both spinner and fly, and even from the shore. We managed to wrap what we wanted in filming action within a day and a half – which was just as well really because that's all the time we had.

The year 1987 was a particularly busy one for me because I travelled from Norwich by train to London once a week as a consultant on the angling partwork *Catch* published by Marshall Cavendish. Fellow consultant was my old mate the late Trevor Housby and we enjoyed a riotous time together helping with page layouts, correcting copy and captioning the photos. It was a known fact amongst the staff that Trevor and John needed to have the current partwork put to bed before everyone went to lunch. Because they couldn't get much out of us in the afternoon once we'd hit the red wine at 'Break for the Border', a Mexican restaurant around the corner. Those were fun days and for me they were not only great weekly breaks from the tackle shop, but a wonderful experience too.

We even found time to venture away from the office periodically on prizewinner days out. I remember one trip to Nythe Lake in Arlesford, Hampshire (now closed), where two prizewinners were accompanied by all the *Catch* staff for a fly-fishing day out after rainbow trout. Unfortunately the sport proved dire due to an uncharacteristically cold and chilly day for May. At lunchtime our two guests had caught nought.

After lunch however Trevor pulled out his trump card and suggested they try the tiny lakes (the stews) behind the lodge where, of course, they couldn't go wrong! We were lucky to get away with it but, as Trevor said, 'Hey, they've come for a day's fly fishing, haven't they?' How could I disagree?

LEFT One of my best buddies, the late Trevor Housby, and I helping to put together one of the weekly angling partworks produced by Marshall Cavendish of Wardour Street in London's West End.

I warmed to everyone on that project, several of whom became firm friends, and respected and valued their professionalism. Simply seeing how my own copy and colour transparencies were used within the partwork was of enormous future help.

When I bought my tackle shop in Norwich back in 1971 after returning from Barbados, along with the stock I inherited from my predecessor, the late Bill Cooper, was a large cigar box full of unsaleable junk, amongst which were some enormous size 8/0 treble hooks. The label read, 'Mahseer Trebles 2/9d'. Weren't they those huge fish inhabiting the rivers of India? I had read a little about these legendary monsters – the great *Barbus tor* – but never thought that one day I would actually be catching them. As chance would have it, in 1980 I was asked to write a piece for the British ABU Tightlines tackle catalogue and was sent the previous year's issue by editor, John Darling, for guidance. It was full of the ABU-sponsored transatlantic overland expedition made by three English guys in a jeep and how they caught mahseer to ninety pounds. The pictures were awe-inspiring and left an indelible image on my memory. The mahseer then cropped up the following year when Paul Boote, another English angler, wrote a fascinating series of articles in *Angling* magazine about his exploits in search of mahseer in southern India.

By now I was straining at the bit, but I had a wife, two children and a tackle business. Swanning off for several weeks to the depths of India was at that time simply not on, so I did the next best thing and read some books about the monster fish – the standard work on the subject by H. S. Thomas, entitled *The Rod in India,* and others by Skene Dhu and Jim Corbett recounting wonderfully those early days of the British Raj in India when mahseer fishing was out of this world all over the country. Unfortunately however since the late forties, due to indiscriminate dynamiting, poaching and netting of all the major rivers, the mahseer had become non-existent in all but a handful of protected locations, mainly in the extreme north and south. I feared it would all be over long before Wilson got attached to a whopper.

After my initial desire to do battle with the mahseer in the early 1980s several years elapsed during which time little was heard in the angling press of this enigmatic species. I was by now starting to feel the pressure of both shop and television commitments and fancied a diversion. The decision finally to do something about mahseer fishing actually came about when friend Andy Davison and I were at a clay pigeon shooting club annual dinner in Dereham near Norwich, feeling decidedly worse for wear. Quite suddenly the subject came up, and there and then we decided we had to go. Andy drove down to Bristol to meet Paul Boote for some advice, and I spent week upon week collecting maps of the famous Cauvery River in the state of Karnataka, where historically many of the largest mahseer had been caught, including those by Paul Boote and by the ABU-sponsored transatlantic overland expedition. We were going in search of mahseer and that was that. We allowed ourselves a five-week holiday during which time Barbara agreed to look after the tackle shop. And so it was, following over a year of painstaking research and putting together what we hoped would be suitable tackle combinations, that in the middle of February 1988 Andy and

I boarded an Air India flight from Heathrow to Bombay and on to Bangalore, there to meet Colonel Naidu of the Wildlife Association of South India.

Spending an entire five weeks in the company of just one person necessitates that he should be one hell of a good friend. The previous occasion that Andy and I shared a fishing holiday was some ten years back touring along the Tay Valley, in Scotland, grayling fishing. We were cooped up in a caravanette with two other friends, Ron Wells and Doug Allen, and although the trip was enormous fun for a week, it did make us all realize that no matter how good the bond of friendship, eventually you get on each other's nerves. Stuck in that tiny caravanette along with damp, stinking nets and tackle, not to mention smelly socks and maggots that were for ever escaping, brought out the worst in us all.

It resulted in Doug and Ron, real 'meat and veg' merchants, usually content with tinned meat pie and peas every night, being totally revolted at the eating habits of Wilson and Andy. We were not prepared, however, to allow the remoteness of Scottish grayling rivers to affect the quality of our cuisine. On one particular evening, for instance, we served up chilli con carne and beef-filled enchiladas with lashings of hot garlic bread, all washed down with two large bottles of Chianti.

The enchilada cases I made from seasoned flour and water, rolled out on the flip-up table top with a Heinz tomato sauce bottle (no rolling pin on board) and for a while there was flour and black pepper everywhere, much to the disgust of Ron and Doug who departed for the nearest pub long before we had the gourmet meal bubbling away on the tiny stove. And there they stayed until last orders were called and the aroma within the van had subsided. Doug swore he could still smell chilli over a week later when he cleared the van up before returning it to the hire firm. Truth is, I believed him too!

I wouldn't recommend to anyone the hassle of arriving at Bombay International Airport and clearing customs before attempting the switch-over to the domestic terminal for the final flight to Bangalore. The amount of unnecessary red tape (left by the British) anyone carrying cameras or fishing tackle has to endure is outrageous. Nowadays there are flights straight through, fortunately, but then I guess it was all just part of life's rich tapestry. Anyway before long we had checked in to the West End Hotel for our first night in India. We left for the river in Colonel Naidu's broken-down jonga the following morning complete with sufficient supplies for our five-week stint which included a dozen live chickens. No freezers in the Indian jungle!

I'm tempted to say at this point that until you've travelled on Indian roads, you have never experienced the pain, heat and exhaustion of third-world travel. Sixty miles of being bumped about, plus the continual blast of hot air mixed with dust from the narrow roads was almost choking. Yet this was at the same time utterly fascinating. We passed troops of monkeys, mud hut villages and the most stunningly dressed Indian girls gathering water from remote village wells. The peasant women dressed in colourful saris had fresh flowers in their ebony hair and wore a kind of pride not seen in the West these days. We passed the simple kilns and workings of brick and tile manufacturers, had a ride on an oxen cart and spent an interesting half-hour with a group of road workers, mostly women, chipping and brushing away at the gravel road in readiness for tarmacing. Goodness knows how many rolls of film Andy and I got through on that first memorable drive from Bangalore to the Cauvery (or the Kaveri) valley at Sangham.

As we motored down the steep hill via several hairpin bends towards our final goal the Cauvery was every bit as magical as we had imagined. Strewn with boulders even in midstream, some larger than a car, the entire centre channel ripped forcibly over more boulders, through a series of rapids and deep swirling pools. This was where we had come to do battle with the mighty mahseer. With steep, thorn-scrub-coated hills picking out the route of the river along both banks we followed the flow upstream, through dry creeks and ravines until we reached what was to be our camp at Gari Bora where a huge rock of granite, half the size of a house, presides over the Cauvery River.

We met guides, Bola and Suban, and camp cook, Ivan, and a most interesting hunter by the name of Don Anderson, whose father the late Kenneth Anderson was one of the most famous of all modern-day shikaris (hunters). His book, *Nine Maneaters and One Rogue*, is a must for anyone remotely interested in hunting and a gripping read. Don kept us captivated with tales of the Indian jungle all through dinner and long into the night, every so often punctuating his stories with identification of the various animal sounds around us: the rooting of wild boar (less than fifty yards away), jackals calling incessantly, and the occasional roar of a bull elephant. How we slept I'll never know.

Then in the early hours a steady, thunderous roar seemed to drown out everything else. Don said, 'Oh dear, they've opened the dam,' which instantly put paid to any

BELOW If there is one place on this planet I have come to love enough to think of as my second home it is the majestic Cauvery River Valley in the state of Karnataka, southern India.

mahseer action for ten days. The state of Tamil Nadu further downriver was like a dust bowl and the government had bent to pressure and was flooding the entire river valley in order to irrigate the farmers' paddy fields. Hence literally overnight, which just happened to be the first night of our trip to the river, the Cauvery rose fully thirty feet in just a few hours. Don said it was as close as we would ever see the river, second only to the full monsoon rains which raise it even higher throughout the summer months. We just had to be patient until it receded. At least this gave us time to explore the valley with Bola and Suban. We tracked elephant herds, located the marks of big crocodiles that basked on the mud slopes and hunted poisonous snakes. Sometimes we used a coracle which was kept at the camp to reach the other side, sometimes we swam across. Everything Bola did, Andy had to do, and so a forty-year-old Wilson suddenly found himself attempting to do things that would have seemed downright dangerous back home, but when in Rome as they say . . . It was a wonderful chance to behave like a boy again and we both thoroughly enjoyed ourselves. So what, I hear you ask, has this odd, almost prehistoric carp-like fish got that all the others haven't? Well, to start with, mahseer specifically choose to live in the very fastest, most turbulent reaches of these big wild mountain-fed rivers. They select rivers up to 300 yards wide which every so often abruptly narrow down to just thirty yards, forcing their torrent through rocky gorges into unbelievably powerful rapids. In such a volatile environment you would quite reasonably think no fish could swim. But it does. In currents doing ten to fifteen knots which rip around great chunks of black rock from which the entire river bed is formed, in a lather of spray and white water, the biggest mahseer are to be found. These massive river fish weigh anything between forty and a hundred pounds or more, with scales and fins so large they seem disproportionate to their body size. The mouth is also enormous, coconut-size with thick-rimmed rubbery lips quite devoid of teeth. But back in the throat is the mahseer's secret weapon, its awesome pharyngeal teeth, capable of crushing to pulp both the fish and crabs which live amongst the rocks, plus the strongest of hooks should you be unfortunate and hook one in the throat. The mahseer has, in addition, seemingly endless stamina. Hour-long fights from fish in the 50–70lb class are commonplace, without the slightest indication of the creature tiring or that you might be getting the better of it. At any time during the fight the mahseer may suddenly rip off fifty to over a hundred yards of 30–40lb test mono as though on its initial run. Often on that first frightening run, reels like the ABU 7000 or 9000 are stripped to the point where you either jump in and follow the fish down the rapids or hear the line crack like a pistol shot. Then quite suddenly, without any warning, after having given its very all, the fish bellies up with its great mouth wide open, ready to be hauled out, and even this is no easy job in water doing ten knots or more.

With hands still shaking, a soft retaining cord is passed through its gill and out through the mouth to form a loop-like stringer and the fish is held steady in the flow with its head upstream until it regains its breath. Then and only then are trophy shots taken. With a strong sense of compassion for the great fish you wonder at its physical enormity as you cradle it lovingly in your arms before returning it from whence it

came, to cheer the soul of another angler on another day. I ask you, how many freshwater fish can strip off 200 to 300 yards of line from a multiplier against the power of an eleven-foot 3lb test curve rod and leave you feeling like a nervous fruit jelly within seconds?

When the river subsided, the kind of fights Andy and I enjoyed were simply unforgettable. Each day there was a fish to top the performance of the one before. Slowly we stepped up line strength from 20lb to 30lb and finally to 40lb test. The current speed, the rocks on which the line all too quickly became frayed, necessitated such tackle and it was none too light. Where the biggest fish resided was too fast for even a four-ounce lead to hold bottom. So the method was to use just a little lead coil wound around the line, twelve inches above a 6/0 hook, and to encourage it by casting across the stream and giving a little slack to catch around a rock. You then tightened up and waited, your nerve ends tingling in anticipation of the violent take of a big mahseer. Even moderate-size fish would have pulled the rod in, so it was held at all times. Whether using a huge ball of paste made from the staple millet grain flour of southern India called ragi, a river crab, or an eight-inch livebait (any small rock fish will do), the take when it comes can only be compared to the hook suddenly being transferred to a lorry doing forty miles an hour.

Your thumb burns as the spool revolves at high speed and you frantically try to knock the reel into gear before setting the hook. Many big fish do in fact almost hook themselves, such is the force at which they belt off downstream. Very quickly your groin aches from the pain where the rod butt digs in. You change hands frequently throughout the fight to rest a tired arm and your buddy helps you gulp from the water bottle in between rattling off unforgettable shots on the camera. And afterwards if it is a big one, you are content not to cast again – lest you hook another! – such is the fight. Actually Andy and I made a pact from the start, agreeing that whenever one hooked into a good fish the other would instantly reel in and grab both cameras. This worked a treat. More than at any other time in our lives we learned to be unselfish.

Actually all species of fish grow large in the Cauvery River. It is so rich in all forms of life, from snails and aquatic insect larvae clinging to the underside of every rock, to the millions of tiny fry along the margins which peck at the bits of ragi paste as you rinse your hands after baiting up. Water temperature was an incredible 87 to 89 degrees Fahrenheit during our stay with the full Indian summer still to come!

In some of the steadier stretches of the four miles we covered, our guides would row us out by the coracle to a rocky outcrop in mid river where the current was fastest. We then got back into the coracle if a big fish set off downstream or upriver (most go down) and gave chase, finally clambering out on to the shore or a rock plateau during the closing stages of the fight. Without question seeking fish in the rapids provided the most thrilling, unforgettable – if not hairy and rather dangerous – sport.

After one week of crashing into unseen rocks without shoes and another of feeling sand and grit rubbing the skin away inside trainers, my feet were so sore I could hardly walk without wincing. Andy then suffered a badly infected left leg from ulcers which turned septic, a huge chunk of flesh and bone – yes, bone – having been gouged by the rocks from his shin bone. I made him take the bus with Suban from Sangham into Kanakapura (the nearest town) to see the doctor. Bandages and penicillin were handed out but a couple of days later, and fully two weeks before we were to be picked up by the Colonel at the end of our stay, Andy's leg was in a really bad way. His calf had swollen up larger than his thigh; even to touch his thigh brought gasps of pain. What to do? Then someone up there took charge. We were just about at our wits' end when suddenly we heard the comforting sound of a four-wheel-drive vehicle coming along the elephant tracks beside the river – the first westernized sound for almost three weeks. It was Susheel and Nanda Gyanchand, a husband and wife hunting and fishing team, whom we had met and fished with within the first few days of our arrival at the river.

Nanda was a practising doctor working at that time in Bangalore, whilst Susheel

BELOW Despite a damsel fly finding my badly abused and painful feet attractive, I doubt there's any chance of a toe job here! This was the result of sand and gravel particles wearing away the skin within a pair of trainers: one reason why I now wear diving boots when mahseer fishing.

owned (and still does) one of the largest granite companies in south India. More importantly Susheel's father – and this was the miracle – was also a doctor and one of the top bone specialists in Bangalore. With a badly infected leg there was not a more welcome couple for Andy to have bumped into miles from anywhere in the Indian jungle. Although Susheel and Nanda had arrived for a three-day mahseer stint with mountains of fresh supplies including an icebox full of cold beers, they took one look at Andy's swollen leg, helped him into their jonga and headed back to Bangalore. There Andy stayed for the following two weeks, leaving me

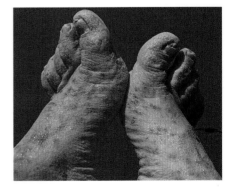

to break camp two days before our flight home. Andy's condition could not in fact have been worse despite his cavalier attitude. He had cellulitis of the bone, which apparently was only one step away from gangrene. Had our newly-made friends not arrived when they did I shudder to think what the consequences would have been. I guess with a whole host of nasties such as deadly poisonous snakes, scorpions and spiders – all regulars around our campsite – plus huge crocodiles in the river, you can understand why we had the entire river valley to ourselves for most of the time. The isolation was indeed wonderful for the soul but it was a bit inconvenient to be so far away from civilization when medical help was required.

We built up a marvellous relationship with our two local guides, Bola and Suban, who swam out eagerly regardless of currents to disengage our lines from hidden rocks to stop a fish in its bid for freedom. We did have to suffer pretty basic Indian food for five weeks (during which time I actually lost two stone in weight!) but it was worth it. We counted no fewer than twelve different birds of prey along just four miles of river. Eagles, vultures and kites actually sat on nests high up in the tall mutti trees together with a family of monkeys right above our campsite, just a stone's throw from the river. In all we took exactly sixty mahseer from five pounds upwards, including a dozen over fifty pounds-plus, the best two weighing 71lb and 87lb. Most came to ragi paste bait and perhaps a dozen or so came to livebaits which the guides caught from the shallow pools in a cast net.

In addition to mahseer we caught, both on paste and worms dug from the river bank, numerous other, much smaller, exotic, peculiar-looking barbel-like tropical oddities, many with weird sucker-type mouths. These they used for sucking on to rocks in the fast water to eat the algae. Their shapes and bright colours were marvellous to behold. Catfish to about five pounds were plentiful and these, when fried and curried, were very tasty. One morning it was my misfortune to hook on ragi paste a very large snapping turtle. It came up hissing loudly, its bright red neck seeming to extend for ever, so I cut the line to be on the safe side. I didn't like the look of it at all. Suban had never seen one before during a lifetime on the river.

Enjoying the spectacular scenery and battling with mahseer in the Cauvery River system was an experience and a privilege never to be forgotten, whether hearing a bull elephant bellowing from across the river at dawn whilst you kit up for another session, watching otters at play or listening to the repetitive rendering of the brain-fever bird (the Indian cuckoo). Small wonder that Andy and I have returned to this wonderful valley time and time again. Needless to say Susheel and Nanda have remained firm friends ever since and whenever Andy and I arrive in Bangalore there is a four-wheel-drive vehicle at our disposal.

Exactly one year later, in March 1989, Andy and I made our first return trip and, due to having Susheel's four-wheel-drive vehicle on loan, we were able to explore the Cauvery for several miles both up and downstream of our camp. One particular morning will remain in my memory for ever because I accounted for the best catch I have ever made in over fifty years of fishing. As usual we were woken long before dawn and quietly moved around the camp gathering everything we needed for an hour-long drive to a favourite hot spot. While Bola and Suban loaded the rods, cast net, cameras and a large bag of freshly boiled ragi into the back of Susheel's vehicle, Andy and I filled our water bottles from the filter unit, had a last look around the camp and told Raju the cook not to expect us back before dusk.

As usual, the dust from the narrow rock-strewn track following the river's path down the valley had covered everything by the time we arrived at the gorge, a wide flood plain, not of sand banks and marginal growth like higher upriver, but jagged, black bedrock – a spot known as Onti Goundu. Since time began the river had carved out its own identity through this primaeval setting and was about thirty yards wide at our favourite spot, immediately above a succession of pools and foaming white rapids. With such strong, swirling currents and depths averaging between twenty and thirty feet most fishermen would never assume that this is where the largest mahseer of all prefer to live, in currents pulling as hard as a staggering fifteen knots – but they do. Humpbacked, fully-scaled monsters, seemingly part carp, part barbel (although the mahseer is in fact a barbel) and here attaining weights of more than 140 pounds.

Andy and I had taken our fair share of whoppers from several spots along the valley – from the deep pools, from the rapids, amidst a mixture of boulders and white water. These were hard-earned fish indeed, all of which provided long, exhausting fights on our eleven-foot, 3lb test rods and 40lb reel line. We fought battles that will be savoured and remembered for ever. But it was here in this hot desolate part of the valley, uninhabited except for monkeys, snakes and the odd wild boar, that both Bola and Suban felt our best chance of hitting a real monster existed.

OVERLEAF I doubt I'll ever beat this phenomenal catch, shared with guides Bola and Suban, and made in just a few hours from the Cauvery River. A magnificent brace of mahseer weighing 81lb and 92lb. My finest ever angling achievement.

It took the four of us more than thirty minutes to work carefully across the network of swift-flowing streams and rock pools on the outer flood plain, before reaching a mouth-watering spot where the river, running right to left, speeds around a double S bend with a long, deep straight between. Andy and Bola crept down to the bottom bend, while I settled quietly on top of a flat rock, above the upstream bend, with Suban at my side. A duck-egg-size ball of ragi paste was carefully moulded around the 6/0 hook and with two ounces of lead strip squeezed on to the line eighteen inches above the bait to catch on the rocks and hold bottom, I made a twenty-yard cast downstream and across.

The bait was quickly gripped by the current and swept across the bottom of the pool towards an outcrop of rock at surface level where a defined crease suggested that a mahseer holding spot was immediately downstream. And it was! Quite suddenly the rod tip buckled over and the free spool beneath my right thumb became a blur as an unseen force rushed downstream at what seemed like 150 miles an hour. Disregarding the painful line burns, I slammed the 9000 into gear and watched helplessly as over a hundred yards of the 40lb line disappeared in no time at all. Under full pressure the fish finally slowed down when it reached the end of the straight and circled around the wide bend where Andy and Bola sat, allowing me to screw the clutch down and regain some line.

What incredibly powerful creatures these big mahseer are! You would imagine that maximum pressure from a powerful rod and 40lb line would slow them down. But this stubborn fish managed to work up and down the long straight, almost at will, for close on three-quarters of an hour, characteristically ironing the line to the rock-strewn bottom as barbel do. Then quite suddenly it came to the surface, virtually beaten to a standstill, to reveal its enormous pig-like girth and cavernous open mouth. Suban climbed down to water level and gently cradled the great fish in his arms. It looked bigger than him and subsequently pulled the spring balance down to exactly 81lb. Gently, Suban sleeved a soft cord through its gills and out through the mouth tying a large loop, so that the fish could move about easily, and tethered it close into the bank around a stake. Big mahseer are always best left on such a stringer for half an hour or so to get their strength back before returning them to face the full force of the powerful current.

Andy and Bola had by now returned fishless from downstream to photograph the fight and so we all decided to retire to the shade provided by a large tamarind tree for a rest from the sun which now blazed overhead to a ferocious 100 degrees Fahrenheit. On our return to fishing Andy and Bola again went downstream to the lower bend and before returning my fish I decided to make just one last cast. This time I used an eight-inch deadbait which Suban had caught in his cast net. As mahseer feed naturally upon small fish and freshwater crabs, a freshly killed deadbait bumping along the bottom from rock to rock is liable to be snuffed up immediately. And on this, Wilson's luckiest day ever, that's just what happened.

No sooner had I feathered the bait down to the bottom following a long cast from halfway along the straight, where a huge slab of rock hung out over the river, than there came an arm-wrenching pull, which almost had me off balance and into the swirling water. Instinctively I knew immediately that this fish was big, very big. I had never before felt such awesome power and I immediately started to worry that it might zoom off downriver and over the rapids, a situation I would have been powerless to stop with such a large fresh fish. Fortunately, however, it reacted and fought totally differently from that first fish, spending the best part of the hour-long battle under my own bank, within a huge undercut, where current force over countless years had carved out a veritable underwater cavern. Try as I might, and I tried by heaving on the 40lb outfit until my arms ache, I could not prise the unseen monster from its lair and out into open water. I was at a complete loss, using up most of my own energy and powerless to stop the line shredding each time the mahseer lunged with its huge tail and bored further into the undercut. My arms were aching, my wrists were aching and my stomach was extremely painful where the rod butt dug in. I never believed that a close-range struggle could be so tiring, and every so often I had to ease off the pressure to relieve the pressure on my own spine – I obviously wasn't as fit as I had thought.

Eventually after more than an hour the fish did budge, and quite suddenly made a couple of rushes directly across the flow, before turning belly up completely exhausted only a few yards from where I sat. By now Andy and Bola were also crouched on the rocks with cameras rolling and it was Bola who offered to climb down to water level and heave the huge mahseer on to terra firma. It was something he did with unbelievable strength and agility. That was amazing because Bola couldn't possibly have weighed much more than the mahseer which scaled an incredible 92lb. This was indeed my red-letter day. Catching a brace of the world's finest freshwater game fish, weighing 81lb and 92lb, in just a few hours remains – to the best of my knowledge – one of the most notable mahseer hauls in post-war times. It was certainly my greatest ever angling achievement.

BELOW Weighing only slightly less than himself, guide Bola actually runs over the jagged rocks cradling Andy's 95lb mahseer across his shoulders.

A couple of days later it was Andy's turn to strike gold with a huge mahseer weighing 95lb from a spot only 200 yards downriver from where my brace came. And during the hour-long fight he had to swim across the river helped by Bola and Suban to avoid a series of rapids along our own bank. For most of the time I rattled off shots with a telephoto lens including the three of them returning with the huge fish slung across Bola's shoulders. Bola was actually running bare foot (as always) across hot rocks fully supporting a fish of around his own weight. The strength, courage and knowledge of natural history of our two guides, Bola and Suban, was quite phenomenal. My gratitude and respect for them are greater than for any other people I've ever met, sentiments that are shared equally by Andy.

In 1989 Andy returned the wonderful hospitality of Nanda and Susheel Gyanchand by taking them to Lake Turkana (formally Lake Rudolph) in Kenya to catch tiger fish and Nile perch. They hooked into dozens of perch in the 25–40lb range whilst trolling lures, as well as a most rare fish captured by Nanda. This was a golden Nile perch of around 60lb which, in coloration, is similar to our own golden tench, being banana-yellow all over, flecked irregularly with black markings, and with black eyes. In all other respects, the golden Nile perch is exactly the same creature as the common Nile perch *Lates niloticus* and, as far as I know, only in Lake Turkana is this stunningly-coloured variant to be found; I have certainly never heard of any being taken from either Lake Victoria or Lake Nasser, the world's two most prolific Nile perch habitats.

Immediately prior to our last memorable Indian trip I had been involved in a most interesting encounter back home fishing a series of three matches against the England team manager, Dick Clegg. These were organized throughout the 1989 winter by *Angling Times* (then edited by Neil Pope) as a modern re-run of the legendary match between the late Dick Walker and top Lincoln matchman, Tom Sails. It seemed that after almost thirty-five years anglers still remembered the confrontation, and that even now few matchmen could swallow the fact that their hero had been beaten by a member of the 'floppy hat brigade', even if the victor was recognized as the finest angling brain of his time.

(A wonderful match-by-match account of this 1953/54 original epic incidentally was given in the 1960 *Angling Times* publication 'Angling in the News' written by Ken Sutton. The matches took place on the River Witham, the River Bain and finally the Hampshire Avon. The series was won conclusively by Dick Walker, 2–1 with an aggregate of 27lb 4 ¼oz against 21lb 11½oz from Tom Sails.)

Now it was all about to happen again due to a handful of *Angling Times* readers suggesting that John Wilson only caught fish on his *Go Fishing* television programmes because swims had been prebaited for weeks on end and that if he were to fish against an experienced matchman he'd be crucified. So I had to take up the challenge! The stage had been set for the 'rematch of the century', as *Angling Times* called it, and they asked Dick Clegg to fish against me.

The showdown was to follow the original rules as closely as possible. Three matches would be fished with the venues chosen to re-create the atmosphere of the original encounter. Neither angler was allowed to use livebaits or hempseed and four hours only were allotted for each match. 'How much do you want me to win by?' said Dick Clegg when the challenge was issued. I was thinking that at least a comparison of our catches with those made on the same venues thirty-five years back should prove interesting. I was also secretly hoping that those club- and match-fishing days during my late teens and early twenties would stand me in good stead.

Round one took place on the River Witham at

Tattershall, Lincolnshire, a typical Fenland drain where you either built up a netful of roach or went for a 'bag of bits', as match anglers say. I arrived at the match stretch early when it was still dark and sat in the car watching dawn break, whilst looking for signs of roach rolling. There weren't any. So right from the whistle I decided to go for gudgeon and ruffe (pope). Choice of pegs was decided by the toss of a coin and Dick won, selecting the downstream end peg of the stretch. And there we sat about a hundred yards apart for four miserable hours in a chilly wind. Everyone had of course expected Wilson to use the big fish approach so there was no small element of surprise when I rigged up a fourteen-foot float rod, 2lb reel line with a terminal rig comprising a 22 hook to a pound bottom beneath a slim waggler. I was going to take Dick on at his own game and try to stay in touch. Fortunately for me I did rather better and produced what for Dick must have been a real shock result. Luckily I found I could catch more gudgeon by twitching my single pinkie maggot around, so as soon as it had fallen to the bottom of the swim I flicked the rod tip which often resulted in an immediate response. The roach Dick had hoped for were non-existent and by the time he switched over to pinkies to go for gudgeon I was too far ahead, weighing in 1lb 5oz of bits to his 11oz. I had upstaged the matchman on his own patch and poor Dick must have taken no end of ribbing when the first match was given a centre-page spread the following week in *Angling Times*.

As with the Walker–Sails match, the tiny River Bain at Coningsby, Lincolnshire, was our second venue. I won the toss and selected a long run overhung by trees along the opposite bank, a typical chub swim if ever I saw one. Dick however – we had the choice of two swims each – opted for a long straight from which both dace and roach seemed the most likely customers on his stick float set-up. Within an hour of the start however neither of us had had so much as a bite as the rain lashed down accompanied by a chilly wind. Then Dick opened the score with a good dace, on trotted maggots. This prompted me to dispense with the mashed bread and quivertipped breadflake approach intended for chub (which had produced just one missed bite) and to switch over to the centre pin and a light waggler rig. A wise move as it happened, because as the day progressed I managed to stay with Dick fish for fish and in the dying seconds of the match hooked my third eel of this round which clinched victory number two. My final score of three eels, a roach, a dace and a perch took the scales round to 1lb 11½oz, 5oz more than Dick. I had thus stretched my modest lead overall to 15oz with one round left.

As everyone had expected from the start, everything rested (as indeed it had in the Walker–Sails match thirty-five years previously) on round three at the famous Royalty stretch of the Hampshire Avon in Christchurch. Everyone arrived at lunchtime the day before in order to recce the match length which was the tidal stretch of this mighty river immediately downstream of the motorway bridge. Graham Pepplar of Davis Tackle in Christchurch had provided us with an accurate lowdown of this interesting beat which runs straight for around 200 yards immediately downstream of the bridge before dividing around an island. We even had time for an hour's fishing in the late afternoon in order to become familiar with the strong tidal currents. But apart from small chub and sea trout, we were none the wiser as to our prospects. The favourite swim looked to be a decidedly chubby overhang at the point where the river divided. But halfway down the straight there existed a deepish run in which lived a shoal of quality bream. I saw one roll as we trudged back to the cars and this, as it happened, influenced the result. In fact that evening back at the hotel before going down for dinner, I mixed up a huge tub of bread mash and crushed casters in the sink in my room. Wilson was going for bream and that strange straight swim if he won the toss.

Unfortunately, or fortunately as it turned out, Dick won the toss when we gathered at the river the following morning with Roger Mortimer from the *Angling Times* to adjudicate. Roger decided that the two swims to be fished were the straight and the overhang where the river divided and when Dick instantly chose the chub hole I was more than delighted. 'Put me down for a big weight of chub today,' said Dick. 'Wilson's bubble is about to burst.' Within fifteen minutes of the start Dick's prediction looked to be coming true. His carefully trotted stick float probed beneath the overhanging trees and produced a fine chub of 4lb followed shortly by a smaller fish. Dick had quickly forged ahead in aggregate weight while I remained without a bite. Actually for the first thirty minutes I trotted maggots, hoping for the odd dace or two, whilst every so often I introduced golf-ball-size helpings of mashed bread into the head of the long straight. For me it was really all or nothing, and depended entirely upon whether the bream would feed or not. Only with a bag of bream could I expect to beat Dick's chub.

As the tide started to drop noticeably I could see tiny vortexes going downstream in a straight line about fifteen yards out, indicating the existence of a long gravel bar with deep water on the inside shelf. If the bream were going to be anywhere they would be foraging up and down that shelf. It was time to switch from float to ledger. That first cast, presenting a large piece of breadflake covering a size 8 hook and the three swan shot fixed paternoster, decided the outcome. The swan shots bumped across the steep gravel bar and came to settle – just holding bottom. Within ten seconds the quivertip sprang back denoting a drop-back bite and I heaved the Avon rod back into my first bream which weighed upwards of five pounds. In a stroke I had levelled our scores as Dick's swim had died following those two chub, though he did add another later.

For the remainder of the match those wonderful bream fed continually but they were decidedly finicky and I lost as many as I caught. By now depth had dropped to less than three feet – not your usual bream swim – and in such fast shallow water bream really use their deep flanks to good effect. It was so frustrating pulling out of what were bream going up to seven pounds or so and I truly think that, had I landed them all, a hundred-pound catch would not have been unrealistic. When the final whistle blew, however, I had nine slabs plus a chub of around four pounds to put on the scales for a total weight of 35lb 15oz. It was all over. The matchman had been beaten 3–0 and the excuses had to end. What my hero, Dick Walker, had achieved thirty-five years before I had now repeated, the final aggregate weights of our three matches being: John Wilson's 38lb 15½oz to Dick Clegg's 7lb 9½oz.

Dick was more than gracious in defeat, saying that 'John's mashed bread approach was perfect on the day and I can think of very few matchmen who would have had the nerve to try it. And if anglers remembered John Wilson beating me when we get to the year 2024 I'll be delighted.' My sentiments exactly. What a nice guy.

BELOW Hailed as the re-run of the match of the century, following the series of three matches fished by the late Dick Walker and Tom Sails back in 1953, these *Angling Times* clippings from 1989 portray the passion of the event in which I fished against England team manager, Dick Clegg.

A New Beginning

J ust as 1989 had ended that decade on a wonderfully high note, with those huge mahseer and my winning against Dick Clegg, so 1990 started in a very sad way. After twenty years of marriage Barbara and I agreed to separate for a two-year period prior to divorcing. The reasons for our split seem now to be academic and certainly not worth resurrecting, although at the time it was of course emotionally devastating for us both. As with all family break-ups it is the children who suffer most, and Lisa and Lee, now seventeen and nineteen years old, found the situation very hard to accept. Indeed were I granted one retrospective wish, it would be for their father to have been more understanding of their needs. As it was I guess I was too wrapped up in the immediate problems of how I was going to continue living in the house, with a huge mortgage, and keep the shop to continue paying for it all when their mother left.

I made the decision to keep both house and shop; and promised to pay Barbara half the value of our estate within two years, to which she agreed. This was an enormous undertaking on reflection when I now think about the figures involved in the cold light of day. But I like to think I have never been afraid of life and I wasn't about to split in half everything I had worked so hard to build in the past twenty years. (However there is a rather funny postscript to Barbara's leaving – well, all my mates thought it was hilarious. She left her mother behind, who had lived with us for the past eight years! My mother-in-law stayed for six months more until I could persuade Barbara's sister to arrange alternative accommodation for her.)

Fortunately *Go Fishing* was now enjoying its fifth series with the promise of more to come, so I literally put everything into my work. Boxtree wanted me to write a series of single species books endorsed by *Angling Times*, so I worked incredibly hard for the next two years, actually completing a total of nine books and eighteen television programmes.

Obviously for both research and the actually filming I was away an awful lot which meant that, with Barbara gone, I had to find someone else to look after the shop. This was solved by my taking on good friend Andy Jubb as full-time manager, a position he had wanted for some time due to his loss of interest in the car-hire firm for which he worked as a mechanic. This was a good move for us both, as it happened, for the car-hire firm closed down the following year.

In 1991 series six of *Go Fishing* included what I thought were two extremely

OPPOSITE With the help of *Mirimba's*; captain, King, wielding the net here, I am about to land a giant vundu catfish from the Sanyati Gorge in Zimbabwe's Lake Kariba.

exciting programmes shot in Zimbabwe. We visited the Zambezi River at Imbabala fifty miles above majestic Victoria Falls, to catch the legendary tiger fish. Then we boarded a sixty-foot luxury cruiser, called *Mirimba*, on massive Lake Kariba. This is a location I have returned to for the past several years now and one that is immensely popular with anglers enjoying guided holidays abroad, a service I have teamed up with Tailor Made Holidays to provide. But more of this later.

The beauty of Kariba, apart from its wonderful sunsets, exotic bird life and unbelievable game viewing from on board a cruiser, is the diversity of its fishing. Whilst *Go Fishing* viewers will no doubt recall that huge 60lb vundu catfish which snapped my rod in three places following an epic two-hour battle before it was finally hoisted into the boat, Kariba is in fact more highly regarded by both Zimbabwean and South African freshwater anglers as the tiger fish capital of Africa. In fact our filming on Lake Kariba coincided with the famous Tiger Tournament, then the largest freshwater gamefishing tournament in the world, comprising over 1,000 competitors representing over 300 teams. Held over three days this competition boasted some mammoth prizes and attracted teams from as far away as Australia, Canada and the USA. There was even a Barclays Bank team from Biggleswade in Bedfordshire. All had to be ready for the six o'clock start each morning at Chiara Point where an assortment of over 300 competition boats lined up, ranging from

ABOVE I took this shot of the magnificent Victoria Falls on the Zambezi River, which separates Zambia from Zimbabwe, from a helicopter. Truly one of the world's seven wonders.

RIGHT Those who cruise or fish on Lake Kariba may wish to take time off and visit one of Africa's largest crocodile farms.

outboard-powered dinghies to fifty-foot cabin cruisers. Upon hearing the starter's gun each then raced for their favourite hot spots across the lake – a truly wonderful spectacle – which, at 170 miles long and up to thirty miles wide, is one of the largest man-made lakes in the world. I think it is also the most beautiful.

Huge numbers of large tiger fish were caught during this event, the heaviest in the 1991 competition of 20lb-plus falling to the rod of a female competitor. Unfortunately all were killed in order to be weighed in and over the succeeding years anglers fear that just this one annual competition, together of course with heavy commercial fishing, has been responsible for considerably lowering the once high average size of the tiger fish on the lake. But don't get me wrong, Kariba still provides wonderful fishing. It's a hard lesson to learn but nowhere has an endless larder.

I witnessed a similar thing happening over a period of several years on another of Africa's huge lakes, Lake Victoria, the world's second-largest lake. It was featured in series five of *Go Fishing* in which buddy Andy Davison and I caught numerous Nile perch on trolled artificial lures to over seventy pounds. Andy, incidentally, returned to Lake Victoria with his wife, Julie, on honeymoon in 1991 and landed, on a trolled Russelure, a mammoth perch of 191½lb. It held the International Game Fishing Association world record for eight years until it was beaten by a 213lb monster caught by Adrian Brayshaw from Lake Nasser in 1998. Sadly it was the policy at Rusinga Island on the Kenyan border, where we had both fished, to kill all perch caught. I remember asking the then manager, Antony Dodds, if he wasn't worried about the inevitable decline that would follow.

A couple of years later in 1993 I accompanied two prizewinners of a competition in the *Daily Express*, Robert Duff and Geoff Neville, to Rusinga Island Lodge and although we caught plenty of perch to 125lb they were noticeably nowhere as thick

LEFT In his Norfolk home my good friend, Andy Davison, lifts up son William beside his 191½ lb Nile perch caught from Lake Victoria in Kenya, which held the IGFA world record for eight years.

on the ground. Almost every day our lures became snagged on sunken nets and long lines belonging to commercial fishermen. The sight of refrigerated lorries loading up at lakeside villages was, I felt, the first nail in the coffin of the once wonderfully prolific Nile perch fishing available along the Kenyan border.

However, perhaps the fishing will survive. Lake Victoria, which has over a thousand islands, and is roughly the size of Ireland, is shared equally between Uganda and Tanzania, with just fifteen per cent of its massive shoreline owned by Kenya. So overall mass commercial fishing of the Nile perch within the Kenyan sector may not be significant after all. I certainly hope so.

Perch exist in all depths all over the lake and there are massive areas of a hundred feet plus. But working the drop-offs along the shoreline and around many of the jungle-clad, steep-sided islands where the prey fish congregate most heavily, reduces the problem of location. And even the largest of Nile perch will feed in just ten feet of water.

Fortunately for me my two companions were both enthusiastic anglers and Buckley Hunt, who organized the package and with whom I had fished on a number of occasions, made up our party of four, a perfect number for fishing two to a boat. There was all the usual banter and friendly competition arising from two teams and our discussions lasted long into the hot night over dinner. Even with sport somewhat reduced, in our opinion, most days at least one of the boats returned with perch over fifty pounds, plus lesser fish in the ten- to twenty-five-pound bracket.

Following our five-day stay at Rusinga Island we flew to the east African coast to Malindi for two days' big-game fishing before returning to the UK. Unfortunately the

RIGHT No wonder *Daily Express* competition prizewinner, Robert Duff from Ipswich, is smiling. His very first wahoo caught trolling (using my gear, too) out from Malindi, Kenya, weighed over 70lb.

three marlin we hooked (all stripies) each managed to jump off the huge kona head trolling lures. But we did enjoy a variety of smaller speedsters in the form of yellow fin tuna, sailfish, king mackerel, some giant trevally and several huge wahoo. Robert landed the heaviest wahoo at a shade over seventy pounds. What a superbly proportioned specimen it was, fully six feet long and unbelievably powerful.

During this same 1991 to 1993 period I also twice visited the Florida Keys to investigate the possibilities of filming there for *Go Fishing*. I was enjoying a wonderful time in my life because I had met Jo, who was later to become my wife. Actually we started off as badminton partners, though on opposing sides, but quickly became soul mates with so very much in common. Jo was already a keen and accomplished angler, loved animals and she had been brought up in the Suffolk countryside. We were, as they say, made for each other. Moreover, unlike my first wife Barbara who was unfortunately not keen on travel because she had a fear of flying, Jo was a seasoned traveller and relished the thought of exploring and fishing in the tropics. To this day she has shared my journeys whenever possible.

Anyway, a fan of *Go Fishing*, Peter Hazlewood, of Milton, Cambridgeshire made, completely out of the blue, an exceptionally generous offer, inviting me to make up a foursome on a shark fishing expedition to the Florida Keys. (Peter had on two previous occasions boated a tiger shark of 850lb measuring 12½ feet from snout to tail and a mako of 824lb whilst fishing out of Islamorada, and lost an even larger, unidentified monster – possibly a tiger shark – which he played for eight hours and twenty minutes before having to break off. The skipper on board *The Dawn*, Jimmy Taylor, estimated Peter's monster at something like 1,400 to 1,500 pounds.) Obviously I wasn't going to let such an offer pass me by and I am glad I didn't because Pete and I have been firm friends ever since. In addition to sharing exotic trips abroad we also occasionally shoot together. But back to those trips to the Florida Keys.

On our first trip we split the week between deep water action on the Atlantic side of the 170-mile-long Keys and back-country fishing by skiff on the quieter, very much shallower, gulf side. The waters around the Keys are unbelievably fertile. For all the tourism this angler's paradise is rather like old-time America and is geared totally to the pursuits of fishing and scuba diving. How I wish we had something like it within the British Isles!

We stayed in a small hotel in Islamorada and fished from Whale Harbour, some eleven miles out drift fishing from *Afternoon Delight* – then skippered by Jimmy Taylor – for big amberjack over a huge plateau called the 'hump' which from 600 feet rises to within 300 feet of the surface. Using 50lb class stand-up outfits with a live mullet or blue runner presented on a size 6/0 hook and 100lb mono trace, taken down by 1½lb lead tied to a weak link, savage takes from amberjack often came within seconds of bumping the hump and winding up a few turns. There literally must have been thousands of jumbo-size amberjacks down there. Even with another twenty or so boats working the same mark, plus several commercial amberjack boats, who caught them on powered winches simply to be used, would you believe, for fertilizer, we

hooked up every drift through. Most were in the forty- to sixty-pound bracket with the occasional bruiser pushing eighty pounds. Even on a 50lb outfit, the fight usually lasted twenty or thirty minutes unless, that is, a hammerhead came along and grabbed the amberjack – not an unusual occurrence over the hump.

The hammerhead led to us going specifically for sharks as well, and we enjoyed several wonderful scraps with these beasts up to 300 pounds or so. Pete and I were more than a little surprised when, as each shark approached the transom and unhooking time had arrived, out from the wheelhouse would come Jimmy Taylor with a loaded 12-bore to guarantee its destiny. Somewhere along the line sharks must have featured rather nastily in his life! As exciting as sport proved to be on the deep Atlantic side of the Keys, which also included trolling for tuna, dorado and barracuda, Pete and I immediately fell in love with skiff fishing on the Gulf side.

Here amongst the tidal creeks and mangrove swamps, colonized by flamingos and pelicans, we caught an unbelievable number of different species using light tackle, including bonefish, sheepshead, spotted sea trout, barracuda, jacks and an assortment of small sharks. We also saw some huge tarpon and missed out on the chance of a big permit.

So impressed were we that on our next visit to the Keys in 1992, when I took my son Lee along, we made just a couple of charter-boat trips out of Whale Harbour to the hump and its amberjacks before spending the remainder of the week skiff fishing on the Gulf side with various guides working out from Bud and Mary's Marina at the southern end of Islamorada. On the very first morning Lee caught a huge bonefish that was approaching double figures on freelined shrimp. Then a few days later when I had teamed up with Peter, our guide Lonnie put us over an extremely aggressive pod of big tarpon, so we float fished live mullet and both Peter and I had each taken a hundred pounds plus of tarpon before it was time to open our lunch boxes. Not since my time living on Barbados had I fished for tarpon and all the old memories came flooding back. It was great to experience again those epic boat-towing fights, which lasted for forty-five minutes, during which these huge tarpon would fling themselves completely clear of the water every so often.

At the end of March 1993, I was asked on behalf of Varig Airlines and Brazilian Tourism by two friends, Simon Williams and Edward Rodbourne – who ran a sports fishing business at Foz do Iguaçú, called Dourado Sports Fishing – to visit Brazil. So off I went to sample some of the finest freshwater fishing in South America. Think of Brazil and the mighty River Amazon immediately springs to mind. Yet this vast country, which is larger than Australia, equivalent to all the European countries combined, and occupies nearly half the total land mass of South America, contains numerous mind-blowing rivers. These rivers are so awesomely wide, fast and deep and so incredibly powerful that even Ireland's Shannon, the longest we have in the British Isles at nearly 300 miles, seems a mere stream by comparison.

Many rivers run for thousands of miles, through tropical rainforests, beside which the fifty-foot-high canopy of palms, vines and bamboos, lining both banks, is so dense that you can see but a few yards into its mysterious darkness. Here beautifully painted

ABOVE My son, Lee, proudly displays a near double-figure bonefish he caught on freelined shrimp using light tackle 'back-country style' in the Florida Keys.

LEFT With guide Lonnie looking on I finally bring a 100lb-plus tarpon to the skiff following a spectacular half-hour battle. The bait was a live mullet float fished.

butterflies flit from wild bananas to pineapples, and parrots squawk noisily overhead. The rivers are simply vibrating from the constant chatter of crickets and colourful finches, and the golden heron waits patiently among the dense marginal growth of sedges and rushes for a shoal of piranha to pass by. Birds such as egrets, cormorants, storks and cranes all earn an incredibly rich living from an abundance of the most unusual tropical freshwater fish you are ever likely to encounter. There are 186 different species to be precise, from freshwater stingrays to the strange Jau catfish, whose ultimate weight must surely double that of the 150- to 200-pounders which are regularly taken on longlines by local fishermen.

Brazil's seasons are exactly the opposite of Europe's, so it was high summer and extremely hot along the Paraná River, my final destination. The point at which this majestic watercourse converges with the Iguaçú River is the border of three countries, Brazil, Argentina and Paraguay. But even more dramatic, and in my opinion

ABOVE I took this photograph from high above South America's magical Iguaçú Falls below which the Iguaçú River merges with the mighty Paraná River. The borderline of Brazil, Argentina and Paraguay.

more breathtakingly beautiful than Zimbabwe's Victoria Falls, are the truly spectacular Iguaçú Falls, a vast column of white water, split into two main cascades. It attracts tourists from all over South America to Foz like bees to the proverbial honeypot.

Apart from emptying into the famous River Plate system, having flowed for a staggering 2,500 miles, the Paraná also boasts the largest hydroelectric power dam in the world at the southern end of Lake Itaipu. This immense structure took ninety-five million bags of cement and eight years to build, using a workforce of up to 40,000 men. It's five miles wide, 120 metres high, has eighteen working turbines and provides nearly a third of Brazil's electricity. Phew! Yet these statistics alone cannot convey the sheer vastness of the Itaipu Dam where there is an experimental fish farm for species like paco, armado (an armoured catfish) and the famous dourado which are reared in floating cages for both food and restocking. So voracious are the young three- to six-inch dourados that they have to be fed six times a day, otherwise they chew each other up – rather like rainbow trout when retained in the confines of the stew.

It was to sample the fighting qualities of this magnificent sportfish, the golden dourado, that had led me to the awesome Paraná River, immediately downstream of Iguaçú. The river varies between 300 and 700 yards wide, is never less than a hundred feet deep through the centre channel and flows at an unbelievable six to eight knots. Huge vortexes of water churn the surface as a result of the current hitting the rock ledges and pinnacles some forty to fifty feet below. It is not the easiest of fishing locations!

The everyday problems facing even the experienced angler are truly enormous, because the river regularly drops or rises drastically overnight. Within days it has been known to rise forty feet or more due to a prolonged deluge occurring literally thousands of miles upstream. But what a fantastic challenge. Looking at the reading on the Hummingbird sonar screen never ceased to amaze me. Whitebait-size fish soup for a solid twenty feet below the boat, followed just above the rocky riverbed, sometimes over a hundred feet down, by the big boys. These are the massive, beautifully marked tropical cats of the Suribi family, with wedge-shaped heads – designed to suit the strong flow – and incredibly long trailing whiskers sprouting from a strange, elongated expanding mouth.

Within hours of arrival I realized that in just a week's stay I was certainly not going to set the world on fire, so I followed the local technique for combating the depth and current by drifting with the boat side on to the flow (anchoring was simply out of the question) and exploring all the really productive, rocky runs or 'corridors' as my guides, Clemente and Jeorges, called them. The cast is made twenty to forty yards upstream so that the bait then bumps back along the tops of the rocks, where the fish are, at current speed. What an enjoyable method this is. A small barrel lead, up to ¾oz, is sleeved on above a 12-inch wire trace to get the bait down. Reel line is 20lb test. Inevitably many end tackles are lost on the rocks which in some areas are bigger than cars. But that's where the larger dourado and monster cats are most densely concentrated and waiting to grab your live *'morenita'* presented on a 6/0 hook. In Portuguese, *morenita* means 'little brown things' and aptly describes the turiva, a lively scaleless eel-like fish of six to ten inches. It's not native to the Paraná but is sold locally in bait shops, imported from Paraguay. The dourados simply love them.

A slamming take so typical of this aggressive sportfish can happen at virtually any time of the drift and, as most of the runs or corridors are half a mile long, you have to concentrate hard all the time. You must be ready to wind the bait up a little when the rocky bottom shallows off perhaps to just thirty feet deep, and then let out more line when it plummets down again even to a hundred feet or more. It's not unlike working lures over wrecks and rough ground out at sea. If a particular run produces a few hits you simply motor upstream and try again; if not, the guides take you down-river to the next run and you drift over new ground. It's most exciting fishing for an extremely powerful adversary which jumps repeatedly high in the air between dogged runs and dives to the rocky bottom.

The dourado is a species not unlike Africa's tiger fish in the speed with which it moves and jumps, with the same horizontal lines of dark scales along its flanks. While the tiger fish sports red-orange fins, however, the dourado is bathed in golden-yellow, not just on the fins but along the lower flanks and belly too. Its huge tail is marked horizontally all the way across with a distinctive thick black bar. Its jaws are immensely powerful with the crunching power to flatten and straighten the

RIGHT A local angler
proudly displays a
30lb-plus golden
dourado, an
acrobatic predatory
species that can
attain weights of
over 60lb.

galvanized trebles on my favourite 5-inch Rapalas. The teeth are much smaller than
those of the tiger fish, without the overall 'Doberman' look. Even so the dourado has
to be unhooked very carefully indeed. One silly mistake and flesh will certainly be
ripped open. They are most common on the ground in the seven- to twelve-pound
bracket and these are great fun on lures, with big double-figure fish always on the
cards. Twenty to thirty pounders are fish of the week, whilst monsters up to seventy
pounds have been taken by commercial fishermen. As an ultimate goal a forty
pounder is not out of the question, and wouldn't I like to have caught one.

In all the slow, quiet bays and sidestreams off the main river shoals of piranha wait
to chomp your morenita in half, so a step down in hook and bait size is imperative.
There are even exotic, fruit-eating species like the paco, an amazingly deep-sided,
discus-shaped fish, which readily gobble up chunks of banana or orange. The paco
fights like stink and averages four to eight pounds with occasional specimens to thirty
pounds. For mini-lure enthusiasts all kinds of weird and wonderful tropical toothy
fish are there for the taking. However most of all it was the massive catfish lurking
there on the bottom which captured my imagination. The pintado, which grow to
150 pounds plus but is more commonly caught in the fifteen- to forty-pound bracket,
also grabs your morenita intended for dourado. Trouble is, before the warning bells
sound and you have put on full pressure, these crafty cats have taken your line
through a minefield of rocks and boulders from which extraction is more a matter of
luck than judgement. I have to be honest and say that in a week's fishing I hooked
two big cats and failed miserably, losing both in rocks literally within seconds of
setting the hook. The problems they pose are more than exciting, believe me!

Finally I must mention the fabulous nightlife in Brazil. There are numerous excellent restaurants serving international cuisine and charging very modest prices, all within easy reach of Foz. Better still there are numerous exotic, spectacular floor shows depicting local costumes, song and dance groups, with the emphasis on mulattos, those milk-chocolate coloured, scantily-dressed beauties, whose gyrating movements are enough to make any luncheon meat man turn to boilies!

However you do not always have to go to exotic locations in order to catch a species you have not previously seen. I love catching new species so when my old pal, Dave Lewis of Newport, South Wales, invited Jo and me at the end of May 1993 across country to sample twaite shad fishing in his nearby River Wye, I was like a kid in a toy shop. Timing exactly when to fish is of course critical because this rather special British migratory sea fish enters just a handful of our major river systems during the spring for the sole purpose of spawning in freshwater. Only during the months of May and June at locations such as Tewkesbury Weir on the River Severn and on the River Wye, where it joins forces with the River Monnow in South Wales, is the freshwater enthusiast ever likely to see – let alone actually catch – one of our rarest fishes.

Wherever shad congregate, often in their thousands, there is a chance of catching them using a superlight spinning outfit and tiny vibratory spinners in the 00 size range. They can also be great fun to catch on the fly rod using attractor patterns, especially silver-bodied fish fry in imitations. We concentrated on our light spinning outfits however and for a good hour in mid morning, from a shallow run, we caught dozens of shad from around a pound to almost two pounds, all of which were returned. Shad all share the same characteristic of leaping repeatedly in a show of shimmering iridescence, not unlike a miniature tarpon. In fact they are not totally unlike tarpon in their physical characteristics too.

The current British record for the twaite shad is less than three pounds so there is no chance of a monster but due to their acrobatics these lively fish more than compensate for their lack of size. What you immediately notice about this enigmatic species is the notch cut into the centre of its upper jaw, into which fits its protruding lower jaw. This is a purpose-built strainer mechanism designed for plankton feeding. Its cavernous expanding mouth is however also quite capable of swallowing sandeels, sprats and immature herrings, hence its willingness to grab artificial lures. Coloration along the back is a mix of pewter and pale grey, sometimes with a distinct blueish tinge, and one of the shad's most recognizable features is a line of several dark, round blotches along the shoulder. These are often visible in the water but seem to disappear on dry land.

The twaite shad has deeply compressed flanks covered in silvery scales which easily become dislodged (just like those of its cousin, the herring) and a most defined keel along the belly. In fact from the small dorsal fin backwards it tapers rapidly towards the sharply forked tail. Confusion with another species is hardly likely, except with the now incredibly rare allis shad which, due to pollution and the construction of weirs and locks, no longer migrates up into British freshwater to breed. Allis shads grow to over four pounds and are much deeper in the body than twaite shad.

Occasionally around the British Isles one is caught at sea, usually by someone feathering for mackerel, although I have regularly used allis shad for barracuda and shark baits when sea fishing in tropical waters. Incidentally the allis shad is now considered a threatened species and is protected under the provisions of the Wildlife and Countryside Act of 1981. It is therefore an offence to capture one intentionally. But let's be honest – you'd have a better chance of finding rocking-horse droppings!

In September 1993 Dave Lewis and I teamed up again to film one of my programmes in series seven of *Go Fishing*, our destination being the famous 'yellow reef' some forty miles off Hansholm in north-east Jutland, Denmark. Our charter boat was the fifty-five-foot *Thailand* which specializes in wrecking and boasts the largest ever rod-caught cod – a monster of seventy pounds plus. I had researched the yellow reef the year before and lost a massive cod whilst on board *Thailand* but the two anglers working pirks on either side of me both managed to land theirs as we drifted over a particularly productive wreck. Both cod weighed over forty pounds. Boy, was I sick, but looked forward to returning to the yellow reef with video cameras. Actually the programme we subsequently made is probably one that most ardent sea fishermen will never forget. Whilst pirk fishing in water some 300 feet deep, Dave went and caught a massive 55lb ling. It provided simply marvellous action for our two cameramen, Paul Bennett and Ron Tufnell who, in addition to the big ling, also filmed Dave and me catching numerous cod up to twenty-five pounds. The only downside was that as a foreigner Dave could not claim the huge fish as a new Danish record, which seems totally unfair. But so it goes.

On the same programme we also featured trolling for cod Danish-style fairly close inshore over rock and kelp beds in crystal-clear saltwater up to twenty feet deep. For cod to chase our Rapala plugs being trolled at two to three knots, the water just had to be clear and while we were in fact after sea trout, cod on the troll proved quite some novelty to film.

In November 1993 Jo and I accepted an invitation from an old pal, Mark Longster, out in The Gambia, whom I had not seen for nearly four years. His totally unexpected fax simply read: 'John, the bottom fishing right now is fantastic – do you fancy a week's action?' Well, who would need asking more than once? The truth was freshwater anglers in the UK at that time (during October and November) were suffering the worst flooding for many years and my local Wensum valley in Norfolk was totally unfishable for weeks on end. So I really had no option but to accept Mark's offer!

Regular viewers of *Go Fishing* may recall that Mark and I had teamed up four years before when a big lemon shark came along bang on cue for the cameras, providing some of the most exciting footage we've ever shown. The programme also included the usual assortment of weird and colourful critters you would expect to catch from the mangrove creeks. However due to lack of time plus the pressure of putting these sequences together, I felt I had rather missed out on the unbelievable choice of inshore boat fishing over reefs and sand bars that the Gambia River has to offer.

Incredibly, there are in fact over thirty different species within that meaty, arm-wrenching 30–50lb weight bracket that you could bump into, and half of these species can actually top three figures in weight.

Also in addition to at least seven species of shark there are several types of ray and guitar fish. There are several species of the jack family, African pompano, leer fish, cobia, dorado, several different types of snappers, kujeli, mackerel, tuna and even tarpon. In fact tarpon have been caught within Gambian waters to a staggering 380lb which is far in excess of the IGFA line class record.

Mark had specialized more and more on the range of inshore reef fishing options since my last visit, obtaining yet another boat with a particularly low-set cuddy, thus enabling him to pass easily beneath famous Denton Road Bridge (by the now defunct peanut factory) and straight out from the moorings into the Atlantic, literally within a few minutes' motoring distance of numerous productive reefs and sand bars. Those who have already fished in The Gambia will know full well that large craft can only get out through the river mouth and into the Atlantic by navigating a complex network of mangrove creeks which eventually lead to behind the harbour and around the coastline – all of which eats away at precious fishing time. So Mark's investment in *Black Warrior*, a beamy eight-foot-wide twenty-two-footer pushed along speedily by a 75-horse Suzuki, had more than paid off, resulting in continuous bookings. There is of course nothing to stop you hiring a rowing dinghy to fish pieces of shrimp in the mangrove creeks or even, as some do (though it is exceedingly muddy), walk along the mangroves and bank fish. Standard carp-pike gear with a 10–15lb line will handle most likely customers, though you may have to go for the occasional long row or walk with a stingray.

You can stay anchored out in deep water right in the mouth of the river which is some two miles wide, or motor inland where it is twice the width and fish the strong tide flow close to Dog Island and stake it out with big baits on the bottom for sharks. You can troll Rapala magnums around inshore reefs and even eventually find blue water and consequently add still more species to the list of those expected. For this, however, you need a large, fast boat and be prepared to motor at least twenty or thirty miles to evade the colour spewed into the Atlantic by the Gambia River, which is some 400 miles in length with a tidal influence of over half that distance. (Giant catfish and tiger fish inhabit the freshwater high upper reaches incidentally.)

We had already decided that our week was simply for enjoying sport with various battlers around the inshore reefs and sand bars. A trip to the local market close by the Sunwing Hotel quickly gave an excellent indication of what the local fishermen, who anchor over the inshore reefs, were taking on their hand lines. Big jacks, kujeli, snappers and even cobia were all for sale. I was surprised to see cobia (called black salmon locally) because I assumed they were really a blue-water game species. But specimens to approaching a hundred pounds were there for the taking. Unfortunately a biggy never came my way although I did hook into one which characteristically rose up from the bottom (as opposed to most species which attempt to hang your line around the nearest

ABOVE This 35lb
cubera snapper is
but one of
numerous exotic
hard-battling reef
dwellers I contacted
within the fertile
waters of The
Gambia, off-shore
from the capital of
Banjul.

rock) but slipped the hook after all too short a fight.

Known locally as cubera, the most common of the big snappers were successfully lured on whole belly fillets from a bonga. And it's interesting to note that these locally netted plankton eaters, the commonest fish seen in the markets, are to all intents and purposes an allis shad. Now a 30lb outfit to catch a 30lb snapper may perhaps seem slightly over the top but these unbelievably strong warm-water reef dwellers quickly shred through the rocks the lighter lines of anyone feeling more sporting.

It's hit and hold arm-wrenching stuff at the very best. Holding the rod with the reel out of gear and the clutch preset quite firmly usually sees many more slamming takes converted into snappers in the ice box, due to the uncanny wariness of this fully scaled, you might even say carp-like fish. But there all resemblance ends because the cubera's teeth are strong dog-like canines and its fighting capabilities, like all saltwater tropicals, put species like carp to shame.

Talking of fighting, one fish I hoped to get amongst during this Gambia break was the tarpon. Mark had taken them in the river mouth to 190 pounds a few weeks previously but the surface was far too ruffled during our stay to be able to locate their characteristic rolling on the surface in large groups. (I did in fact experience this in the Florida Keys when fishing with Peter Hazlewood earlier on in the year.) When tarpon are really on, anything can happen . . . But they will have to wait for my next trip to The Gambia.

What we did latch on to, however – and what a splendid acrobatic fish it is – was the tarpon's younger cousin, the ladyfish. Locally these silver streaks, looking for all the world like a stretched-out herring, are called nine bones and we boated them up to ten pounds on lures. A Rapala 'Slither' in lime green really did the business when trolled through shallow water no more than six feet deep between huge banks of sand which have built up around the outside entrance to Denton Bridge. Anchoring in these long rolling waves proved useful. We simply made long casts to the side presenting small mullet or herring livebaits on size 2/0 hooks tied directly to 12lb test (with an ounce bomb attached via a link fixed two feet up the line using a four-turn water knot) and used the waves to bump the bait gently across the tide. This exciting technique also took those rather prehistoric-looking flat fish called bastard halibut (which also took Rapalas) and some jumbo-size kujeli (also nicknamed captain fish). These strange fish which have a built-in jelly-like transparent nose are actually threadfin salmon and whilst those we took went to twenty pounds, Mark has seen them topping a hundred pounds.

After several days of fun fishing we anchored in the middle of the estuary mouth opposite Bangul with the hope of encountering some shark action. With over sixty feet of coloured water hiding the entanglement of rocks along the bottom and the tide ebbing strongly, expectations of something big happening along were very high. Before long something made off with a Spanish mackerel of fully four pounds containing a double 10/0 hook rig. The reel started to squeal like a stuck pig with that uncanny suddenness only associated with shark fishing and when I slammed home the clutch to strike I was certainly not expecting a missile-minded barracuda. This metallic projectile veered across the tide going like a bat out of hell and performed multiple Polaris impersonations. This was despite the heavy shark trace and 50lb outfit which should have slowed it down but appeared to have little effect. Moreover the barracuda had completely swallowed the Spanish mackerel; but then it was close to five feet long and better than thirty pounds. It was not a huge specimen by any means but a good one nevertheless, and typical of the quality in surprises you can expect when probing the deep-coloured and incredibly fertile water of the Gambia River.

During the winter of 1993/94 I spent an inordinate amount of time sifting through thousands of colour transparencies and hour upon hour of my taped *Go Fishing* programmes for clips of foreign fishing. The reason for this was that Pearson Publishing of Cambridge were going to produce the first angling CD Rom made in Britain, called *John Wilson's World of Fishing*. This mammoth work contains seventeen exotic fresh and saltwater destinations around the globe with 600 photos and 150 video clips, plus over two hours of my narrative. It contains over a hundred detailed destination fact sheets and a rundown of sixty-eight individual species all of which can be printed out as required.

The project involved far more work than I had ever envisaged but turned out to be most rewarding. When first published in 1995 it was actually far ahead of its time, and it received rave reviews from several dedicated magazines including *CD Rom Today*, *CD Rom User* and *Windows User*. If only they all knew that when it comes to computers I am hopeless and leave the workings of our Apple Mac completely to my wife Jo, bless her. Actually in 1996 Eagle Moss Publications Ltd also produced a CD Rom called *John Wilson and Friends' Complete Guide to Coarse Fishing*. This was a 'how-to' spin-off from the weekly partwork *The Art of Fishing* with much additional material in the way of top-quality video footage in which well-known angling writers, Des Taylor, Bob Nudd, Matt Hays and Keith Arthur, also featured. It remains to be seen however whether CD Roms will ever really catch on with anglers. Personally I think books will always have the edge.

On account of my having to rewrite my book *Where to Fish in Norfolk and Suffolk* again for its fifth update, 1994 was another extremely busy year. My television series, *Go Fishing*, also demanded much of my time both in research and in the shooting throughout the summer months of six more half-hour programmes.

During September I was to make one of my finest catches ever by landing no fewer than nine double-figure bream in one session from a thirteen-foot deep swim in a

RIGHT Weighing over 13lb this bream was one of a catch of nine doubles caught during an early-morning session on a Norfolk Lake: possibly my finest coarse angling achievement in fifty years.

BELOW Brother Dave proudly displays a superb brace of specimen bream weighing 13¼lb and 13½lb taken ledgering in a Norfolk gravel pit.

secluded twenty-five-acre Norfolk stillwater I call the 'forgotten lake'. I marked an area in the middle of the lake with a buoy and heavily prebaited it for the two previous evenings with a mixture of stewed wheat, casters, maggots, chopped lobworms and brown breadcrumbs. I was confident of some action and arranged for the video cameras to be there. A thick mist hugged the lake from dawn until late morning which, although it restricted our filming early on, encouraged the shoal of bream to continue feeding far longer than they would normally have done. This resulted in my enjoying unprecedented sport using a sliding float rig baited with a lobtail. Initially I had started with two 13-foot float rods but quickly put one away as bites were happening within a short time of the lobtail settling on the bottom. I had the choice of accumulating the largest catch of huge bream ever recorded, or taking the time whilst fishing to go through baits and explain in detail my sliding float arrangement with all the inevitable waiting around (when I could have been catching) that filming demands. Frankly I reckon I could have caught twenty or even thirty of those ravenous bream.

Filming is a really slow process, even with two cameras, and I have never regretted choosing the latter option, because not only did I finish with nine bream over ten pounds to 13lb 10oz (a fish which just seven years earlier would have broken the British record), a 4lb 1oz roach-bream hybrid, plus a 2lb perch, but we were able to put together a totally unique video. It was not only one of the largest all-time hauls of double-figure bream ever captured but, more importantly, it was recorded on camera exactly as it happened.

Incidentally, together with a session after big carp on the River Test, this catch provided the basis for the first of five sell-through videos produced under my own label, Kazan River Productions.

I went on to take several more large bream from the forgotten lake during the following two seasons to 13lb 14oz, and a massive roach-rudd hybrid of 3lb 15oz. But never for me, nor anyone else, did that shoal ever feed so enthusiastically again. I did however account for a bag of five double-figure bream to 12lb 5oz in a single sitting on ledgered sweetcorn a year later from a local gravel pit. This was on a morning shared with my brother, David, who took two superb doubles of 13lb 4oz and 13lb 8oz respectively. Strangely, as I have mentioned earlier, during these past few years double-figure bream have become relatively attainable catches from estate lakes and mature gravel pit fisheries up and down the country.

A month after that fantastic bream season I was in a very different setting – the Seychelles. Bordered on three sides by the crystal-clear turquoise of the Indian Ocean, the single runway of Mahé's international airport is not only situated in one of the most beautiful spots on this earth, it is the only terminal in the Seychelles which can handle jumbo jets. So to sample some of the world's most exotic blue-water fishing you then island hop from Mahé to a dozen or more paradise locations including Praslin, Silhouette, La Digue, Bird Island and Denis Island' none of which takes more than thirty minutes to reach via De Havilland Twin Otter aircraft.

With *Go Fishing* in mind, I had researched part of this coral and granite atoll which rises from the depths of the Indian Ocean covering a staggering 250,000 square miles, two years earlier in the company of Buckley Hunt of Hunt Travel. We fished both Bird and Denis Islands plus further south at Desroches in the Amirantes Islands and experienced unbelievable sport throughout. But sadly I couldn't talk the television people into providing a budget for any such programmes . . . and still can't.

The Seychelles was, however, the perfect place in October 1994 for Jo and I to get married, a facility organized by several travel companies and one I can thoroughly recommend. The wedding took place on Mahé, the main island of the Seychelles, and home to ninety per cent of the 65,000 population of the 115 islands. We dragged a couple of fellow hotel guests from the beach for the afternoon ceremony as witnesses and, as though booked to order, a large stingray swam across the clear-water bay below the flower-covered terrace just as we made

BELOW Just a twenty-minute northerly flight from the main island of the Seychelles, Mahé, lies Bird Island which, apart from being home to a world record number of sooty terns and everyone's idea of coral paradise, contains an infinite variety of exciting gamefish in the deep blue water less than half a mile off shore.

RIGHT Jo makes friends with the queen of Bird Island, 'Esmerelda', who at 150 years old and weighing over 700lb is reckoned to be the world's oldest and largest tortoise.

our vows. The champagne flowed, a small band played and we danced into the sunset as it formed a kaleidoscope of yellow, orange and crimson over the horizon.

The following morning we left Mahé to go island hopping and enjoy some fishing. Being the most northerly of all islands in the Seychelles and situated on the very edge of this shallow coral atoll, Bird Island and Denis Island offer unrivalled sport because very deep water is just a few minutes' motoring away. Both islands maintain one fishing boat each, available to guests for bottom fishing or trolling. The accommodation comprises luxurious individual thatched chalets which are only yards from the ocean. Charges for the day are only half what you would expect to pay for blue-water trolling off America's Florida Keys.

There is a never-ending choice of inshore and offshore banks in depths from thirty to eighty feet or you can troll along the tempting irregular line of drop-off separating the last visible reef from a deep blue, seemingly bottomless, void. Although occasional marlin are caught, sport with the spectacular and high-leaping sailfish is available virtually all year round. Sails in the sixty- to eighty-pound class are everyday catches – often in multiples of two or three in just a few hours of trolling, so light 30lb outfits are ideal for maximum sporting enjoyment.

With just two anglers aboard plus a local skipper, the most workable routine is to fish four rods and two heavy cord handlines – one off each corner of the transom. These pull teasers just thirty to forty feet behind the boat, which motors at around six to eight knots and quickly provides enough bonito or tuna for strip baits. For sailfish Seychelles

BELOW Me hoisting a brace of large dorado caught on trolled lures.

LEFT Using a 30lb
class outfit and
mounted tuna belly
behind a colourful
squid skirt, Jo
boated two
magnificent sailfish
before lunch on our
first day's trolling.
(Such is the quality
of sportsfishing in
the Seychelles.)
What a honeymoon!

skippers prefer to add a twelve-inch strip of tuna belly behind a plastic squid skirt. The bait is held in place with elasticated cotton wound around an 8/0 hook attached to a five-foot 100lb wire trace – in case a barracuda or wahoo grabs hold! These are trolled around thirty or forty yards behind and away from the boat on outriggers so they skip tantalizingly through the waves while the other two rods offer either Rapalas Magnums (blue mackerel or red and white) or medium-size Kona heads, or perhaps even one of each. Sometimes a big dorado or wahoo will gobble the tuna belly baits, or a sailfish will suddenly pop up close to the boat and make off with the Kona head or diving plug. Yellowfin tuna are particularly partial to big squid skirt lures or Kona heads trolled just behind the handline lures or single large feathers intended for bonito.

When a reel screams in the Seychelles you never know what's coming. It's the most fabulous nail-biting blue-water sportfishing I have yet sampled. Using my old glass Ryobi uptide rods and S320 reels crammed with 30lb line, Jo and I trolled for two days out from Denis Island bringing to the boat several sailfish and dropping an equal number. We were constantly on the look-out for birds working the surface – mostly terns or the odd frigate bird – which feed upon small shoal species pushed up to the surface by the much larger pelagic species. We enjoyed constant action from dorado to thirty pounds, wahoo of the same calibre, some really large bonito, yellowfin tuna and a lot more. We also dropped a couple of really heavy fish on the big Rapalas, which the skipper reckoned were dogtooth tuna.

On our final day at Denis Island, Sydney, our skipper, suggested that having caught two sails and dropped a third before lunch we might like to try a spot of handline drifting for big red snapper. I never knew that handlining in fifty fathoms could be such hard work. As we had no proper leads aboard we used 4lb scuba diving weights to take the huge chunks of fresh tuna hiding 8/0 hooks quickly to the bottom. Colourful reef battlers like brown spotted grouper and the outstandingly colourful

moonsail sea bass and tomato hind were consistent biters within seconds of the makeshift rigs touching coral. Then I pulled into what Sydney assured me was a really big snapper – at least ten pounds. But I failed to notice a shark which grabbed the huge red snapper on the bottom hook of the handline a split second before I could hoist it into the boat. The shark had probably followed it all the way up through 150 feet of water. My feeling of joy quickly turned to pain as the ten yards of 300lb mono trace and the four-hook rig was ripped through my right hand, the large brass crimps joining cord to mono tearing out several chunks of finger flesh in a well of blood and gore. In just a few seconds my prize was gone.

Our last three days were spent on Bird Island which is not only home to the world's largest colony of sooty terns – over a million of them – but also the world's largest tortoise. Known as Esmerelda, this 700lb giant is said to be over 150 years old. Our Bird Island skipper, Clive, remembered me from a couple of years back and so Jo and I immediately felt at home. What's more the fishing hadn't changed one little bit. On our very first morning out Jo brought to the boat and released two large sailfish while I enjoyed some unrivalled sport on my ultra-light trolling outfit with huge garfish, green job fish, blue-finned trevally, rainbow runners and numerous barracudas.

With over 900 different species inhabiting those fertile blue waters we were totally spoilt for choice. Then all too quickly our honeymoon holiday was over. However I'm sure it won't be difficult to talk Jo into taking a second honeymoon to these bountiful islands in the not-too-distant future.

Life went on and then in March 1995 Jo and I were invited by our friends, Nanda and Susheel Gyanchand to visit India for two weeks of mahseer fishing and wild boar shooting. We borrowed Susheel's four-wheel-drive vehicle for the first week which we spent in the Cauvery Valley with our guides, Bola and Suban. At that time there were absolutely no other anglers on the river; it was truly magical and felt just like coming home. Jo caught her first mahseer and then several others to over forty pounds plus but lost a real monster – certainly of seventy pounds plus by the way it shot off downriver.

After a slow start using ragi (visiting anglers had now become more frequent with the result that mahseer had wised up to this bait), I switched over to a deep-bodied shoal fish, called a petagara, which is much loved by jumbo-size mahseer. On two consecutive mornings bumping these pound-size fish between the boulders in the rapids immediately below our Haira camp I hooked into two superb specimens of 83lb and 91lb. Each provided a fight to remember, not only for the unbelievable power of

this phenomenal fish but also because Bola and Suban were at my side to assist and share in the excitement throughout.

Jo and I slept under the stars on a pair of old ex-army camp beds. We regularly watched otters play amongst the wide shallows opposite our camp and one evening were treated to the magnificent sight of a family of nine elephants plodding through the green, monsoon-fed jungle beside the river and stopping to drink not fifty yards

LEFT Suban helps Jo hoist up my 83lb mahseer for the camera.

away. Our week beside the Cauvery passed all too quickly and it was time to drive back to Susheel's farmhouse, south of Bangalore, to prepare for some local sightseeing and a couple of pig shoots.

Now whilst game shooting in India is technically illegal, Susheel is regularly called upon by local government people to deal with dangerous wild animals. Wherever a rogue elephant needs shooting or a man-eating panther – the leopard is called the panther in India – has to be destroyed within the state of Karnataka, Susheel gets called in. Several years back he built up a substantial reputation by tracking down a pack of wolves that was responsible for attacking babies whilst their mothers toiled in the fields. The wolves lived in a cave from which the bones of numerous babies were recovered and Susheel proved what many of the peasant farmers simply couldn't believe: that wolves were responsible for taking children. So Jo and I couldn't have been in better hands.

After spending a couple of days relaxing around the farm with parties in the evening for me to renew old friendships, Susheel arranged a driven shoot to the south-west of Bangalore near the ancient city of Mysore. (I had been there on several previous occasions. Once was to visit the world-famous taxidermists the Van Ingens, two brothers of Dutch ancestry, who had been responsible over the last half a century for preserving many of Africa's and India's game fishes and animals. The world-record mahseer of 120lb caught from the Cubbiny River, a tributary of the Cauvery, was taken by Dewett Van Ingen back in 1920.)

Without any form of government control to restrict the numbers of wild boar which regularly raid the paddy fields, and ragi and maize crops of poor farmers, the beasts are poisoned, mutilated in ancient traps and even hunted by spear. None of these is an effective method of culling them. Whenever Susheel arranges an organized shoot, with up to six guns, all the peasant farmers are only too pleased to act as beaters, because not only are the boar which ruin their crops culled but also everyone gets to eat pig meat. Meat is a luxury for these farmers who rarely have the money to enjoy more than a chicken every so often as a supplement to their otherwise vegetarian diet.

The huge hillside around which Susheel had arranged the beaters to work was unbelievably thick in thorn scrub, so rather than shoot from a low position which could easily become restricted, Susheel suggested a high rocky bluff at the very end of the beat from where we should be able to get off killing shots as the boar broke from one piece of thick cover to another. So we climbed carefully up the hillside and sat perfectly still amongst some huge boulders with a great view downwards to where Susheel said the pigs would break. Even before we settled down and steadied ourselves in readiness to put our 3006 rifles into action the yells and screams of the beaters could be heard as they worked their way towards our position. Fire crackers were let off every so often and soon peacocks and jackals could be seen breaking cover from the dense thorn scrub across an open area about one hundred yards wide where Susheel said I should expect to direct my aim.

There then came much unexpected screaming and shouting at what we later found out was the beaters climbing trees to avoid a female panther whose cubs appeared to

be under threat. We actually thought the beat was over, completely ruined by the presence of the panther, when all of a sudden a large boar came running from the thorn scrub across the very spot predicted by Susheel around 150 yards away. How he does it I just don't know. It's as though he thinks like a wild boar, and I didn't let him down, giving it a good lead and dropping the boar with one well placed shot immediately above its shoulder on the run. Susheel then thumped one into another smaller pig, which I just hadn't seen at all, and our shoot was over. Afterwards everyone sat beneath a large tamarind tree and sipped coconut milk in the midday sun while three beaters dismembered the two boars and shared out the meat. It had been a most successful hunt.

A couple of days later I accompanied Susheel and friend Sachi on a night-time lamping shoot. This consisted of chasing across paddy fields in the 4x4 trying to pick out the forms of feeding boar with the aid of a million-candle-power lamp connected to the twelve-volt battery. Talk about exciting! As usual Susheel and Sachi wanted me to get

BELOW Using Susheel's 3006 rifle I bagged this huge wild boar during a chase across terraced paddy fields in his 4 x 4 whilst lamping at night.

the first shot off and, after several unsuccessful hours of driving from one farm to another, I managed to oblige when a huge boar suddenly appeared in the searchlight. Trying to steady myself when the 4x4 lurched to a stop over the ruts of a paddy field however was not an easy task. I don't think I have ever been so hyped up before or since. It was so very different from shooting a pheasant or a rabbit.

(Incidentally, killing for food certainly brings out the hunter in me and makes me realize how important it is that we constantly remind ourselves to be responsible for the food we eat which generally someone else kills for us. I have absolutely no qualms about shooting a live animal to eat. The necessities of man to enjoy hunting, shooting and fishing date back to our forefathers and it saddens me that a proportion of today's society wishes to suppress this heritage. While I do not go fox hunting for instance, I certainly don't wish to stop those who do. While those in the countryside do not preach to town folk, why is it that a townie might see fit to tell those in the countryside that hunting or fishing is wrong? Let's leave those living in suburbia to manage suburbia and those in the countryside to look after themselves.)

Much of the summer in 1995 was spent filming series ten of *Go Fishing* which included some fun carp fishing on the float at my local Catch 22 fishery at Lyng Easthaugh, tope fishing out from Brancaster Staithe in north Norfolk and trips for barbel and bream at the famous Throop Mill Fishery on the Dorset Stour near Christchurch, Hampshire. I also decided to include celebrity and life-long angler, Roger Daltrey. Actually Roger and I had discussed teaming up for a *Go Fishing* programme a few years earlier and in order to provide viewers with an accurate image of Daltrey the angler, trout fishery owner and trout farm mogul (he owns four trout farms), we started filming in one of his trout farms in Dorset. Manager Graham was in fact an acquaintance from way back when he managed the Nythe Lake trout fishery in Arlesford, Hampshire, a location I often made to fish with my old mate, Trevor Housby, during the early 1980s.

RIGHT During the filming of series ten of *Go Fishing* I teamed up with my old pal, Terry Houseago, for a real common carp bonanza at the prolific Catch 22 fishery in Lyng Easthaugh, Norfolk.

Roger was nothing less than passionate about the quality of the brown, rainbow and brook trout he breeds for stocking. These are destined for his own four-lake day-ticket fishery called Lakedown in deepest Sussex, just ten miles south of Tunbridge Wells, and for numerous other trout fisheries up and down the country. I think this aspect well and truly came across in our programme. For the vast majority of viewers who only ever thought of Roger as a rock singer and actor, our programme must have been quite an eye-opener, because his involvement in trout fishing actually takes up the greater part of his working life. Lakedown Fishery, for example, conceived and built by him, is not only one of the most picturesque I've ever fished, it's incredibly well laid out and managed, with a comfortable lodge where guests can enjoy refreshments adjacent to the water. Whilst shooting the aerial introductions for the programme with cameraman, Paul Bennett, from a helicopter, we both agreed that Roger's lakes were by far the most beautiful we had ever filmed.

Once we got down to catching some trout after all the preliminary filming, I forgot to tell Roger not to bash a

trout on the head on camera. It's stupid, I know, because how on earth does a live trout finish up on your plate if it's not dispatched. But in television filming we have to work within certain rules and guidelines, whether we consider them stupid or not. But lo and behold when Roger caught his first trout of the day, he got his priest out, bashed the trout over the head and immediately gave an address on how as hunters we should be responsible for dealing with the food we eat. No wonder the man's such a pro! Needless to say I left it all in and no one made the slightest comment. To top it all Roger then went and caught a superbly proportioned double-figure rainbow (the largest he had taken from his own fishery incidentally) to end what for me and my son, Lee, who had come along to help out, had been a most enjoyable shoot.

Later on in 1995 my hitherto partner in Kazan River Productions, Paul Martingel, decided to end our partnership to pursue a new direction in life. As Paul lived in Twickenham, south London, and I in Norfolk it was indeed difficult to retain a close day-to-day working relationship, although it has to be said we had been exceptionally successful together producing six series of *Go Fishing* for Anglia Television.

Anyway, this enabled my wife Jo to become my partner, taking over all the bookwork and business side previously looked after by Paul. It was at around this time at the end of 1995 that East Midland Allied Press engaged our services to make a series of hour-long specialist angling videos to be sold through their eight angling magazines. So over the next few years – right up to the present day in fact – we have produced for *Sea Angler Magazine* tapes with the titles *The Video*, *The Sequel*, *Mastercast*, *Cod* and *Bass*. In addition we filmed a barbel and carp video for *Improve Your Coarse Fishing*, a fly-fishing extravaganza for *Trout Fisherman* and an epic for *Angling Times* entitled *The Lake Nasser Safari*, a production I shall elaborate upon later.

RIGHT Roger Daltrey was not only a wonderful host and enormous help in putting together our trout programme, he went and caught the biggest rainbow, too.

A large proportion of material shot for both the cod and the bass videos allowed me to team up again with good pal and Lymington skipper, Roger Bayzand, who single-handedly runs *Sundance II*. Roger had produced the goods for me on many occasions on both photo shoots for *Angling Times* and during the filming of series eleven of *Go Fishing*. He came up trumps again in the bass video which on paper had promised to be our most difficult challenge yet. There was Roger catching a splendid double-figure bass almost to order, just like the huge cod and pollack we subsequently enjoyed from pirking and jelly worming over one of his favourite south-coast wrecks. When you have only a day or two to film saltwater species there is no one better than Roger to find them.

Just before Christmas 1995 I received a fax from Dr Ian Fox of the Falklands Tourist Board, suggesting that these two islands might make a wonderful location for *Go Fishing*. I replied that I was sure they would but at present filming was restricted to the Anglia and Meridian viewing areas. Ian replied with a positive proposal nevertheless and invited Jo and me to the Falklands in March 1996.

This led to us boarding a Tristar at Brize Norton, Oxfordshire, and making the excruciatingly long flight to the Falklands: seventeen and a half hours broken only by an hour's stop at Ascension Island. Legend has it that you can experience all four seasons in just one day on the Falklands. What they failed to mention is that you can get snow, rain, sleet, hail, and sun accompanied by near gale-force winds – *every* damned day. Setting out each day well togged up and totally prepared for anything that comes your way is imperative.

Actually our flight seemed to pass comparatively quickly. I have certainly endured far shorter, yet considerably more uncomfortable journeys. When we finally arrived

LEFT Jo and I in the office overlooking our lakeland setting where the majority of my writing and scripting for video editing is done.

ABOVE My old mate and the best charter boat skipper in the UK, Roger Bayzand, nets a cod for the cameras during a deep-water wrecking programme way off shore from his home port of Lymington in Hampshire.

RIGHT With Falklands Tourist Board guide Nick Bonner looking on, Jo displays a weird-looking Falklands mullet she caught spinning. These are in fact a species of Antarctic rock cod.

at Mount Pleasant Airport we were instantly whisked away to the capital, Stanley, surveying *en route* the barren scenery of rolling hills and grassy plains covered by rocky outcrops with tussock grasses, lichens and squat bushes covered in bright red berries. Immediately I drew a comparison with the Northwest Territories of Canada, where above the tree line there are no indigenous trees, although in the Falklands there is a handful of wind-breaking conifer varieties planted around most of the settlements. Against such a persistent wind they need them, believe me.

There are two main islands, east and west, divided by a narrow strip of sea which, together in land mass, easily equals that of Wales. With a resident population of fewer than 2,000 people (although there is a similar number of British military personnel stationed at MPA), you immediately realize that fishing in the Falklands is going to be both peaceful and unhurried. Some of the smaller outlying islands contain the greatest concentrations of penguins, seals and exotic birds. Sea Lion Island is an absolute must for visiting naturalists. We saw both gentoo and rockhopper penguins plus large numbers of seals, dolphins, giant petrels and black-browed albatross while staying at Blue Beach Lodge in the San Carlos estuary with William and Lynn Anderson on East Island.

The Falklands are indeed a stark, bleak, barren mixture of raw beauty and solitude that very quickly grows on you. The bird life is extremely varied, from the flightless

steamer ducks, to turkey vultures, caracaras, and red-backed buzzards. Barn owls, short-eared owls and cassius falcons were present too, plus a galaxy of colourful smaller birds such as black-chinned siskins, long-tailed meadow larks and black-throated finches.

Several spate-fed rivers such as the Malo, Warrah, San Carlos, Chartres, Murrell and Pedro rise high up in the mountains from an amalgam of peaty ditches and streams. Throughout their length only rarely does the width exceed thirty yards so a single-handed 10- or 10½-foot fly rod is ideal for the superb annual run of seatrout which are a direct result from the stockings of brown trout from Chile and Britain between 1940 and 1952, further stockings being made between 1961 and 1964.

Our first taste of the fishing was with local guide, Nick Bonner, on the Murrell, a wide shallow estuary just half an hour's Land Rover journey from Stanley. Jo and I soon got into spinning Toby lures for seatrout and Falklands mullet; which is in fact an Antarctic rock cod. It looks more like a cross between a common carp and a bass, although it does have the characteristics of mullet, it feeds high up into the river's freshwater reaches with the tide and it fights like stink. The food larder within Falkland estuaries is simply enormous, the two main items being the orange-red krill and smelt. Watching both seatrout and mullet smashing into the huge concentrations of young smelt (delicious when fried as white bait) in shallow water is a common sight.

Though I flogged away with my fly rod for the best part of our day along the Murrell I simply could not strip it fast enough to trick the seatrout into grabbing hold in the crystal-clear water, regardless of pattern. So I borrowed Jo's spinning rod and promptly accounted for a dozen or more superbly marked seatrout in the two- to five-pound range, most of which only slammed into the three-inch Toby at the very last moment. We then experienced similar sport on lures at our next destination on the San Carlos River estuary following an overland drive of some two hours. These islands demonstrate the need for which 4 x 4 vehicles were designed. Roads are so few and far between it would be simply impossible to be able to get around, let alone right down to the river bank, without one.

Though the record Falklands seatrout of 22lb was caught in 1992 by Alison Faulkner from a pool way up the San Carlos River, with autumn river levels being pathetically low (not a common occurrence apparently), we experienced only mediocre sport above the first tidal pool. But that's spate river fishing for you. Ever-hungry wild brownies in the four- to twelve-ounce range grabbed both fly and spinner wherever we tried. From several locations in the tidal reaches, where the estuary is still relatively narrow, I took seatrout to close on six pounds, the most successful pattern by far being a General Practitioner. The orange hue and shrimp-like appearance of the GP comes nearest to the trout's natural food in the salt, namely krill, which comes inshore in such dense concentrations that the sea turns red.

During the most productive part of the tide, the last two hours of the ebb and first of the flood, a ten-gram Toby quickly located groups of seatrout, whereupon I then usually switched over to the fly, depending on wind. Calm days in the Falklands are few and far between, so your approach to fly casting and presentation has to be altered accordingly. One useful option is to cast downwind with your back to the water (in a facer) and lay the fly down on the backcast. But this is simply not practical while exploring clear rain pools that are barely flowing, using the standard wet-fly technique of downstream and across when a howling wind is blowing directly upstream or straight into your face. The best answer is to start at the downstream end and stealthily work up, after first carefully wading over to the most approachable bank from which to get a line out. I also found that stepping up at least one line size helped combat the continual wind. As previously mentioned the GP, a size 8 double, proved an excellent pattern as did a size 8 or 6 Dunkeld. Black flies appeared to be the next best choice – patterns like Stoat's Tail and a black marabou-tailed mini leadhead on a size 10 or 8 long shank. The weighted pattern helped enormously in straightening out the long cast, also providing me with a visible plop, thus giving its whereabouts.

From Blue Beach Lodge in the San Carlos estuary we flew by Islander over to the West Island to stay with guide, Robin Lee, at Port Howard Lodge on the banks of the River Warrah estuary. Again we were blighted by lack of rain, but fortunately most of the pools contained a handful of stale, yet catchable, fish in each and I started with a 6lb cock fish again on a GP. I also saw the first double taken, an 11lb hen fish to the rod of Jim Jackson from New Jersey who was on a fishing holiday with his son, Darryl.

Incidentally together with my wife, Jo, we four were the only visiting anglers in the Falklands during the last two weeks of March. Now you can't beat that for solitude! The season for seatrout starts in October and ends in April. The lovely River Warrah really was a joy to explore and one afternoon a totally unexpected occurrence had us completely gobsmacked. Well you don't expect several hundred pounds of sea lion to come zooming upriver pushing a wall of water in front like a torpedo while you are fly fishing, do you? But this dark brown monster, as thick as a wheelie bin, did exactly that.

I experienced another strange encounter one evening whilst spinning in the Warrah estuary. I looked down through the clear water beneath my feet to see a large octopus moving about – something which in cold water took me completely by surprise. I had of course speared numerous octopus whilst living on Barbados but here in the Falklands its presence seemed bizarre. So I lowered down my Toby lure, yanked and there I was connected to a superb meal. In fact I severed the legs from its body before taking it back to the lodge and our host's cook prepared the octopus in chunks fried in breadcrumbs, exactly to our requirements. What an unexpected starter!

Only a ninety-minute drive overland from the Warrah is what I considered to be the most prolific seatrout fishing in the Falklands, namely the lovely Chartres River. It was certainly the clearest river by far, holding large numbers of both fresh run and dark fish in all the pools we visited for several miles up from the estuary at Little Chartres. We stayed with sheep farmers Lyn and Tony Blake, and Tony acted as our guide. His understanding of the river was extraordinary. He seemed virtually to know what each and every pool contained and where the fish were lying. He had an

BELOW Ex-patriot Paul Chapman, now settled in the Falklands, took me seatrout fishing in the tiny River Pedro near Stanley and landed this magnificent 12¼lb seatrout on a small Toby.

uncanny knack of spotting fish movement even when the wind whipped the surface. My best of three days exploring the Chartres resulted in no fewer than fifty-one seatrout from a total of eleven pools. The bulk averaged between one and two pounds with the odd fish approaching four pounds – and all on the fly. Tony was also a past master at preparing and frying up the milt and eggs from out-of-condition seatrout. He didn't care how 'black' a fish was, and I must admit to enjoying his fried goodies on several occasions.

Jo and I returned to Stanley by Islander for one last day's fishing on the renowned River Malo which is controlled by the local Stanley Angling Club. Being an early river, most of the seatrout had already gone upstream during spates in February, but I did manage a 7½lb hen fish on a Toby. What I also enjoyed was taking mullet from two to six pounds one after another during that magical last two hours of the ebb from the estuary. All came to orange and red leadheads with marabou tails, fished down and across as the tide ripped out.

Due to our RAF Tristar running a day late, I was treated to an extra and totally unexpected day's fishing on the tiny River Pedro. Ex-pat Paul Chapman, from Sheffield, invited me to join him on a rarely fished beat which meanders for

mile upon mile from the estuary and through boggy marshlands – and it enjoys a really super-late run of big fish. Due to an overnight downpour Paul suggested that spinning would produce the best results, and he was absolutely right. Toby lures produced thirteen seatrout totalling 96lb, the best three of 9lb, 11lb and 12¼lb falling to Paul's rod. My best went a shade over eight pounds and like all our fish went berserk on light tackle in the confines of small turbulent pools.

After spending over two weeks at various settlements comprising three or four dwellings each, Jo and I both felt not just a little sad on returning to the comparative civilization of Stanley, which itself is little larger than an English village. Not only are the island people exceptionally hospitable and helpful, but the clear fresh air, remote farmhouse accommodation and total isolation all added up to a unique experience. I just hope we'll return one day in the not too distant future.

During the summer of 1996, having researched two large clear-watered clay pits at Elstowe near Bedford during the close season for series eleven of *Go Fishing*, I finally achieved a life-long ambition and caught a rudd over three pounds – and live on camera at that! It was all down to my nephew, Martin Bowler, really. He had previously not only caught numbers of huge carp from Elstowe to over thirty-five pounds but had also been extremely successful in tracking down the small shoals of huge rudd for which the No. 1 pit was renowned. Strangely most syndicate members only ever bothered with the carp.

My best of several beauties over the 2½lb mark weighed 3½lb and came on a simple waggler float rig baited with a couple of maggots, presented alongside a dense reed bed: classical rudd fishing no less. Martin also provided the location along the

RIGHT With much research help from my nephew Martin Bowler, I caught this stunningly coloured rudd of 3½lb from Elstowe Clay Pits near Bedford during the filming of *Go Fishing's* eleventh series.

upper reaches of the Great Ouse controlled by the local Vauxhall Angling Club for a real barbel bonanza shown in the same series. I really warmed to fishing the Upper Ouse again after, believe it or not, a thirty-year lay-off and was surprised to find it flowing clear and fast over a gravel bottom. It is as fine a barbel river as you will find anywhere within the British Isles, and I was rather curious to know why.

Although barbel have been stocked by local clubs throughout much of the Upper Ouse during the past twenty years to supplement a small stock of resident fish, they really have taken off in leaps and bounds. This is due in all probability to the fact that all of the treated effluent from Milton Keynes is piped into the Ouse through a series of settling pits at Cotton Waterworks. This injection doubles the force of water and invigorates a river which otherwise, like many others, could now well be suffering from the effects of water abstraction. It's so nice to hear of a positive arising directly from sewage treatment.

Series eleven of *Go Fishing* was the last produced by my company, Kazan River Productions. The following three series reverted back to in-house Anglia Television productions. It was a move I actually welcomed because this kind of change injects new life not only into the programme but also into the presenter. The changeover certainly had a great effect and after series twelve and thirteen went out in January 1999, director Ron Trickett sent me some most satisfying statistics. In terms of percentage share (which is how shows are rated) *Go Fishing* was not only Anglia Television's top-rated programme but currently the longest running. It had taken me ninety half-hour programmes, with all the associated problems of putting fish on the bank to order, to finally arrive. For me it has been perhaps a strange set of transitions

LEFT Taken during a week's vacation on board *Mirimba,* friends Andy Benham and Ed Pope display the stamp of high-leaping tooth-laden tigerfish for which Zimbabwe's Lake Kariba is justly famous.

from hairdresser to printer to tackle dealer to angling author and then to television presenter and producer. But it has been a fascinating learning curve that I wouldn't have swapped for anything.

Earlier on whilst recollecting filming experiences for series six of *Go Fishing* on Zimbabwe's Lake Kariba, I mentioned its immense value as both game reserve and exotic fishing location. It is certainly one of my favourites and I look forward each year to escorting parties of up to eight anglers, organized by Christine Slater of Tailor Made Holidays. I renew my love-affair each autumn with what is arguably Africa's most enchanting and diverse water wilderness.

Our base and home for the week is a sixty-foot luxury cruiser/houseboat called *Mirimba*. It comes complete with King, the captain, plus a cook, a crewman and four fourteen-foot tenders with outboards in which everyone sets off game viewing and fishing into all those inaccessible spots.

Bordered on most of its northern shoreline by Zambia and by Zimbabwe along the southern bank, Kariba's charisma originates from the mighty Zambezi River. During the 1950s, to provide hydroelectricity for both Zimbabwe and Zambia, the river was dammed across the gorge in the township of Kariba, resulting in close on 200 miles of pristine nature reserve, where both game viewing and tropical sportsfishing are truly spectacular, but may be enjoyed by boat only. It is an offence – and downright dangerous incidentally – to go ashore because huge crocodiles bask on mud and sandbanks craftily camouflaged by clumps of reed and flotsam on their backs. Otherwise it is in fact possible to get so close to the wildlife, elephants in particular, that a telephoto lens is an optional extra!

A good pair of binoculars is however essential for maximum enjoyment. Lunchtime is a wonderful time for game viewing, when you return to the houseboat from an early morning session in one of the tenders in search of vundu or tiger fish, just two of the exotic freshwater adversaries found in the Zambezi system, along with predatory bream, barbel, eels, electric catfish, tropical pike – over a hundred species in all. Elephant, buffalo, baboons, hippo and water buck can all be comfortably viewed from mere yards away along the lush and thick marginal canopy of water hyacinth from the safety of your fishing tender.

To safari fishermen Kariba is arguably amongst the most exciting of all tropical freshwater sportsfishing locations. Only in southern India, with its magnificent rocky, mountainous rivers and giant mahseer, have I experienced comparable challenges. But in truth Kariba has more overall appeal whether you choose to view the bird life or game animals through binoculars or tussle with Africa's largest and most powerful freshwater catfish, the vundu. This is prolific in the twenty-five- to fifty-pound range, but grows to well in excess of the 100lb Zimbabwean rod and line record. And would you believe their favourite baits are luncheon meat and blue soap – yes, soap. The river gorges and entrances around the lake's southern perimeter seem to be the best vundu hot spots and the preferred method is to drift slowly with the wind gently bumping the bait along the bottom until a vundu picks up the scent and gobbles it

up. Gear of 30lb test and a size 6/0 hook are none too strong for this extremely strong fighter, which is given a little slack line when it mouths the bait and is allowed to run for several yards before you bang the hook home. Vundu have no canine teeth as such, but are well equipped with crushing pads in both the top and bottom of their capacious jaws and in their throat, each pad being armed with thousands of tiny pin-like gripping teeth. A glove therefore is essential for unhooking vundu, to avoid painful scraping of the skin across your knuckles, back of the hand and wrists. Even my son, Lee, who has never really been a fanatical angler, was in absolute awe of the vundu's animal strength, landing specimens to close on sixty pounds.

One of the best fights I have ever enjoyed was in fact a vundu shared with a lady guest, Ruth Taylor. I hooked what was obviously a big fish and handed the rod over to Ruth who hung on for spells of five and ten minutes at a time, before handing it back to me again. This went on for the best part of an hour as we drifted fully half a mile from where the monster was first hooked. Finally its massive flat head and long whiskers broke surface. Then there were a couple of heavy swirls, where I just had to grab the rod back for fear of Ruth going over the side, and our prize finally rolled into the net. It was an incredibly long vundu that pulled the scales down to 95lb.

Once everyone has enjoyed their string being well and truly pulled by at least one big vundu, efforts are then concentrated close in around Kariba's irregular shoreline for the high-jumping, tooth-laden tiger fish. These acrobatic speedsters hunt talapia and the lake's smallest fish, a sardine called kapenta, amongst the petrified tree tops of what were once large forests of hardwood trees, prior to the Zambezi valley being flooded. So-called 'fishing the sticks' is perhaps best compared to the unlikely situation of casting amongst tree tops from the platform of a hovering helicopter, except you are in a boat floating above them. Lines are of course always hanging over branches, which makes the extraction of each and every tiger fish a battle to remember. However, many are lost amongst the woodwork because tiger fish simply never know when to give up or when to fight fairly. Anyone who lands two from ten hook-ups is not doing too badly! In addition to tigers, squeaker catfish and barbel, even the occasional vundu, are hooked on bunches of freelined kapenta, but few are ever extracted from the entanglement of skeleton bushes and tree stumps.

From a Harare taxi driver to the kapenta fishermen of Lake Kariba, that special Zimbabwean zest for life prevails in the friendliness of the people, in their humour and especially in their willingness to share such a beautiful and bountiful country with visitors. Immediately from the first blast of hot air against your cheeks whilst disembarking from the plane, the love-affair always resumes. It is an infectious, delicious and decidedly haunting experience based upon a love of exotic flora and fauna, combined with that exhilarating perfume which is Africa. It is a mixture of spices, dust, heat and pollen, as unique to the continent as the trumpeting, somewhat unnerving brass band sound of a bellowing hippo at dawn or the haunting cry of a fish eagle. It is what brings me back time and time again.

(Of my last three books written between 1992 and 1997, two contain snippets of Zimbabwe's magnetic fishing, *Go Fishing Techniques*, and *John Wilson's Coarse Fishing Method Manual*. Each, like most of my books, contains numerous diagrams drawn by my good friend and angling buddy Dave Batten, who in my opinion has no equal in putting across technique in line drawing form.)

In October 1996 the *Daily Express* contacted me and asked if I would consider writing a weekly angling page for the sports section. I accepted and have since enjoyed immensely the exposure and platform which a page in a national newspaper provides for angling. But what with the never-ending workload of researching, filming and helping to edit six yearly *Go Fishing* programmes for Anglia, producing specialist angling videos for Emap through Kazan River Productions, writing monthly for two angling titles and periodically for others, not to mention all the work involved in our two carp syndicate lakes – now wonderfully mature and providing superlative fishing – trying to find time for John's Tackle Den became almost impossible. I think I was on the point of working myself into an early grave. Throughout the summer, following each hectic week's filming away from home, I then had to go into the shop on a busy Saturday in order for my manager, Andy, to have a day off. Quite simply, after twenty-five years of serving the anglers of Norfolk and Suffolk, the shop had to go. So I asked Andy if he was interested in buying me out and that is exactly what happened. For the first time in my working life I suddenly felt free and it took some time for me to adjust to my changed circumstances.

Having always worked on Saturdays, both as a hairdresser and shop-keeper, for the best part of forty years, it now seemed rather strange to have the day off – I felt as though I was cheating. However within a few months I soon warmed to the reality of more free time and not being constantly under the pressure of the retail trade. Besides

I felt that in latter years much of the fun had gone out of shop-keeping, due not only to the escalating crime of shoplifting but also because of the unsympathetic attitude of local government. For instance, when I fitted roller steel shutter blinds to my shop window the council sent someone round the next morning, ordering me to take them down. The shop was a listed building with some half-rotten squiggly woodwork at the top of one of the vertical window supports. The council were not happy that the box in which the roller blind retreated out of sight during shopping hours covered up part of this woodwork. They failed to take into account that during a twenty-year period my shop windows had been broken on some eighty occasions. Yes, eighty times. I was a local joke when it came to broken windows! With a pub at both ends of Bridewell Alley in Norwich where my shop was situated, you can guess what happened when the drunks rolled out at closing time! On three separate occasions I had my windows broken twice in the same week.

Early break-ins were from louts stealing air rifles and pistols which I then sold. So I simply stopped selling air weapons. But even with two-inch mesh grills solidly welded to heavy angle iron frames which each had to be lifted off and stored in the churchyard opposite every morning, come rain or shine the glass still took the impact and shattered. So while nothing was stolen, my insurance company finally reached the point of putting my excess up to what it cost to replace a glass window, so I had to fork out for every breakage. How I didn't give the shop up during that ghastly period I don't know.

Instead, I decided to fight the bureaucracy of the local council who took me to the local magistrate's court about my roller shutter. This was strange because numerous shops all over Norwich had (and still do have) roller steel shutters fitted, many of them to properties actually owned by the local council. So one Sunday just before the court hearing I walked through Norwich when all the shop blinds were down and used up two thirty-six-exposure rolls of print film photographing each and every shop front – just like mine, hidden by shutter blinds. After the three magistrates had listened to the council's prosecutor and had then tried to find my shop on the four three-foot by two-foot boards I submitted, covered in photographs of all the shops in Norwich that had roller blinds, they chucked the case out!

I did, however, finally have to submit a year or so later when the council again tried to take me to court, this time on a technical point covering listed buildings – and a point of law from which I could apparently not escape. So I compromised and had to have six upright fibreglass 'wood-like' shutters made, to replace the roller shutter which still had to be removed every morning. What a waste of everyone's time and money . . . except the design company who charged me six grand for manufacturing and installing the shutters!

Much of this aggravation occurred way back in the late 1980s and early 90s before Andy took over at John's Tackle Den, but I hope it illustrates part of the trials and tribulations of running a tackle business and why I was not sad at letting it go. Indeed far from it . . .

I could now accept offers of fishing in exotic places without having first to think of the shop. Indeed in March 1997 I relented because of the extreme pressure put upon me by brother Dave and good friends Len Head and Jason Davies, and booked our flights to India for a fortnight's mahseer fishing. Each had heard all the stories of these great fish and could not wait to experience their exhilarating power first hand. Fortunately the Cauvery River was in fine form during our stay, running fairly clear and dropping steadily from the previous summer's monsoon rains, which gave everyone the chance of contacting big fish.

As luck would have it I managed to land a superb specimen of 91lb on only our second day on a deadbait bumped through a rocky glide immediately upstream of the Haira rapids. It led me a real song and dance for almost an hour. At one point it became stuck solid amongst several huge boulders in midstream, necessitating Suban to row me across to the other side in the coracle in order to apply pressure at a new angle on the hooked fish. Three days later I did it again with a mahseer of 78lb (pictured on the front cover) caught from my favourite swim called Centre Rock. Here a fast rip roars downstream around a large rock in the middle of the river upon which I sit (hence its name) and changes direction fully 150 yards downstream by going at right angles over a series of mini rapids. The exercise is to stop a hooked fish before it makes the rapids. On this occasion I did but in past years I have lost some real thumpers.

Meanwhile Dave, Len and Jason were slowly coming to terms with the very different problems and techniques of mahseer fishing. Len lost a huge fish one evening not far from camp as did Jason much lower downstream at a place we call Red Rocks. The look on his face when the hook inexplicably pulled out just when he was getting the better of what was obviously a big mahseer said it all – so near, yet so far. I then left the three of them on the river for a few days and joined my good friend

BELOW The Cauvery River, India. Everyone takes hold to hoist my 91lb mahseer up for the camera. (*Left to right*) Len Head, Jason Davies, Chick Raju, Boss Raju, myself and brother Dave.

Susheel and his wife, Nanda, for a few days' pig shooting up in the hills – bagged a boar too.

On my return to the river Dave was grinning from ear to ear, having landed a 68lb mahseer, while Len was equally happy with one to 57lb. Unfortunately only moderate-size mahseer came our way during the remainder of our stay and Jason had to settle for memories of his lost leviathan plus mahseer landed to 35 lb, which is nevertheless still an incredibly worthwhile capture.

For my part it was most gratifying to share in my friends' success and sleep beneath the stars beside the majestic Cauvery River once again. It's a part of the world where little changes from year to year except river levels which, like the farming expectations of the local peasant farmers, are totally dependent upon the monsoon rains.

Earlier on whilst recalling the formation of my second lake back in 1985, I finished the chapter with the newly excavated fishery, landscaped, planted with trees and marginal shrubs and stocked with a variety of both fish and lilies. There was now, together with the small lake, around two and a half acres of water which needed time to mature. And over the years that have elapsed since I am proud to say my dream has grown and blossomed beyond all my expectations. It's required not just a little help along the way of course, and pruning back both trees and lilies which can grow all too rampantly within the confines of what is, after all, a relatively small fishery is an on-going job. Beauty does in fact come at a price and each summer my diving wet suit comes in very handy for the work of cutting back lilies and submerged tree branches plus replacing the front support logs of each swim as nature rots them away. But it's a real labour of love, and there is invariably someone available to help who owns a similar fishery and requires a selection of lily roots or young saplings.

Initially just about all the carp could be landed successfully using just a 6lb reel line. But as both lily beds and the size of carp have grown, an 8lb outfit using a heavy Avon-style rod is now required, with the exception of catfish that is. For extracting these and the larger carp from beneath submerged trees (mainly in the old, smaller lake) beefier tackle is imperative. But overall a fun 8lb line outfit will suffice in the majority of swims. To date incidentally, in case you are wondering how the fish have matured, the lakes have produced eels to 6lb 4oz, chub to 6lb 2oz, wels catfish to 20lb, golden orfe to 6lb 6oz, grass carp to 21lb 5oz, crucian carp to 2lb 14oz, plus mirror carp to 24lb 1oz, common carp to 20lb 8oz and metallic carp to 18lb 12oz. In fact the lakes contain such a prolific stock of various carp with most fish into double figures, plus the odd twenty, that there is no need to bivvy up for days on end to enjoy catching carp. Most of the syndicate members prefer to spend just a few hours or so at the waterside, which was my original intention. The bank sides consequently never look bashed or even well trodden. After all it is our front garden in addition to being a fishery around which we walk our four dogs several times each day.

For the first twelve years of the new lake's life I owned and took a long time in training a wonderful German Shepherd called Buzzy, a large black and tan, big-boned

ABOVE Nestled amongst the woods adjacent to the house, it seems as if the new (fourteen-year-old) lake has always been there.

dog with such a friendly nature, yet incredibly strong and instantly aggressive and protective if he thought those he loved were in danger. It is a trait born into most German Shepherds which I guess is responsible for the breed being used almost exclusively by the police and security firms. With Buzzy sadly gone however we now have two more German Shepherds, one white and one black and tan, a West Highland Terrier and a huge Rhodesian Ridgeback-Bull Mastiff cross who has the habit of returning to the house every so often with someone's tin of half-used luncheon meat or a bag of floating carp pellets. Funnily enough no one ever seems to complain, although that could have something to do with the fact that Max weighs in at close on thirteen stone!

I think one of the greatest successes of the fishery is the way in which the metallic carp have flourished and added that hint of mystery and beauty to everyone's catches. With such a high stocking density I never expected them to all become thirty pounders. From the outset it was my wish for most of the carp to grow into double figures and thus provide exciting sport on relatively light tackle. There are enough under-stocked big carp fisheries around as it is, where everyone knows the name of the fish they are after. This is not my idea of carp fishing. It is perhaps interesting to note that I kept many of the (now large) metallic carp in my garden ponds prior to moving to Lake House so these are all over twenty years old. Whether I shall live long enough to see them all reach their optimum age is doubtful – carp can live for up to fifty years. Come to think of it my African Grey parrot, Cheeko, who is also around twenty years old, will in all probability outlive me too.

Keeping a record book of how the lake has progressed these past fifteen years has also highlighted how weather patterns are changing. Today it seems everything is in extremes: the coldest this, the hottest that and so on. For instance, November 1994 was the mildest ever since records began. The 1988/89 winter was the mildest for 300 years and the driest in the south-east of England for a hundred years. We had fresh

ABOVE Jo with the loves of her life Max, Bola, Toby and Sam, at our lake's south-eastern end.

LEFT Grass carp like this twenty-one-pounder have fared particularly well in the new lake, together with the stock of golden orfe, wels catfish, chub, big eels and numerous king carp.

lily pads up on the surface during February and flowers actually out during March. Conversely, the October 1987 gales were the worst in living memory, though fortunately only a few elderly alders and birch fell around our lakes. And February 1986 was one of the coldest in living memory with an average temperature of just -9°C. The lakes were frozen over for the whole of February that year which necessitated my having to keep an area (by the bridge) clear of ice each morning to allow the rising gases from rotting vegetation to escape. Unfortunately many owners of small, overgrown, shallow and well-stocked fisheries that winter who failed to appreciate possible deoxygenization lost their entire stocks.

The earliest that carp have ever spawned in the lakes was on 1 May 1993 and they kept at it for three days. This was followed by later spawnings during June and once more in July. In my experience carp never get their reproductive cycle over in one go. They usually spawn from the early hours of the morning until the sun is well up, and many anglers never get to appreciate that there are several spawnings each summer. Also breeding successfully in the small, now wild, pond is a colony of the rare and protected great crested newt which spends much of its life in the water. These were actually featured in one of my *Go Fishing* programmes filmed around the two lakes and they share their sub-surface home with smooth newts, frogs and toads, all of which reproduce annually in profusion.

The number of different species of birds which now annually use our lakeland setting for breeding is simply staggering. Four or five pairs of greylag geese fly in to start sorting out their nesting sites during March and once their goslings are but a day or two old they walk them across our drive and down through the woods to someone else's eight-acre lake which is at the bottom of our lawn on the opposite side of the house. It's as though they know our lakes are simply too small for so many geese but that the islands are perfect sites for nesting. In recent years the odd pair of both Egyptian and Canada geese have spent a day inspecting the islands for nesting but the greylags are too intimidating. There are of course resident moorhens, mallards and at least one pair of tufted ducks that reproduce each spring.

The poplars and conifers have grown to more than twenty feet high and the hundreds of willows and alders provide numerous nesting sites as do the self-seeded gorse bushes. Fortunately all around our property is dense, mixed woodland so together with what I have planted around the lakes, there is now a superb habitat. Resident birds include wrens, tree creepers, robins, whitethroats, chiffchaffs, blackbirds, song and mistle thrushes, wood pigeons, collared doves, tree sparrows, kingfishers, chaffinches, greenfinches, goldcrests, reed warblers, herons, great tits, blue tits, coal tits and long-tailed tits. There are also green woodpeckers, great spotted woodpeckers plus the occasional visit from kestrels and sparrowhawks. It is indeed vastly different from when I purchased the property back in 1982, when the majority of it was silver birch scrub providing little in the way of suitable nesting sites.

I have however found one very good use for mature birch trees, say from eight to nine inches across and larger: birch sap wine. This delightful tangy wine, which clears quickly and is similar to a fruity vodka, is quite drinkable within three to four months of being taken off the yeast. After a year or so it will blow your head off. In fact in Russia entire birch woods are destroyed by the over-zealous tapping of mature birch trees. To obtain enough sap for a gallon or two you do in fact need to drill into the bark of a tree. This must be done – indeed it can only be accomplished – during late March or early April when the birch sap is rising. Choose your tree and use a brace and one-inch diameter bit to drill through the bark. Make the hole around two and a half feet off the ground, angling the bit slightly upwards, and stop when the sap starts pouring out. Sap rises up the tree on the outside of the wood, immediately beneath the bark, so be careful not to go right into the tree.

Now fit half a drilled demijohn cork (cut in half crossways) into the bark and gently push in around two feet of quarter-inch clear tubing. This goes straight into a clean demijohn and, hey presto, within twenty-four hours you can obtain up to a gallon of the clear sap from just one tree. If not, simply drill another, remembering to plug each hole afterwards with a solid cork bung. The next step is to boil the sap together with the pared peel from three oranges and three lemons for around twenty-five minutes. You then add 3lb of sugar and stir until it is dissolved. Then set aside to cool. Once it's cooled add the yeast and the juice from the oranges and lemons, and leave for three days (covered by a muslin cloth) stirring twice daily. Then strain off the liquid and funnel straight into a demijohn. Fit with an air lock to ferment off. For those who have never made their own wine, it might be worth investing in a basic book on the subject and then follow these simple steps. You won't regret it!

I have also made elderberry and blackberry wine from our own fruits and in recent years have acquired a taste for wild mushrooms. Those which commonly appear are the parasol mushroom (*Lepiota procera*), which has a lovely nutty smell and is deliciously rich to eat, and the shaggy inkcap (*Coprinus comatus*), also excellent eating when no more than a day (or two) old. We also eat the St George's mushroom (*Tricholma gambosum*) when it appears at the end of April.

Incidentally Jo makes a delicious spicy mushroom pâté from the large parasols. She starts by melting 4½oz of butter in a saucepan to which three chopped shallots (or one medium onion) are added and cooked for four minutes until soft. Then 12oz of chopped mushrooms plus two teaspoonfuls of Worcestershire sauce and half a teaspoon of cayenne pepper are added and cooked gently for half an hour with the lid on after stirring well. Then put into a blender, whiz until smooth and return to the saucepan and add a beaten egg. Cook gently (on a low heat) until thickened. Then put into a small dish, so it almost reaches the top, and chill in the fridge. When cold, pour an ounce of melted butter on top and pop into the fridge again. It's absolutely delicious.

Watching the lakes grow up has also increased my interest in and love of lilies, surely one of nature's most beautiful aquatic plants. I have been surprised at the durability of most ornamentals within an angling environment. Those most breathtaking of all, the reds, suffer no less when a hooked carp goes charging through

RIGHT You spend the first five years planting marginals and lilies in a new lake and then the rest of your life keeping it all in check. Friend Phil Gray and I removing surplus yellow lilies (*Nuphar lutea*) which are not wasted but passed on to other local fisheries.

their stems than the common yellow, *Nuphar lutea*. In preference I would choose William Falconer and Attraction, with the deep red of James Brydon as the most beautiful of all the red lilies. I have also been extremely impressed by Commanche, which is a coppery-orange, and two pinks, Rose Arey and Helen Fowler, the last having large beautiful flowers held well above the surface. Of the twenty-plus varieties of ornamentals in the lake I also like *Marliacea chromatella* which has distinctly variegated pads and creamy flowers. Many water gardening books list this particular lily as a yellow. But having had it now in both pond and lake for over twenty years, the flowers have never been what I could call yellow. Obviously planting such an array of ornamentals in addition to the common yellow lily means annual cutbacks and clear outs, as I have already mentioned, to keep them all in check. Nevertheless the entire project has proved such an enjoyable and rewarding part of my life, I wouldn't change anything for the world.

In fact in May 1997 Jo and I were invited to the Café Royal in London for the Sand and Gravel Association's annual restoration awards presented by Richard Simmonds CBE, Chairman of the Countryside Commission. There were six winners, each recognized by SAGA for the quality of restoration work turning ex-gravel workings into nature reserves and fisheries. I am exceptionally proud to say that on behalf of Atlas Aggregates, who shared the honours, I accepted an award for our own lake in Great Witchingham. The award report described our lake, and I quote, as 'an idyllic tranquil masterpiece' and 'a jewel in the landscape'. The SAGA award plaque is now proudly displayed in the cedarwood summerhouse which provides a panoramic view across the lake.

LEFT Much of what I have written during a period covering twenty years of water gardening has appeared in specialist magazines such as *Coarse Fishing Handbook*, *Practical Fishkeeping*, *Water Gardener* and *Koi Carp Magazine*.

What I find even more exciting is that, through these awards, gravel companies are at last not just rewarding landowners for restoration work; there is an awareness in planning habitat-rich waters which will provide a future for freshwater fishing in this country. As our rivers sadly decline through water abstraction and damage from farming chemicals, what I have been saying for many years is now coming true: that we shall be relying more and more on gravel pits to provide quality freshwater fishing in the future. So if, in some small way, the creation of the lake can act as a blueprint for small stillwater fisheries of the future I will be a very happy man indeed.

August 1997 was the beginning of what was to be a hectic few months of foreign reconnaissance fishing trips, with a destination that can only be described as desolate. Thank goodness Jo is such an understanding partner. She understands my needs, through writing commitments, to be for ever zooming off here and there to places far and wide – often leaving her at home. Following a long haul from Heathrow to Halifax, Canada, plus an internal prop jet flight from Halifax to Deer Lake and from Deer Lake to Goose Bay, my journey into the province of Newfoundland was almost at an end. But not quite. Canada's far north is one hell of a country. I was met at Goose Bay by Englishman, Jon Cumming of Friends of the Innu UK and following a quick tour of the native Innu settlement we met Canadian photographer, Ted Ostrowski, and loaded all our gear into a De Havilland Beaver float plane – our final destination being Mastastin Lake. Called Kamastastin by the Innu native Americans who for over 8,000 years have laid claim to this land, the lake is situated due west of Davis Inlet and south of the 56th parallel. Measuring some fourteen by eight miles it is a massive sheet of cold, unbelievably clear water. But more importantly it is home

OVERLEAF My favourite view and piece of natural history that I had both the opportunity and privilege of creating.

to huge lake trout and the most exquisitely coloured arctic char. The climate of the area is in fact sub-arctic, where the ice and snow which covers everything all winter doesn't melt until June and then it starts freezing over again come the end of September. We had but a few weeks left until the harsh annual cycle started repeating itself.

Until being encouraged into living within government-run settlements, the Innu had led a completely nomadic life for thousands of years, hunting porcupines, bear, goose and caribou, in addition to catching and smoking fish. Labrador is a large peninsula and does in fact boast the biggest concentration of caribou in the world, estimated at in excess of half a million animals. But few Innu hunt them now. Suckered into an easy, predictable but boring life in the settlements, the nomadic self-supporting ways of these gentle people are fast eroding, with the result that alcoholism and suicide are very real problems. Like so many situations the world over, from the Australian Aborigines to the native Americans, their unique culture has been repressed by the greed of the white man. And being white there are times when I genuinely feel ashamed in that it was my forefathers who started slavery and the decline of such peoples.

The Innu, however, are fighting back and hoping to set up country wilderness camps for hunting and fishing to attract tourists, which is more or less where I came in. I had been invited by the Innu to help research fishing potential of the Kamastastin lake and river system from which summer camps could possibly be managed. During the two-hour flight from Goose Bay to Kamastastin where our guides, John Pierre Ashini and ex-pat Tony Jenkinson, had gone ahead to set up camp, my eyes were continually drawn to the wilderness through the clouds several thousand feet below. I contemplated the immortal words used by the famous explorer, Jacques Cartier, who described Labrador as 'the land God gave to Cain'. It certainly did look cold, harsh and forebidding.

The roads ended only a few miles north of Goose Bay leaving a true wilderness landmass best described as being similar to a mixture of both the Falkland Islands and British Columbia, where I fished several years back. And though in mid summer areas of snow could still be seen, water in the form of lake and river systems was everywhere, interspersed with tundra, bog and forests of black spruce, birch and red willow. I just wanted to put the plane down everywhere so I could sample it all: thousands of square miles of virgin game fishing. There was however time

BELOW On the banks of the Kamastastin River in Labrador, with Innu guide John Pierre and a handsome, unbelievably coloured arctic char I caught spinning.

enough, for we were soon skipping over waves at the eastern end of Kamastastin lake where three white tents and a pile of cut logs were the only sign of civilization I had seen during our 250-mile flight. Talk about being isolated!

We were greeted warmly by John Pierre and Tony and their families, who much preferred the isolation of Kamastastin to the inherent problems of government settlement life, and shown to our trapper-style tent where the traditional carpet of spruce tips had been arranged to cover the ground. With a basic iron stove for both warmth (at night) and cooking, it took us no time at all to fall into the Innu way of life and our very first meal consisted of smoked arctic char.

During the following week we grid-searched the marginal contours along the lake's shoreline with my portable Hummingbird fish finder unit and found that in places the lake floor actually ran off the 120-foot depth limit, less than the equivalent distance out from overhanging cliff faces. But although quite awesome to contemplate, the lake's depth did fluctuate enormously and by far the best hot spots for char and lake trout were where rivers entered in relative shallows of between five and twenty feet. Here we caught on both wet fly and spoons superbly coloured char to eight pounds and lakers to over fifteen pounds.

But in truth during a week on Lake Kamastastin you can only scratch the surface. My favourite location was at the lake's outlet where it becomes the Kamastastin River which cuts through a steep-sided pine-stacked gorge. Here the arctic char provided unbelievable fights on a wet fly or on lures in the countless pools. The most effective lure by far was an 18g Toby.

However, I must warn anyone planning such a trip during August that, in addition to mosquitoes, you have the fierce biting black fly to contend with. Frankly it is not everyone's cup of tea but I loved it. I'm sad to report that there is no happy postscript to this adventure because, due to the discovery of an incredibly rich nickel deposit at Voseys Bay, there is a Canadian government plan to dam Lake Kamastastin across its outlet to provide power in the form of hydroelectricity. Now far be it from me to stop progress, but what is more important – the native Innu re-establishing their culture in the land they have roamed for thousands of years or the 'get rich quick' attitude of the Canadian government? I'll leave you to decide.

Now we swing from one extreme to the other because in September 1997 I had the opportunity to come to grips with the most exciting battler of them all. For less than a mile offshore from the second tallest cliff face in Europe – an awesome granite feature separating landscaped terraces of fruit trees, vineyards and flowers on either side – the sea bed continues to shelve steeply downwards to over 2,000 feet. Here the warm sea is a majestic purple-blue, and flying fish and dolphins skip the waves. Go a mile further out, to where small groups of commercial tuna boats chum live mackerel on the drift in search of big eyes, and the depth more than doubles. Such is the incredibly deep and fertile habitat along the south coast of Madeira, which lies some 360 miles off the west coast of Africa, just north of the Canaries. It is a truly magical island, perhaps most loved by tourists for its winding roads and panoramic views,

ABOVE Big game trolling boat *Lara Jade* in a lumpy sea just off Funchal, the capital of Madeira, one of the world's top locations for monster blue marlin throughout the 1990s.

exotic flowers and wines, yet revered throughout the 1990s by big-game fishermen everywhere as the blue marlin capital of the world.

To do battle in the fighting chair against these mammoth creatures which average between 600 and 700 pounds, blue-water fishermen come from Cairns in Australia, Fort Lauderdale in America and most places in between. There are more 'granders' (marlin topping a thousand pounds) off Madeira's southern coastline at the moment than anywhere else on this planet. This is a phenomenal statistic indeed when you also consider that most are taken trolling within just two to seven miles of the picturesque shoreline, which is dotted with white-painted houses with terracotta roofs as far into the hills as the eye can see.

So after just ten minutes from leaving the marina in Funchal, the Madeira Islands' capital, giant kona head lures are run out behind the boat and the chance of a jumbo-size marlin begins. But, as my boat partner and I were to experience, such gladiators do not happen along willy-nilly, and towards the end of our fourth day nothing had so much as even poked its bill out above the waves to inspect the carefully arranged formation of six marlin lures being trolled at around nine knots.

Fellow angling journalist, Dave Steuart (lead writer for *Angling* magazine during the 1970s) and I had been invited along by angling fanatic, Frank Perry, who was a British karate champion for several years and now runs Madeira Sportsfishing with two superbly equipped big-game fishing boats out of Funchal marina: *Margarita*, a thirty-five-foot Maine Coaster, and *Lara Jade*, a thirty-three-foot Cyfish which actually holds the world record for catching more granders than any other boat. Frank's business was previously owned by my old mate, Roddy Hays, who was responsible for putting Madeira slap bang on the marlin map a few years ago with outstanding catches of huge blues all caught and released during the season (which runs from May through to November), many exceeding that magical thousand-pound barrier.

Regular viewers of *Go Fishing* may remember that Roddy and I initially teamed up for a wreck fishing programme when he lived in Alderney in the Channel Islands, accounting for numerous twenty-pound-plus cod and big double-figure pollack on pirks from a deep water wreck some eleven miles off shore. Then several years later we got together for some big eyed tuna action in Madeira from his old boat *Anguilla*. But the vision of sportsfishing in Madeira waters goes back further still to the pioneering exploits of another very dear friend, the late Trevor Housby, whose catches twenty-five years ago indicated the island's untapped potential. By sheer coincidence Islda Housby (Madeiran by birth) and Trevor's seventeen-year-old son, Russell, were holidaying on the island during our stay and it was like going back full circle for me, having Russ actually crewing on our boat. But Russ couldn't make those marlin move any more than Frank could.

To change our fortunes we even tried a day's shark fishing on *Lara Jade*, skippered by Anibal Fernandez and Richard Howell, with four big mackerel baits set at different depths beneath partly inflated balloons, drifting along away from the boat in a superb slick of mackerel rubby dubby. But nothing! Then we had a go at drifting for broadbill swordfish at night using large, whole squid presented deep down beneath clear plastic bottle floats, each illuminated from within by a different coloured light source. It was great fun and I especially enjoyed catching the squid for bait using mackerel tail and jigging lures. But nothing again and I could sense Frank's frustration at those big blues not wanting to play ball. He was certainly up for Dave and me sampling some 'Madeira magic'.

On the positive side even during our short stay (while fishing from *Lara Jade*) – and four days is not nearly enough time for marlin – a monster blue of 950lb was taken on *Margarita*, skippered by Mark Ryder Haggard and Mark Ryan. So when I fished from *Margarita* and finally that 80lb line class reel screamed into action like a scalded cat, with just two hours remaining on my last afternoon, for an instant I thought the miracle just might have happened. As we were trolling around the commercial tuna boats however, pulling a mixture of both marlin and tuna lures in the hope of last-call action, commonsense suggested that a big-eyed tuna had grabbed hold and immediately sounded deep. But I was far from complaining and was into the fighting chair like a shot, quickly clicking the bucket seat straps on to the reel lugs. The fish

was by now a fair way behind the boat still ripping line down into the blue depths, so I slowly increased the lever drag to slow it down before pumping the rod quickly up and down to gain line. Lovely stuff! Suddenly the world was a better place. As the converted know only too well, tuna really do wrench your arms out of their sockets and for ten or fifteen minutes I really had my 80lb string well and truly pulled, savouring a great scrap and tug of war with what materialized into my largest big-eye ever, a corker of 220lb.

No sooner had I arrived back from Madeira than an invitation arrived through the letter box from Linda Patterson of CSS International Ltd in London. She was asking me to compete in the first world invitational Bonefishing Championship (fly only) as the UK entrant alongside anglers from Japan, Italy, the United States and the Bahamas. How on earth could I refuse? The Bahamas have in fact the largest bonefish habitat anywhere in the world. Situated in the south-western corner of the Atlantic, due east of Miami, this coral archipelago wonderland comprises 100,000 square miles of shallow ocean plateaux from which sprout over 700 exotic islands – which, incidentally, were under British rule until independence in 1973. Add sumptuous seafood, exotic colourful cocktails, the friendliest people in the world and you are only just starting to appreciate this group called the Bahamas.

The highest point is just 200 feet above sea level and the average all-year-round temperature is in the mid-eighties. It is indeed a tropical paradise with unrivalled hospitality and friendliness. It sports over twenty dedicated world-class bonefishing resorts separated by coral reefs, caves and mile upon mile of sparkling white sandy beaches and mud flats. When illuminated by sunlight, the crystal-clear sea takes on all manner of breathtaking colours from shimmering jade green to cobalt blue, from aquamarine to turquoise or emerald green.

Following the flights from Heathrow to Miami to Nassau and to Exuma, it was difficult to believe that over thirty years had flown by since I had last fished in the Bahamas. My mind instantly returned to those carefree early years in the Merchant Navy when on board P & O cruise ship SS *Oronsay* I enjoyed some fabulous battles with sharks in the warm blue waters off Nassau. Now I had returned for this, the first championship of its kind. It was held in the middle of the Bahamas on Exuma, a ninety-mile-long chain of islands of James Bond fame (both *Thunderball* and *Never Say Never Again* were filmed on location here) which has 365 separate cays (pronounced keys) offering a wide diversity of bonefish habitats from the classical wide sandy flats to dense mangrove inlets, swamps and lagoons where goliath herons, sand pipers, egrets and even ospreys are sighted daily.

The local Bahamian guides have unbelievably sharp eyesight plus a vast knowledge of their particular patch and whilst wading, drifting or poling you along, they are continually pointing out barracuda, tarpon, permit and any one of several species of sharks which also hunt bonefish along the same shallow flats. However, unlike the fly fisherman, these predators do not practise catch and release. Huge stingrays are also regularly encountered, sometimes in mere inches of water, and on one occasion I was treated to the exceptionally rare sight of a huge sawfish, fully twelve feet in length, digging aggressively into the bottom muds for crabs using its tooth-laden saw.

The competition was exceptionally well organized and run over four consecutive days from the club Peace and Plenty by the most enthusiastic Ministry for Tourism team. Every entrant was allocated a different guide and a different observer (to see fair play) each morning which ensured that the same ground was never covered twice. Only specimen bonefish measuring more than twenty-two inches from nose to tail fork counted for points in the competition (we are talking of bonefish weighing six pounds and upwards here), so the guides were continually searching for schools or pods which contained the odd sizeable fish or they were on the lookout for those single, lone bonefish which generally averaged a larger size. This necessitated continually zapping across the flats and reefs at speeds approaching thirty knots from one favourite hot spot to another, and covering anything up to forty or fifty miles during a day which started with lines in at 7.15 am and lines out at 3.15 pm.

The reason bonefish are held in such esteem by international fly fishermen is that they not only accelerate faster from a standing start than any other light-tackle sportfish but scream your entire thirty-yard fly line out in a matter of seconds followed instantly by anything up to and over 150 yards of braided backing. Their power is truly phenomenal, and, combined with the fact that in these crystal-clear shallow waters you must track, stalk and then systematically sight cast individual fish often over distances of twenty-five yards plus in a stiff breeze, they are indeed a most challenging adversary.

To combat the prevailing exceptionally windy conditions I used a ten-foot Masterline, Avantage Venom rod and a WF9 floating line joined to 300 yards of Pro micron backing. Competition rules dictated a tippet strength not exceeding 8lb and my choice of adding around eight foot of fluoro carbon to the upper half of a big butt leader helped turn over enormously. I tried all the favourite local fly patterns, and the acclaimed Gotcha special – tied with a pearl glitter tail and body, long pink throat hair and chain eyes, to imitate a shrimp – really did the business. Whether being stripped in using slow even pulls or allowing it time to sink, those bonefish inhaled it like the last shrimp in the sea. Hook-ups were no problem; it was landing them all that proved difficult. Trying to stop a bonefish, for instance, from winding your line through an entanglement of mangrove roots when it's doing twenty miles an hour is not easy, believe me.

The classic time for hunting these wily speedsters is at low tide on the mud flats in water mere inches deep where their tails and dorsal fins stick out above the surface, as they search nose down for crabs. As the tide floods you then swap location and drift along the edge of the mangroves into which the bonefish eventually move for the rich pickings and to avoid capture by sharks. It's all simply wonderful fun. How did I do it? Well the list of lost fish and hard luck stories would, I am sure, bore you sick. It included losing a real monster literally, on my very last cast on the final day, which is one reason why I just can't wait to get out on those flats again. But everyone experienced the same problems and I did in fact manage to get amongst the prize money by finishing in third place behind Buck Buchenroth of Jackson, Wyoming and Henry Roberts of the Bahamas (both bonefishing guides incidentally) which for a self-confessed bream basher is better than I had ever hoped.

Exactly one year later in November 1998, Jo and I accepted an invitation to go on a media trip as guests of the Bahamas Ministry for Tourism and were shown exactly what these fabulous islands have to offer the international fly fisherman. I can tell you honestly there are not enough days left in my life to be able to experience it all.

ABOVE One of the superb bonefish that helped me into third placing in the 1997 world invitational Bonefishing Championship held on Exuma in the Bahamas.

Following flights from Heathrow to Miami and on to Grand Bahama, we stayed at the Port Lacaya, a resort near Freeport, with our first destination along at the island's eastern end at the renowned deep-water Cay Club which provides excellent accommodation and facilities, managed by husband and wife team, Paul and Alison Adams. By coincidence our guide was Henry Roberts who pipped me into second place in the tournament the previous year and he poled the skiff for hour upon hour over some of the most beautiful and challenging flats I have ever fished. They had some enormous bonefish too: specimens in the seven- to nine-pound bracket were common, though I also saw several whoppers well into double figures and only wished we had had time to do them justice. Alas the weather stayed overcast and windy throughout the day with only modest-size fish landed, the big fish seeing us first and spooking before an effective cast could be made. Then again, as a bonefish of just three or four pounds will strip off your entire floating line plus a hundred yards of backing in just a few long surges, every fight gets the adrenaline flowing.

The following day fishing was provided at the North Riding Point Club situated on Grand Bahama's southern shore and managed by Ben and Judy Rose. Here boats are trailered to a galaxy of flats, inlets and mangrove cays covering several hundred square miles along the island's northern shore. In just a three-hour afternoon session with the help of the experienced eyes of Ken, our guide, I hooked and released eight bonefish to around six pounds, having pricked or lost even more. Again also sighted were some jumbo-size bones plus the occasional tarpon.

After enjoying the Las Vegas show at the Princess Casino that evening we left Grand Bahama and island hopped to Abaco the following morning, our host being a larger-than-life woman in the form of Nettie Symonette who runs a unique ecotourism resort called Different of Abaco where, in addition to enjoying her menagerie of animals which include wild boar and iguanas, guests live in superb accommodation along a powdery white beach and get to explore an outstanding assortment of marls along the west side of the island. I teamed up with good friend, Terrie Yamagishi, Japanese editor of the *American Fly Fisherman* magazine, and we hooked into a whole bunch of hard-battling bones which came most aggressively to our Crazy Charlies virtually all day long. The following morning our entire group of eleven anglers travelled south to Sandy Point to the Bonefishing Paradise guest house managed by Stanley White, and again the fishing was superb. Despite only two hours of actual fishing time, my guide Kendall put me over so many pods of quality bonefish that I was happy to hand my rod over to organizer Nalini Bethel of the Tourism Office in Nassau, so she could experience the exhilarating power and speed of a hooked bonefish.

There is a story behind the legendary Crazy Charlie flies that is well worth mentioning here. In 1974 on the Island of Andros, a Bahamian bonefishing guide by the name of Charlie Smith invented a devastatingly effective fly that was to revolutionize the sport of bonefishing. In fact just about every pattern of bonefish fly that has been created since follows the Crazy Charlie theme with a pair of bead brass or lead eyes tied on top of the shank (so it fishes upside down and doesn't foul bottom weeds) to resemble the shrimp upon which bonefish feed. So actually to meet Charlie Smith on this particular trip and watch him tie some bonefish flies was indeed a privilege. In fact Charlie tied two shrimp imitations for me but I know I will never take them out of my fly box in case I lose them.

After Charlie we visited the famous Andros Island Bonefishing Club managed by Donna Reeny and I teamed up with Cordell Thompson from the ministry to fish a fabulous flat interspersed with mangrove cays at Behring Point on the east side. Our guide, Nick, predicted that bones in plenty would leave the mangroves where they feed on blue crabs and head in our direction once the tide started dropping away – and he was spot on. For an hour I literally had trouble in choosing which fish to single out for sight casting. What a whirlwind week!

There was, however, more to come that autumn, as I had been invited with friend and fellow angling journalist, Dave Lewis, to Tanzania on Africa's East Coast by Annie Ayton of Safari Plus. We were to make a reconnaissance trip, incorporating game viewing and tropical freshwater fishing at the famous Selous which lies a little southwest of Dar es Salaam. Following our long haul from Heathrow, to reach our final destination at the panoramic Sand Rivers Lodge, which overlooks the coloured waters of the fast-flowing Rufiji River, required an hour's flight in a light aircraft from Dar es Salaam to Kiba airstrip. In fact the mighty Rufiji River actually borders the Selous after gathering stature from an amalgam of wild, sandy rivers like the Kilombero, Great Ruaha and Luwegu, thus creating the largest river basin in Africa. Opened by the Germans in 1905 and said to be a birthday gift from the Kaiser to his wife (some present), this 30,000-square-mile nature reserve is the largest protected wildlife sanctuary in Africa, possibly the world, yet it is inhabited by fewer than 200 people – a fact I found quite staggering.

LEFT My good pal, Terrie Yamagishi, editor of the Japanese edition of *American Fly Fisherman*, casting to bonefish on the flats in front of Andros Island Bonefishing Club. Florida sportsfishing writer, Walt Jennings, looks on.

Dave and I had but a week to explore the exotic freshwater fishing of what was pristine wilderness comprising woodland, grassy plains, swamps and marshes interlaced with natural lakes. There was also the muddy shallow, and the exceptionally fast-flowing Rufiji in which there were more hippos and large crocodiles than I had ever seen in my life before. The comfortable lodge was managed by an English couple, Alex and Harriet Edwards. Alex was extremely knowledgeable about the local natural history and the perfect guide for game viewing sorties into the bush where elephant, buffalo, giraffe and a galaxy of the most breathtakingly coloured birds were daily sightings. On one occasion we had the good fortune to study the feeding habits of an entire family of the now quite rare African hunting dogs only minutes after they had brought down an impala. All manner of fish were on offer here including several species of catfish plus the legendary tiger fish. At some of the more remote locations, using a variety of baits from luncheon meat cubes to small freshly killed fishes, we caught several weird and wonderful species of tropical catfish. The bottom of this unusual river is simply paved with pussies from the spined and heavily armoured catfish called squeakers (similar to those I have encountered in the Zambezi incidentally) to monsters of five feet long, though what the species is called I am not sure.

Tiger fish strike everywhere and I would have dearly loved to have stayed attached to two huge fish in particular which, like so many, stayed on the hook for just a few seconds before jumping off. Presenting huge chunks of buffalo meat on strong wire traces in the hope of really big quarry certainly produced some screaming runs on my 30lb class multiplier outfit but in every case fish were not responsible for these runs. It seemed bizarre to be standing beside the river on a sandbank playing crocodiles

which simply sat on the bottom after grabbing the bait! Fortunately they either bit through the wire trace or we pulled for a break lest they walked up the sandbank towards us.

We also enjoyed some exciting sport in one of the many adjacent lakes. In addition to numerous tiger fish in the four- to six-pound range and similar-size sharp-tooth catfish caught using freelined deadbaits and artificial lures I also, for the second time in my life (the first was in India), landed a snapping turtle. This one had an exaggeratedly deep shell and must have weighed the best part of twenty pounds. Fortunately the hooks came out cleanly and it plodded off into the depths of the lake seemingly none the worse for its experience.

The Rufiji is certainly one of the most exciting rivers I have ever fished. Simply travelling upstream with a guide winding the aluminium punt through pods of decidedly hostile hippos would for some prove excitement enough. These particular hippos openly disliked the whine from the outboard engine to such a degree they were for ever charging across the shallow flat in mock attack (we hoped). Should the punt have been overturned however the chances of making it to the shore with so many large crocodiles about, basking on the sandbanks, let alone those not visible, were, I would think, very slim indeed.

Naturally, before, in between and after this string of exotic locations I was still fishing locally. In fact during the 1997/98 winter I teamed up with my two nephews, Richard and Martin Bowler, for a concentrated assault on the big perch inhabiting the upper reaches of the Great Ouse above Bedford. Both had caught perch from the meandering overgrown reaches of this habitat-rich river during the autumn to over three and a half pounds on lobworms. But once low winter temperatures set in sport died away to very few bites. My first two trips in fact resulted in complete blanks but at least I had the opportunity of both walking and, more importantly, plumbing depths along a most interesting two-mile winding beat enticingly overhung by gnarled old willows and large blackthorn bushes.

Then at the beginning of February whilst sharing a wandering day with Richard with the Ouse running slow and quite clear, I managed to catch a nice brace of stripies on trotted worm from a deep hole on an acute bend, weighing 2¼lb and 3¾lb respectively. Just a week later I again fished the same swim with Richard who on quiver-tipped lobworm managed to induce a perch bite from amongst the hoards of signal crayfish which along this part of the Ouse almost pave the bottom. They are in fact a horrible nuisance but obviously responsible for the phenomenal growth rates of the adult perch. Richard's prize perch fought strongly in the now heavily pulling river and was in absolute spanking condition. It pulled the scales down to 4lb 5oz.

A week later during a particularly promising mild spell I was back on the banks of the Upper Ouse though rather disappointed to find it bank-high and coffee coloured. Three days of incessant rain had turned every ditch and side stream into raging torrents, but at least for February the weather was surprisingly mild, despite a continual downpour which started when Martin and I arrived at the fishery at 7.30 am, and was still coming down when we finished at 5.00 pm. Never before in fact can I remember actually sheltering beneath the brolly for the entire day. Strangely however it did not deter the big perch from biting, although our initial decision of concentrating upon the same deep bend where Richard and I had scored only weeks before proved a total failure, due I am certain to a farm drainage dyke immediately above the bend spewing its filthy water into the river. A complete lack of bites save for the attention of bait-robbing signal crayfish, which are continually active (except when perch are on the prowl), meant that the perch had been sickened by the filthy orange water which no doubt included a proportion of silage.

So at around midday I walked to the top of the meadow well above the farm dyke and catapulted a couple of dozen broken lobworms into an acute deepish bend. Here a huge mat of brown rotting bullrushes lining the inside bank would have provided a superb hide-out habitat earlier on in the season throughout the summer and autumn months. My intention was to move in just above the bend for the remaining few hours of the day. It was the best bit of forward planning I have ever done. On arrival back at the deep bend Martin was about to lift out a crayfish firmly attached to his lobworm. That did it for me. Ten minutes later I was nicely settled in at the upstream end of the bend with my 13-foot rod presenting a stret-pegged worm close beside the bed of decaying bullrushes in a depth of seven feet. Once the float had settled at a half-cocked position indicating that the bait was static on the river bed, I cast out a second rod presenting a three swan shot ledger into the middle of the bend pointing it directly at the huge lobworm and clipped on a bobbin indicator between butt ring and reel.

When I looked up again I found the float had disappeared and my instinctive strike resulted in a lovely throbbing, head-shaking resistance deep down, so characteristic of a big perch. With just a 2½lb test reel line on the centre pin I was afraid to bully it and so enjoyed a spirited fight until it was up on the surface and ready for the net, all 2lb 2oz of it. A fine start, that. As soon as I had popped it into a pre-soaked sack at my feet the ledger bobbin jerked twice and slowly climbed to the butt ring in that classical, confident way big perch inhale a lobworm. And what a big perch it felt too. Taking line against the clutch, it powered upstream for a few yards before turning back downriver across the swim, boring deep all the time, and it stayed close to the bottom while I pumped it cautiously upstream to where I sat beneath an old willow tree watching the rod tip didn't catch in the branches above. It seemed an age, but finally my perch came up through the coloured water into view and thrashed the surface displaying its massively deep flanks and fat belly. Perhaps with more pressure than I should have used I quickly bullied it straight into the waiting net and heaved it ashore. On the scales it weighed exactly 3lb 10oz which made it my second-largest perch ever. What a day – and it was far from over.

After introducing some more broken lobworms into the middle of the bend I eased another worm on to the size 4 hook and plopped it out to exactly where the big perch had come from. Within less than a minute the bobbin shot up and I struck into yet another biggy which after just four or five seconds unfortunately slipped the hook. I automatically feared that this would unsettle the shoal which it certainly did for a good hour or so. Then almost simultaneously bites came on both rods as the shoal again moved over the carpet of broken worm pieces. The float was first away and I struck into what felt like another whopper which bored away downstream taking several yards of line before I managed to turn it level with the end of the rush bed. Unfortunately it veered inwards towards the near bank and became stuck fast in the bed of decaying bullrushes. When I pulled steadily the hook came free. Was I gutted, though I had little time for self pity because from the corner of my eye I witnessed the ledger bobbin jerking slowly upwards to the butt ring. This time the hook set firmly as the fish belted off downstream against a firmly set clutch, obviously another whopping great stripey by its head-shaking antics and dogged resistance. My Avon quiver tip rod and 6lb reel line were stretched to the full with this fish which led me a merry song and dance by screaming off upriver past where I sat, just missing a sunken willow branch, before I could get it back again under control and beneath the rod tip ready for netting. It was by far the largest perch I had ever seen on the end of my line in over fifty years of angling. It was a monstrously hump-backed specimen sporting wide, dark brown stripes, beautiful crimson fins, an incredibly fat belly (full of crayfish no doubt) and a huge mouth. It pulled my dial scales down to 4lb 1oz exactly, and boy, was I over the moon.

By now Martin had moved into the sedges bordering the next bend downstream but his ledgered lobs could attract small perch only. I experienced yet another lull for over an hour before the float suddenly shot away again resulting in my last perch of

the day, another superbly fat specimen of 2lb 3oz. It too was stuffed full of broken worms, coughing up the remains of at least twenty into my hand after removing the hook. So I'd got four perch weighing together exactly 12lb. It was difficult to believe that I would ever better such a catch. At least those were my thoughts as Martin and I trudged wearily yet happily back to the cars across muddy meadows with the rain still falling heavily. Little did I know then that the following winter would produce totally staggering results.

At the start of 1998 I was asked by Polish publisher, Jerzy Markiewicz, if I would visit Warsaw to be the guest of honour at their annual angling exhibition in mid February. As Warszawski Dom Wydawniczy had already translated several of my Boxtree books to be published in Poland, and taken four of my Kazan River Production fishing videos also for translation into Polish (I'm called Johna Wilsona out there – honestly!), I was indeed very proud to attend.

I flew out to Warsaw with Jerzy's son, Bartek (then studying over here at Warwick University), who acted as my interpreter and was totally gobsmacked by my popularity amongst Polish fishermen. Following television interviews and book signings I was escorted around the exhibition by Jerzy and his manager, Janusz Dobrzelecki, who speaks good English and was most surprised to see posters from my books and articles all over the place. Manufacturers were continually giving me samples of their floats and excellent plugs and spinners, and when I stopped to look at a Polish copy of a British reclining carp chair, little did I know that very item would be wrapped up and waiting at my hotel the following morning. Their generosity and hospitality were second to none and it was a good job I didn't look at any boats. But when it came to eating out on boiled mirror carp and jellied grass carp, would you believe I tried my best to assure them that although an angler I didn't like eating fish. Which is perfectly true. But I nevertheless did down a few mouthfuls of each (ugh) just to be polite. Apparently at Christmas in Poland the national dish is not roast turkey but – yes, boiled carp!

I was later presented with a large polished box full of wonderfully hand-crafted artificial lures at yet another dinner where I met the editor of *Wiadomosci Wedkarskie*, Poland's most successful angling magazine, which has a staggering monthly readership of 140,000, and fellow author in the form of Tadeusz Andrejczyk (translated to Ted Andrews) who like me also wrote about scuba diving in freshwater for *Angling* magazine back in the 1970s. So there was much to talk about.

What with a quick sightseeing trip around old Warsaw to witness how superbly some of the old buildings had been restored and even totally rebuilt to their original specifications following Hitler's madness during the last war, followed by lunch at a Mexican restaurant (my choice) only to find they served up chocolate chilli con carne – yes, it really did taste of chocolate – my all too brief visit to Poland was over. It was fascinating to say the least.

When viewers sit back to watch *Go Fishing* I am certain they never fully appreciate the frustration and trauma that go into bringing fishing into their homes on the small screen. Naturally they only ever see the sun, sand and specimen fish. So even now after fifteen years of presenting, directing and producing through Kazan River Productions the fishing videos and Anglia-Meridian programmes for British television, I often ask myself why I still enjoy the hassle of something which is tantamount to knocking your head against a brick wall. Because it is only great when you wrap and go home with sufficient 'in the can' as they say. Due to weather and water conditions, plus that old luck factor, our favourite subject has no equal in unpredictability. Sports such as football and boxing, in fact most organized events, are by comparison an absolute doddle to film. At least you know at what time the action is going to start and in most cases even when it will end. But can anyone ever predict when a fish is going to bite? I reckon it is this unpredictable factor which gives me such a buzz and keeps me for ever looking for new challenges.

I was therefore really looking forward, at the end of March 1998, to our planned trip to Lake Nasser in Egypt in the company of Emap's then fishing publishing editor, Andy Benham, to make a ninety-minute safari-style video about this 300-mile-long water wilderness, home to the world's largest freshwater gladiator *Lates niloticus*, the Nile perch. Just as easily however, being the producer, it could have also turned into my personal nightmare. Had we taken the right generator along for charging camera batteries? Had we sufficient tape stock? What if our camera went down out on massive Lake Nasser, hundreds of miles from nowhere? Would our delicate filming equipment and precious rod tubes all even arrive in Aswan via Cairo in working order? I once had my fishing rods sent to Japan instead of back to Heathrow from Canada where I had been filming *Go Fishing*. Fortunately this was on the way back. But should it ever happen to the flight out, what a disaster!

I had first fished Lake Nasser back in April 1996 with my wife Jo, plus Christine Slater and her daughter, Emma, on a reconnaissance trip for Tailor Made Holidays. We were guests of Kenyan-born Tim Baily who, as The African Angler, operates six specialized fishing boats on the lake plus two supply vessels. We had a fabulous time, starting our safari at Abu Simbel where the huge statues of the Pharaohs built by Rameses II to impose fear upon the Nubians preside over the water, and slowly motored in a northerly direction up the lake towards Aswan catching dozens of perch

RIGHT The history of
Egypt is evident
throughout the
length of Lake
Nasser: these huge
statues of the
Pharaohs were built
by Rameses II to
impose fear upon
the Nubians.

to seventy pounds trolling around the islands and rocky shorelines. This trip led to
my accompanying guests on further safaris, right up to the present day in fact.

There is indeed something rather enigmatic and mystical about Lake Nasser which
is of course the valley of the River Nile flooded all the way from the Sudan to Aswan,
where the high dam protects the city from the waters of this enormous man-made
reservoir. Of course the Nile itself is an amalgam of the Blue Nile which originates in
Ethiopia and the White Nile whose source is none other than Lake Victoria. But
enough of the geography. Let's return to our meeting Tim Baily in Aswan airport at
the start of our Lake Nasser Safari video shoot.

I had chosen the end of March because usually at around this time of the year the
weather is wonderful. I was expecting clear blue skies, daytime temperatures in the
nineties and warm, sultry humid nights that barely necessitate a sleeping bag while
you drift comfortably into oblivion admiring the stars, sleeping on the open deck of
your twenty-five-foot fishing boat which is literally your home for the week. So when
Tim gave us the news of some most inconsistent fishing due to completely
unprecedented cold, windy weather and sand storms, it was hardly a promising start.
Unfortunately I had told cameraman, Dave Allen, and sound recordist, Dave
Runciman, that all they need bring along were a pair of shorts and a few T-shirts. They
were not happy bunnies. El Niño had a lot to answer for.

Worse still, once out on the lake with the camera starting to roll, one of Tim's front
teeth suddenly dropped out. Never mind, I thought, a quick drop of Superglue should
do the job. Within minutes, despite almost sticking his lips together, I had fixed it
back in place as good as new. Fortunately we were tied up to the shore well away from
the white horses out on the lake in a quiet cove at the time, shooting an intro to the
video in which Tim obviously did not fancy looking like Goofy. But halfway through
the second take his tooth flies out again and plops overboard straight into the lake

several feet from the boat. Immediately a plastic bottle marker float and lead line (used for buoying underwater pinnacles) was thrown over the spot. Mohammed, our ace diver, who thinks nothing of recovering expensive lures caught up in submerged tree tops in twenty feet of water, was quickly over the side after the elusive tooth. Alas, an hour later, Mohammed was completely knackered and had reluctantly to allow Tim's tooth to rest in peace. So minus his front tooth Tim and I eventually started the video's introduction. It was now forty-eight hours from checking in at Heathrow with not an inch of action in the can.

Fortunately, Lake Nasser is blessed with a truly fantastic head of Nile perch which breed most prolifically and enjoy a diet of tilapia, small perch and tiger fish. They exist all around Nasser's countless islands and irregular contoured shoreline, so Andy and I were into some exciting action once the wind finally started to drop on the following morning. By trolling CD Rapalas and Buchertail depth raider plugs at between two and three knots close around rocky headlands in depths of between fifteen and thirty feet, where clusters of boulders the size of a family car provide the perch with a variety of ambush points from which to dart out and grab their prey, we were soon providing cameraman, Dave Allen, with some spectacular footage. The great thing about Nile perch is that each and every one of them including the 'buffalos' (hundred-pound-plus fish) treat you to a head-shaking, gill-flaring exhibition of tail walking at the end of the fight once they finally hit surface, following a powerful, deep and dogged battle. They are certainly one of the most obliging sportsfish it has ever been my privilege to film.

LEFT Tim Baily, myself and guide Mohammed being filmed by (*Left to Right*) Dave Runciman and Dave Allan during the making of Lake Nasser Safari video, which I presented, directed and produced through Kazan River Productions.

We literally lost count of the specimens between thirty and fifty pounds taken on the troll and so decided to dedicate part of the video to shore fishing which to the ardent lure angler represents truly amazing prospects. Where else, for instance, can you stand on the shore from amongst the rocks, or cast from a position high above sheer-sided rock faces and hook into freshwater gladiators possibly of over a hundred pounds? Even, would you believe it, two hundred pounds! Several monsters approaching two hundred pounds have in fact been landed from the shore on Lake Nasser, using little more than stepped-up pike tackle.

We also caught a few perch fly fishing, and whilst working deadbaits sink-and-draw style. A supply of freshly gill-netted herring-like fish and some small tiger fish were swapped for a bottle of Coke and a few hooks with the local fishermen, and once rigged on a pennel set-up incorporating two size 7/0 single hooks tied direct to a 100lb mono trace (wire is not necessary for perch) these naturals really scored when retrieved slowly. They glinted most attractively through the clear, blue depths (where visibility often reaches ten feet) and suddenly to observe the dark shape of a big perch following the bait was nerve-racking to say the least. Takes were extraordinarily savage and nearly ripped the rod from my grasp. So after a while I knocked the ABU 10,000 multiplier into free spool when drawing the deadbait upwards, which was often when the perch made a grab, engulfing the fresh fish in its huge jaws. Several yards of line could then be given without the perch feeling resistance before lowering the rod tip, engaging the clutch and slamming into the perch when all was tight. Great stuff.

Using lures we also hooked into numerous tiger fish averaging between three and

LEFT What a whopper! My 120lb Nile perch was quite some lump for me and guide Mohammed to hold up for the camera.

six pounds, accidentally hooked the strange-looking freshwater puffer fish every so often and lost a couple of huge vundu catfish. There are some enormous vundu in the lake but few are ever landed because they dive to the bottom having grabbed a lure on the troll or being worked from the shore and immediately wind your line around and even under the rocks. Tim has however taken them to over seventy pounds. There are also some bagrus catfish which reach forty pounds and the horrible electric catfish which is capable of generating electrical pulses and discharging over 300 volts. Fortunately being coloured in pale grey with large black spots, this particular species is easily identified and not to be messed with. The two I have caught of around three and six pounds respectively both fortunately worked themselves off the lure without my having to consider a way of unhooking them.

During the making of this video I also finally fulfilled a personal ambition of catching a freshwater fish exceeding that magical hundred-pound barrier. Following goodness knows how many mahseer and vundu catfish to over ninety pounds and dozens of perch to close on the same weight from both Lake Victoria and Lake Nasser during the previous decade, plus a couple of lost monsters that were far in excess of a hundred pounds, I became soundly attached to a whopper on the troll, which really made the 35lb reel line sing in the wind while it did its best to reach the sanctuary of the rocks on the bottom of a fifty-foot deep gulley. My powerful voyager rod was dragged over into an alarming bend for a good twenty minutes but eventually the pressure told and the great fish finally hit the surface in a shower of spray close alongside the boat, wallowed a couple of times and lay there totally exhausted. It was an immense creature, so incredibly deep in the body, which measured five feet long and weighed exactly 120lb. Was I over the moon or what!

The bird life on Lake Nasser is wonderfully diverse which is not what most visitors expect from, what is after all, a flooded desert. Daily sightings might include egrets, Goliath herons, vultures, kites, Egyptian geese, pelicans, owls and terns, even flamingos plus numerous colourful, land-based finches which congregate around the shrub-like bushes along the shoreline. There are of course no trees as such but it's certainly not difficult to fall in love with such a seemingly barren environment. For those who look there is a truly fascinating ecosystem. Sightings along the shoreline and on the larger islands include camels, goats, donkeys, desert fox, jackals, giant spiders, scorpions, snakes and lizards. Some of the monitor lizards, which are woken from having a snooze upon a flat rock as your boat trolls close by, are up to six feet in length and quickly crash dive into the lake like mini dinosaurs.

Being part of what was once the River Nile, Nasser also contains huge crocodiles which, unlike those I have encountered in other African rivers such as the Rufiji and Zambezi, are not to be feared. In fact it is most difficult to approach them close enough to obtain a photograph. This is because they feed mainly on fish and, due to the total lack of game around the shoreline, are not used to gorging on herd animals such as wildebeest and zebra in shallow water. So for the most part a dip in the lake to cool off every so often is not only safe but extremely pleasant.

Though we had shot an enormous amount of footage during our week's stay on Nasser in March we were still short of some general views such as sunrises and sunsets, plus various aspects of natural history. So as I was returning with guests on escorted trips in April and again in May, on behalf of Tailor Made Holidays, I took up Dave Allen's offer of purchasing his compact digital video camera, a Panasonic AG-EZ1E, complete with standard and wide angle lenses. I also bought an underwater housing for the camera plus a super wide angle lens, to enable me to take a few sub-surface shots when we returned. Until now I had always stayed away from getting involved with the filming side of my videos, preferring to produce good stills rather than mediocre video footage. But I was pleasantly surprised by the results which were no doubt helped by the fact that as I was both directing and paper editing the video, I knew exactly what clips were required.

An unusual and rare opportunity presented itself one particular evening when on seeing some jackals not far from where our boats were tied up, Tim walked ashore in the pitch black helped by a torch beam and deposited the left overs from dinner on top of a mound not forty feet away to see if these normally inquisitive but naturally timid animals would come closer. Having taken my Samalight HD lighting unit along (what a superb piece of kit) should such a situation occur, I positioned the powerful main beam of light on top of the dinner scraps and set the camera up on a tripod on the sandy beach just a few feet from the supply boat, to see if the jackals would play ball. I am glad to say they did. At one time no fewer than five were captured in the light beam and by using maximum gain on the digital camera I recorded this truly

memorable occasion of wild animals feeding, seemingly oblivious to more than a dozen humans staring in wonderment. You could have heard a pin drop.

Jackals and the desert fox are in fact regular campsite visitors around Lake Nasser during the quiet hours of darkness once everyone has turned in, as their footprints seen in the sand on the following morning testify. But rarely do you get the chance of actually seeing them at such close quarters, let alone recording the occasion. It was a privilege indeed. Our encounter with a noisy frog however was entirely different. Once all the tit bits had been cleared and the jackals moved on it was time for everyone to resume drinking before thinking about getting their heads down. But not three feet from the bows of the boat on which I slept there was a large frog squatting in the mud, puffing its cheeks out every few seconds and creating the loudest, most irritating 'RIVET' you have ever heard. He didn't seem to mind me picking him up and depositing him in the reedy margins fully fifty yards away and I walked back to the boat, making sure there were no snakes in the torch beam, to continue some serious drinking. It was a sultry, warm intoxicating evening, the kind where your mind is truly at peace. Ten minutes later, in exactly the same spot to the inch, I swear, sat exactly the same frog which of course brought a hail of disbelieving laughter from everyone who thought I was batty anyway moving the frog in the first place.

Up I got again, and this time I walked fully a hundred yards before dropping him into a dense bed of marginal reeds and again returned to the boat. Yes – you've guessed correctly. Twenty minutes later (a determined frog this one) a loud indignant 'RIVET' told everyone that he was back again. I suffered in silence while everyone laughed themselves silly. Not long afterwards however the riveting was finally halted by someone who got up, walked along the bows of the boat to just above the serenading frog and urinated all over him. And I'm not saying who that person was.

Even before I got around to editing our Lake Nasser Safari video, which had become easily the most exciting television I have been involved with, in June 1998 I was off abroad again. I was making a long-awaited return trip across the Atlantic to see my old mate, Stu Makay, at Lockport Bridge Dam, near Winnipeg in Canada on the fabulous Red River. This is a fishery simply stuffed full of common carp, most of which have yet to see a baited hook, and the unbelievably hard-battling channel catfish. Both species incidentally average high into double figures in this part of the Red River, a phenomenon I first encountered around ten years ago whilst travelling back from researching the lake trout fishing on Lake Nuletin in northern Manitoba. I can remember then saying to Stu, who runs the fishing and accommodation at Lockport, that he was sitting on a gold mine. In complete contrast to how we British anglers put tremendous value on the carp as the supreme freshwater adversary, with species like zander at the bottom of the list, North American anglers put walleye (their zander) at the top and, for the most part, are not the slightest bit interested in catching carp regardless of their size and how they fight. Odd, isn't it?

In fact most Americans and Canadians would really rather catch a bundle of 2–3lb walleyes, which merely flap around like a bream of similar size, than have their string pulled by long, lean and unbelievably hard-battling common carp which are so plentiful in the 10–25lb range, their sheer density in numbers takes some believing. I thought I had experienced prolific river fishing for carp when I first sampled the Rio Ebro in eastern Spain for my *Go Fishing* programmes. Its coloured water is simply stuffed full of common carp and barbel, but most are on the small side and double-figure carp are not regular catches. Whereas on the Red, doubles are the norm. My old mate, Fred J. Taylor, likens the river to a fish factory, and he's right.

Lockport Bridge Dam with its churning maelstrom of white water offers quite staggering boat and bank fishing. Channel catfish and common carp to over 30lb exist here plus the exciting freshwater drum, a predatory bream-like fish that is always willing to have a go at your fish strip, worm or fly. Add shiners, goldeye (a roach-like silver shoal fish and catfish bait *par excellence*), walleye, saugers, sturgeon, white bass, bullheads, pike and other oddities, and you can understand why parties of British anglers are now regularly visiting the Red River during the summer months, June until September being prime time. From October until early May it is completely iced over, such is the severity of Canadian winters.

Our party of eight, including Christine Slater of Tailor Made Holidays who organized the trip, stayed in Stu Makay's anglers' accommodation which commands a wonderful panoramic view across the river, with the custom-built boats less than a stone's throw away.

But before getting afloat everyone had a whiff of Stu's stinking corn, the carp bait supreme. What is stinking corn, do I hear you ask? Well you tip 50lb of hard maize into a large plastic bin which has a lid. Several bags of sugar are then added – you don't have

to be accurate, say 10–20lb – and the whole lot is covered by a few inches with boiling water and stirred thoroughly to dissolve the sugar. You then put the lid on and leave it for several weeks, or a few months if you like, for a ripe fermentation to take place. Those who make their own wine will understand the process here which benefits from a thoroughly good stir once a week. It is wise to put your bin full of stinking corn at the end of the garden well away from the house because when ready, and you will know, the smell is next to unbearable. You then scoop out a bucketful, a lid is also imperative here during transportation, and go carping. Loose feeding and styles of fishing are then the same as for baiting with sweetcorn, maize being the hard variation of corn on the cob anyway and ridiculously cheap to purchase from the local corn merchant.

Strangely your Stinkers will not have softened to any great degree and the best presentation is to use two to four grains on a hair rig whether ledgering or float fishing. Alternatively it is possible to side hook one or two grains. Either way, don't forget an old piece of towelling for wiping your hands on. Now stinking corn works anywhere, believe me, and on the Red River those carp simply queue up once they've got a sniff. Incidentally a large ladle-type spoon lashed to a stiff two-foot cane serves as an ideal throwing stick for loose feeding.

On our first carping session Stu ran the eighteen-foot aluminium boat hard up on to a shallow gravel bar, where a wide drainage dyke joins the Red River not 200 yards from our accommodation, and scattered several scoopfuls of maize just thirty feet out. Within minutes there were so many tails sticking out of the surface knocking our peacock quill 'lift' floats, it was sometimes difficult to distinguish between line bites and the real thing. True, Stu had prebaited the evening before, but what followed was quite staggering. Having seen it all before Stu sat back, with a grin on his face, to see how his three guests would enjoy Canada's carping hospitality. To cut a long story short, although we fished for but only four or five hours, it was the most hectic sport with double-figure carp and cats (they take maize too though prefer fresh fish cutlets) that it has ever been my good fortune to experience. What a wonderful change from the over-fished carp waters of our British Isles.

Incidentally, tell a Canadian that you love catching carp and he will give you a quizzical look for sure. But mention that you actually catch the same fish twice back home and even give them names, and he will drop his beer from laughing in disbelief. It is simply beyond his comprehension, because most Canadian carp have yet to see an angler's bait. This probably explains why in just a few hours and from little more than two rod lengths out from the boat, my two guests, Roberto Ferrario (who had travelled from Italy) and Richard Ward from Southampton and myself accounted for exactly fifty superbly conditioned common carp between 11lb and 24lb, nine channel catfish to 23lb and eight drum to 7½lb. All came to stinking corn and breadflake baits and on several occasions two rods were bending simultaneously. At one stage all three were fully bent! We only stopped when we did in mid afternoon because Stu said, 'Hey guys, let's call it a day at fifty, eh!' He was right of course. The fishing is so prolific there is no point whatsoever in trying to fill your boots on every session.

Throughout the week we sampled carp in other locations off the Red River system including creeks, vast swamps, and wide channels, all with similar results. Beautifully proportioned common carp simply knock the spots off a pot-bellied mirror of twice or even three times the size. Their strength and stamina were quite phenomenal.

We all enjoyed equal success with channel catfish and it was fun at the start of each session to waggler float fish pieces of worm to catch goldeye for bait close alongside the boat jetty. Each goldeye is then sliced into five or six cutlets and just one gently nicked on to a size 4/0 barbless hook. By the way, barbless hooks are compulsory in Canada as is the use of one rod only at all times. Mind you, the fishing is so fast and furious how anyone could look after two rods simultaneously (let alone three) is beyond my comprehension. Holding the rod and feeling for bites is imperative or the pussy lets go of your bait. A foot or two of line is given the second that a cat mouths the ledgered bait, followed immediately by a quick wind down and firm strike. Pound for pound the carp fights faster, but channel catfish (and I used 14lb mono and an eleven-foot 2lb test curve rod for both) will pull harder and for longer. Incidentally, regular viewers of *Go Fishing* will perhaps remember that I featured the channel catfish of the Red River with Stu Makay several years back in series six and, unlike sport in our British waters, I am pleased to say that it hasn't changed since – not one little bit.

Due to heatwave temperatures, anchoring the boat amongst the deep swirling waters of the dam weir produced the most consistently hectic action with channel cats during the daytime. You can night fish of course but this was supposed to be a leisurely holiday and as two anglers sharing a boat often accounted for four or five cats apiece between ten and twenty pounds in just a few hours, there was little point in losing valuable drinking time during the evenings. Best pussy of the week was a 27½-pounder to the rod of Richard Ward who boated another of 25lb.

An additional treat was in store for our guests that week because my old mate, Fred J. Taylor, who spends several weeks with Stu each summer, just happened to be at hand to organize some of his legendary riverside cook-outs. So most evenings saw us watching the sun go down in wonderful company, having a good old guitar-backed singsong around the camp fire. There was yet another surprise for me personally in the form of jolly Keith Sharp from Fergusen Lake Lodge in the Northwest Territories, who was now noticeably slimmer than his former twenty-three stone when we were last filming *Go Fishing* together eight years previously and he fell through the ice – a story I mentioned earlier. Keith was staying at nearby Winnipeg recovering from a triple bypass operation and had popped along to Stu Makay's place completely unannounced. How wonderful it was to be in the company of such great friends. There most certainly followed a night to remember, although in the morning I couldn't remember much about it. Christine said if she hadn't caught him from falling forwards off his seat, Fred J. would have toppled over into the fire. Fred said I wouldn't stop singing even though he couldn't remember the chords to the Grand Coolie Dam, and apparently Stu sat there totally out of his tree but contentedly happy all evening.

Upon returning from Canada in time for the start of the river coarse fishing season I got well and truly stuck into filming series thirteen of *Go Fishing* visiting some wonderful locations. I fly fished for mullet and bass at Kimmeridge Bay in Dorset with fellow journalist, Dr Mike Ladle, battled with conger eels inhabiting a south-coast wreck with skipper, Brian Joslin, out from Rye in Sussex, took some fine chub over four pounds and pike to twenty pounds from the Hampshire Avon near Ringwood and actually managed to catch on cue from the Upper Ouse a big perch for the cameras which weighed 3lb 12oz. But the most beautiful fish filmed in the series that summer was undoubtedly the near twenty-pound golden coloured ghost carp I caught on float tackle from Heacham Park Lake in north Norfolk.

In the middle of the filming, at the end of July to be precise, Christine Slater of Tailor Made Holidays asked Emap's publishing director, Andy Benham and me if we fancied making up a foursome together with Roberto Ferrario (who came to Canada) on a research trip. This was to be to Africa's south-west coast in Namibia to catch sharks from the beach and then head inland for some tiger fishing along the upper reaches of the Zambezi in Zambia. Obviously we jumped at the opportunity, and what an exciting whirlwind trip it turned out to be. I can never recall cramming so much travelling and fishing into such a short period of time. In fact we travelled 21,000 miles in just five days.

Our first destination was to Windhoek (pronounced Vintook), the capital of Namibia. We then chartered a six-seater Cessna 210, piloted by JC, for a one-hour flight heading due west to Swakopmund on the Skeleton Coast. Here we were introduced to Ottmar of Levo Sports Fishing, a short, most enthusiastic and rather eccentric German guide who for several years has been taking visitors shore fishing by Land Rover and offshore ground fishing on board an eighteen-foot ski boat powered by twin Honda 90s. The sea was extremely rough with huge rollers crashing up the

sandy beach which stretched for mile upon mile in both directions for as far as the eye could see.

Ottmar decided to drive our party of five, which now included Peter Sawyer of the Namibia Travel Connections, twenty miles north to where a huge reef broke the force of the waves 400 yards out leaving a large area of fishable water between it and the beach. He provided all the tackle and soon had us all rigged up with one-piece, fourteen-foot South African-style surf rods, multipliers loaded with 40lb test and a simple swivelled paternoster rig combining a 6oz lead with a fresh mullet head on a size 6/0 hook: his standard shark terminal rig, until the big boys put in an appearance. When they do the mono trace is replaced with 80lb wire and 8/0 hook. In case you are wondering, the 'big boys' are bronze whaler sharks weighing anything from 100 to 300 pounds plus. Cow sharks of between eighty and 150 pounds also feature in everyday catches here. Trouble was, our visit being in July (the African winter) conditions were not really conducive to these particular sharks coming close inshore. Anytime between January and April, we were told, would virtually guarantee action with bronzes, as Ottmar affectionately calls them. I had no reason to doubt his words because we caught everything else he said we would, including three black spotted gully sharks of between fifty and seventy pounds plus a couple of forty-pound-plus hound sharks which are not unlike our tope. Add three more lost of similar size and it was pretty impressive action for just an afternoon's sport at the wrong time of year.

When the water warms big kob, steenbrass and three species of ray are also regular captures from the shore along the prolific Skeleton Coast. My old mate, Dave Lewis, from Newport, together with fellow angling journalist, Clive Gammon, who regularly wrote for *Angling* magazine during the 1970s, had been after the sharks only a few months before our trip. They travelled further up the coast and got stuck into several 150-pound plus bronze whalers, the best weighing 250lb. What marvellous and unique beach fishing.

Exactly one year later in February 1999 Dave accompanied a party of ten British shore anglers to the Skeleton Coast and in six days they landed a staggering total of 15,000lb of sharks. This included no fewer than eighty-eight bronze whalers between 145lb and 280lb-plus smaller sharks and nine other species. That is certainly the best haul from the beach I can ever recall being taken anywhere. But back to our whirlwind tour.

Following a night in the superb Swakopmund Hotel, where we enjoyed a magnificent meal including wine for around £8 a head, we were collected by Ottmar at seven o'clock to go out fishing on his boat. We were back in again by ten o'clock having caught fifty or so catfish and kob to around four pounds on cut sardine bait at anchor. Honestly, it was amazing light-tackle sport. Then we boarded the Cessna for our next leg of the journey. Well I did say it was a whirlwind tour and I meant it!

Heading in a north-easterly direction over desert and the savannah, JC brought the plane down four hours later at Mpacha airport in Katima. Here our Land Rover transfer was waiting to take us over the border into Zambia where we followed the course of the mighty Zambezi River upstream for eighty miles along a dust track to the lodge at Mazeba Bay. This bumpy route should have taken around three hours but was nearly doubled on account of two punctures, the second within just five miles of our destination which left us without a spare. So Shaun the driver had to thumb a lift and returned an hour later with another wheel. By this time it was pitch black and quite chilly, so we lit a fire in the middle of the track and huddled around it. After a warm welcome from our hosts André and Janine Van der Merwe and a much-needed evening meal, everyone crashed out only to rise the next day at six for an early morning session by inflatable boat up the fast-flowing Zambezi.

Now whilst I have enjoyed catching the tooth-laden tiger fish in Zimbabwe from the Zambezi River immediately above Victoria Falls and way below in massive Lake Kariba, until now I had neither seen nor fished the Upper Zambezi. Tales of its remoteness as it cuts through the Zambian jungle, and of narrow but deep swirling pools and eddies where monster tiger fish lurk, had always captured my imagination. It sounded so very different from the wide, reed-lined expanse of the lower reaches where hippos wallow on the sandbanks and muddy pools, and where animals of the savannah come down to drink.

Accommodating just twelve visitors at any one time in unique A-frame thatched lodges set high off the ground, with breathtaking, picture-book views across the Zambezi, Mazeba Bay offers anglers unparalleled sport with specimen tiger fish to twenty pounds, barbel of thirty, plus several species of colourful predatory bream. Much of the river here runs through a rocky gorge and so is never netted by the locals. Consequently it is simply full of fish and there are some mouthwatering pools screaming out to be fly fished. Most of the rocky runs however were best fished by trolling from the lodge boats or shore casting using big single hook spoons or Rapala shad rap and CD 14 magnum plugs, the rear treble of which is replaced by a strong size 4/0 single hook to improve the ratio of fish hooked and lost to fish landed. When you do hook a tiger fish in these fast currents the ensuing battle can only be described as spectacular. Their initial run, always followed by an explosion of spray as they catapult themselves high into the air in order to throw the hooks, is like no other freshwater sport fish. My outfit consisting of a small multiplier loaded with 17lb test and 30lb wire trace, and an eight-foot fast tip spinning rod, was certainly none too heavy for these tigers. From a couple of dozen hits on our first session we boated and released just six deep-bodied specimens to around six pounds. But don't run away with the idea that Mazeba Bay is all fishing. You can take a flight up the valley to view the falls from above in André's microlight, go game viewing by Land Rover in a nearby national park, tackle white-water rafting, or simply take it easy and enjoy the exotic bird life through binoculars.

By nine, the sun's brightness terminated any further action from toothy predators, so we beached the boat and walked way upstream through the bush to marvel at the magnificent Ngonye Falls (a mini Victoria Falls), one of the major attractions at Mazeba Bay Lodge, although I am sure some guests would give me an argument in favour of Lilundu, a four-year-old orphan elephant. She has been raised by the Van der Merwes from just a few months old, and visitors get to share their afternoon back at the lodge with her – a fascinating experience to say the least. Sightings of fish eagles, hornbills, pied kingfishers, crocodiles and breathtaking views across the Zambezi valley, accompanied by two further tiger sessions with fish to seven pounds in the boat and a lost beauty of double the size saying goodbye in a kaleidoscope of spray, terminated our stay. Will I return? You bet your life I will.

Following a long hectic summer continuing the making of my *Go Fishing* programmes, I decided to devote time to catching those jumbo-size perch of the upper reaches of the Great Ouse above Bedford once autumn settled in. Its a 250-mile round trip from my Norfolk home necessitating an early start. This is a long haul for a day's sport but as I had caught a four pounder there last February and was optimistic of the chances of more to come, I felt the loss of sleep was well justified. My first session in mid October proved the point. As I have already said, the reason for the Ouse producing these huge perch in such numbers is due to the proliferance of the dreaded signal crayfish.

Unfortunately neither of my nephews, Martin and Richard (whose company I had enjoyed along the river here last winter), could spare time to join me for the day, which simply cried out big perch due to a strong, warm wind from the south-west accompanied by a cloudy sky through which the sun occasionally shone. Changing light values are so important in my opinion for keeping predatory fish willing to feed throughout the day. I settled into a favourite swim half an hour after dawn.

Flowing left to right the river here is about five feet deep through the centre run with an old willow lapping the surface on the opposite bank about forty yards downstream. All along my own bank are thick beds of yellow lilies whose sub-surface lettuce-like leaves provide sanctuary to dense fry shoals. That is one very good reason I am sure why big perch patrol along the cabbages, as they are called. As is my usual preference when fishing for perch along the Upper Ouse, I fished with two rods. With eyes glued to the sensitive tip of my Avon quiver-tip rod, one of the lobworms (on fixed paternoster rigs holding three swan shots) was placed halfway down the run, with the second worm cast into a clearing amongst the cabbages, and a bobbin indicator clipped on the line between butt ring and reel on the Heritage quiver-tip rod which has a softish tip. In both set-ups line strength was 6lb test with size 2 hooks tied direct.

Fishing two outfits in this way, both in different parts of the swim, I find I can locate perch far more effectively than by using just one rod. Moreover because I am continually twitching one worm, whilst allowing the other to remain completely static for up to half an hour before recasting, the perch are given a choice depending upon their mood on the day. This is most important. On so many occasions, having remained biteless for twenty minutes or so, has an immediate response resulted from lifting the rod or pulling the bobbin line down to move the worm a few inches. It is as though the perch is lying there daring the worm to get away before pouncing in – exactly the way a cat behaves with a mouse or small bird it has caught.

I missed the first bite, but the second resulted in that satisfying, head-shaking feeling of a big perch doing its best to rid itself of the hook. They are able to do this with surprising ease if the slightest slack is given. But this one stayed on and after a begrudging dogged fight, so typical of big perch, it was safely in the landing net – all 3lb 14oz of it. What a start! There then followed one of the most extraordinarily productive catches of specimen fish it has ever been my fortune to experience, a catch I rate amongst my top three in over fifty years of fishing.

Strangely those fish never really went mad, and I invariably had to wait fifteen, even twenty minutes for a bite. But the swim remained active literally all day long as various groups of perch and pike moved through attracted by my continually catapulting out broken lobworms. And do you know, not once did I experience that continual twitching on the quiver tip which denotes that crayfish are on to the worm – such was the predatory aggression within the swim. The next bite produced a magnificent perch weighing 4lb 2oz and shortly afterwards a pike of around five pounds grabbed my ledgered lobworm. I then pulled out of a good fish on the strike (which could have been perch or pike) but fortunately the next stayed on and in came a perch of 4lb 1oz. Two four-pounders in one session! I just couldn't believe my good fortune. But there was more to come in a glut of pike, with fish of around six, ten and fourteen pounds (I didn't bother to weigh the pike) roaring off with the ledgered lobs. For a minute or so I actually thought the largest must have been a barbel, such were its speed and power.

It's funny how you can thoroughly enjoy the fight of a big fish on light tackle for several minutes until it rolls on the surface and reveals itself to be a pike, whereupon

its stature suddenly becomes somewhat diminished. In fact I thought the next bite was from another pike and so bullied it upstream through the swim towards me in cavalier fashion only to have a huge perch slide into the net. Another four-pounder no less, weighing a massive 4lb 7oz – my biggest ever by far.

I was by now wondering whether this was all really happening but there was still more to come in the shape first of another fish lost halfway up the swim which I thought would put the kibosh on any further bites. But it didn't. The next perch weighted 3lb 5½oz and at around 2.30 pm my last, another four-pounder, pulling the dial scales round to 4lb 1½oz. Three of the six perch had come to static worms and three within seconds of twitching the lobworm, of which I used well over a hundred. Was I in a dream or what? Four perch over four pounds in a single session plus the two three-pounders which collectively made the catch amount to 23lb 15oz. It was quite a remarkable catch to say the least.

It was no good, I just couldn't fish on. At 3pm I decided to set up the camera on the tripod to photograph the catch, always a frustratingly lengthy operation when fishing alone, before the sun started to drop too low. And I'm glad I did. In retrospect I am sure a few more bites were left in the swim but there comes a time, though I must admit it has arisen on only a handful of occasions with this angler, when your soul has been so well and truly satisfied that continuing is impossible. My two huge mahseer from the Cauvery River in India mentioned earlier weighing together 170lb and a catch of nine double-figure bream to 13lb 10oz in a single session from a Norfolk lake immediately spring to mind. They were times when I simply had no interest whatsoever in fishing on. Another similar and memorable catch happened in the mid-1980s whilst stret pegging at night with a betalight float on a favourite stretch of my local River Wensum at Drayton. Using breadflake I took a mirror carp of 10½lb followed by a barbel of 12¾lb, then a roach of 2lb 7oz, followed by a chub of 4lb 6oz on four successive casts. After this I just couldn't cast out again.

Following this unique catch of huge perch I was asked by the national Perch Fishers' Group to write about my exploits for their magazine which I was only too pleased to do. Having compiled record lists of all the big perch caught within the British Isles since the turn of the century, it was most gratifying to know that the Perch Fishers considered my catch of whoppers quite unprecedented and the most remarkable haul of four-pound plus perch ever reported to them. What with my 120lb Nile perch caught from Nasser whilst making the Safari video there for Emap back in

March and then in October to catch four perch over four pounds in one sitting, you might say 1998 was one hell of a big perch year for me.

It is indeed most satisfying every so often to improve on your personal best, if like me you have a leaning towards the pursuit of larger and larger specimens. Being on a bit of a roller at the end of 1998 it actually came as no great surprise to experience similar good fortune whilst grayling fishing. Although I had caught three-pounders (and that's a big grayling) from Canada's far north, plus numerous two-pound plus specimens over the years from the Tay, the Test, the Kennet, the Dever and from the Frome, I had never caught a British grayling over the three-pound mark – my best weighing 2lb 14½oz from Dorset's tiny River Frome. So when in December my good friend Trevor Stroud invited Bruce Vaughan and me along for a day on the Frome, which is his local river and noted for biggies, I was all keyed up and ready to go as usual.

To break the long drive down to Dorset from Norwich I motored across country to Oxford in order to collect Bruce and then on to Dorchester where we stayed overnight. Now being both a chalk stream and a spate river, I have always been puzzled why the Frome throws up so many huge grayling. In looks and sheer breeding power Hampshire's River Test would seem to possess all the credentials for record-breaking grayling, dace – even roach – potential. But this isn't so. Instead lesser-known fast-flowing rivers, due to unidentified factors, can have the ability to produce specimens of truly huge proportions which is strange in this case because Frome trout are nothing out of the ordinary.

When my old mate and one of the greatest British all-round anglers who ever long trotted, the late Trevor Housby, first took me grayling fishing on the River Test I was like a boy in a sweet shop. I photographed everything we caught and I even took two large grayling home with me (they were unwanted on the exclusive trout beat of the Test we fished) for preserving. They weighed 1lb 10oz and 1lb 14oz and they stare down at me from their bow-fronted glass case high on my office wall as I write this. I feel proud of them because not only did I catch them, I also stuffed them. I later preserved a 2½lb grayling that Trevor caught which still hangs on the wall in the house where his wife, Ilda, and son Russ live. That grayling encompasses all our feelings not only of the angler we loved but of this enigmatic species.

Inevitably these and many more memories ran through my mind as I belted a bait pouch around my waist and filled the two pockets, one with redworms, the other with maggots. Sadly the light values never climbed above a thirtieth at 2.8 (keen

BELOW A 'flash back' photo taken during the 1980s of an unusual catch I made whilst stret pegging the Upper Wensum after dark. It contained a 12¾lb barbel, a 2lb 7oz roach, a mirror carp of 10½ lb and a chub (not shown) of 4lb 6oz that I had already returned.

photographers will identify with our problems) throughout the entire day, so any kind of action photography was out. It was a case of fill-in flash trophy shots or nothing which was a pity because the river is so attractive and with the flow extremely fast and the water clear, some quality grayling were certainly on the cards.

Despite our casual start following a prolonged evening meal at a local Indian restaurant and a late night, we systematically wandered the river trying numerous swims for perhaps thirty minutes at each run or so before either scoring or moving on. This of course is the way to treat grayling fishing. If they are having it, a fish usually comes in your very first or second trot through – thirteen-foot trotting rods, centre pin reels loaded with 3lb test, and Avon and chubber type floats carrying a heavy shotting load being order of the day.

On one particular acute bend where the flow angles sharply across to the far bank, leaving a defined crease on the inside line along which I steadily guided the double maggot bait, an instant bite produced a superb grayling of 2lb 11oz. I expected nothing more but on the second trot through, gently holding back on the 7AA Avon float, the tip dipped positively again and when I struck the rod arched over to the vibrating pulse of what was obviously not a trout or grilse, but a big grayling. It is the way they hang in the flow and twist whilst you try and force them upstream, which makes you realize that on the end of your line attached to just a 16 hook, is a specimen 'lady of the stream'. So your heart is in your mouth throughout the entire fight, right up until it glides over the net. Weighing in at 3lb ½oz this particular grayling, a male complete with splendid sail-like dorsal fin edged in crimson, was just one of four biggies I caught that day. A specimen of 2lb 10oz and a brace of 2lb 11oz

RIGHT Long-time fishing pal Bruce Vaughan and I display some of the monster grayling we caught long trotting the upper reaches of the River Frome in Dorset.

completed what for me was the best quartet I have ever landed in a day's fishing. I told you I was on a roller, didn't I! Indeed, that three-pounder was for me the pinnacle of half a lifetime of long trotting in swift, clean-flowing rivers for this, one of my favourite freshwater species.

Not far into January 1999 I was back on the upper reaches of the Great Ouse once again in search of big perch. I had made one more trip in the meantime following that memorable quartet of four-pounders, taking one three-pounder whilst fishing with Martin Bowler who caught a surprise 5lb chub just before we packed up and headed for home. Martin was also on a roller during this period due to his exploits with the monster Ouse barbel inhabiting the famous stretch immediately below Adams Mill, which were regularly making the angling press. After several huge doubles Martin finally broke the British record with a 16lb 13oz beauty caught on a paste-covered boilie, ledgered on the bottom of a slack in appalling conditions with the Ouse in full flood and all over the fields. Unfortunately the very same fish was caught just two weeks later by another angler (now weighing a staggering 17lb 3oz) before Martin's record claim could be endorsed. Nevertheless, albeit for a short period, Martin was the captor of Britain's largest ever barbel. The very same barbel became the current record when it was caught for a third time by Ray Walton at 17lb 6oz a few weeks later, just prior to the end of the river season on 14 March.

Now with an entire day to myself again and the river nicely up and heavily coloured, I tried the productive cabbages swim and in the first two hours caught perch of 2lb 12oz and 4lb 4½oz, both on static lobworms. The thought that I might be in for another bumper haul did, I admit, cross my mind. But by early afternoon I had not had another bite. So I carried on moving back upstream towards the car trying several favourite swims *en route,* all to no avail. With an hour or so to go before calling it a day my final choice of swim was a large slack that had formed behind a huge sunken willow on the opposite bank – a veritable floodwater haven to any perch living close by and a swim I had not before fished. Within minutes, quite literally, the quiver tip buckled over as something big (I suspected a chub) grabbed the worm and screeched line from the reel as it made off downriver. After several heavy runs and much head shaking I drew yet another huge perch over the landing net. It weighed 4lb 4½oz, exactly the same as the four-pounder I had caught earlier over a mile away. There was then barely time for me to set up the tripod and take a few trophy shots using the self timer and fill-in flash before darkness loomed over the Ouse valley.

Martin's brother, Richard, visited the river a few weeks later and accounted for a fabulous catch of specimens, both on ledgered lobworms. They were a perch of 3lb 13oz and a chub of 6lb 10oz. What a brace!

A few weeks after this in mid February Richard and I teamed up for a day which though mild enough and seemingly pregnant in big perch potential, due to a strong south-westerly wind, produced little until later afternoon when light values started to stop. We put this down to a now low and quite clear river which had a visibility of at least two to three feet following several weeks of extremely cold weather. Fishing several yards apart in a deep bend of the river amongst sunken branches along the opposite bank, Richard had three bites in quick succession, connecting with two, both of which were perch of around the pound. I then struck and pulled out of what felt like a good perch but hooked into a small pike on the very next cast from the same spot. I then lifted into what I thought was a crayfish bite in order to shake it off and the crayfish materialized into a chub of exactly 4½lb.

With an hour or so to go before we called it a day and rain now starting to spit, the bobbin on my near rod jerked up to the butt ring positively and I struck into another whopping great perch which fought as hard as I have encountered from any four-pound fish in British freshwater, making several unstoppable runs against the clutch until the Avon rod eventually got the better of it. I lifted the monster out and we quickly recorded its weight on Richard's scales – 4lb 7oz, exactly matching that of the largest I had caught last October and bringing my total of four-pound plus perch caught in less than a year to eight. Some kind of record in itself. Having read over and over again the legendary perch captures of the late Dick Walker from Arlesey Lake back in the 1950s, little did I ever believe then as a teenager even in my wildest dreams that I should be emulating his remarkable achievements forty years later. Just for the record concerning famous Arlesey Lake in Bedfordshire, Dick did, in fact, share with Bob Rutland during the 1950/54 period dozens and dozens of 3lb-plus perch on long-range ledgered worms, with a total of seven over four pounds. Dick's largest was 4lb 13oz and Bob's was 4lb 10oz.

At the beginning of February Jo and I flew off for a week in The Gambia quite literally on a whim. I had just completed a retrospective piece about fishing in The Gambia for my page in the *Express* when Jo said, 'Hey, why don't we have a week there?' And away we went, meeting up again at Banjul airport with good friends, Tracey Day and her partner, Mark Longster, with whom I made two *Go Fishing* programmes several years back as I described earlier.

It was great to be back in The Gambia again, where Mark runs his fishing charters from the river at Denton Road Bridge, and the beach hut at the Sunwing Hotel where we stayed. With exotic seafoods readily available, it was indeed tempting simply to lie by the pool or on the beach and stuff on grilled lobster and the biggest

BELOW What an unusual brace of specimens to come from the same swim on the Upper Ouse. A perch of 3lb 13oz and a chub of 6lb 10oz are proudly displayed by Richard Bowler. Both fell to quivertipped lobworms.

jumbo shrimps you've ever seen in your life, whilst knocking back the piña coladas. But I'm no Del Boy (although Jo would give you an argument) and so we split the week between relaxing and fishing. As I'd had my fill of fantastic reef fishing on past trips with kujeli, cassarva, barracuda and cubera snappers, we decided to go for broke by attempting to track down those monster tarpon for which the Gambia River is justly famous. In recent years monsters weighing up to a massive 385lb have been caught here but not ratified by the International Game Fishing Association. In just three days' fishing, however, anchoring in the river at its widest point, some four miles across at a location known as Dog Island, I was over the moon just to experience on one of those days a truly unforgettable occasion with literally hundreds and hundreds of hundred-pound plus tarpon all around the boat. I have never seen so many huge fish in one area before. They could be seen wallowing and crashing through the glass-like surface and stretched for at least a couple of hundred yards in all four directions around the boat. But could we get a run? Could we hell. One of our bottom-fished live mullet had been grabbed by a forty-pound flat-headed catfish prior to the tarpon moving in an hour before the top of the tide, but

though we put livebaits out on floats way behind the boat, wobbled baits using an erratic retrieve and even presented baits at mid-water, those tarpon were frustratingly not interested. Then Mark decided to put a general outfit over the side as our 50lb class rods were doing nought. Within just a few minutes of him lowering jumbo shrimp down to the bottom on 20lb gear, it was grabbed by, yes you've guessed it, a huge tarpon.

Immediately Jo helped wind in all the rods while I rushed up front to buoy the anchor as Mark's tarpon did a hundred-yard sprint followed by two high, acrobatic jumps when it completely cleared the surface in a kaleidoscope of shimmering spray. It was an immense fish which we both put at 200lb-plus. But on 20lb line?

Getting on for three-quarters of an hour later, the great fish, having been slowly and skilfully played by Mark, was now on a short line and literally walking him around the boat with me in close pursuit trying to record a jump on camera. It really looked as though the impossible was going to happen. It was now slack water and we were inwardly thinking about all sorts of line class records. Then the inevitable suddenly happened with the line cracking off like a pistol shot. Swearing loudly as we both did achieved nothing, for the 20lb monofilament was heavily frayed for several feet and I suppose the outcome was inevitable from the beginning. But full praise to Mark who really hung in there. So my big Gambia tarpon will have to wait a while, and by big I do mean record fish and hundreds of them to boot. The memory of fish upon fish rolling within yards of the boat permitting appreciation of their enormous bulk while we drifted slowly in pursuit of Mark's tarpon will stay with me for ever. Like a drug The Gambia – not forgetting the company of Mark and Tracey – will have Jo and me returning again real soon.

Back home again and it's 1 March with just two weeks of the river fishing season remaining. I rose at 4 am and headed for Bedfordshire once again. My passion and quest during the past two winters for the big perch of the Upper Great Ouse had not waned an iota despite the long drive. The day however did not start particularly well when I saw in the rear mirror that irritating flash of a speed camera recording my number plate as I obviously exceeded the speed limit going through a sleepy village. The rain was lashing down heavily but it was due to clear later and, most important of all, the outside temperature gauge read a warm 11°C. I just felt it was going to be a good day for perch.

Martin Bowler had visited the stretch a week previously and taken a marvellous brace of perch weighing 4lb 5oz and 4lb 14oz, so the chance of a five-pounder was not such an impossibility. He was in fact due down at the river to join me for the afternoon session through until dark, so from dawn until around two o'clock I decided to have a lone roaming stint fishing numerous swims for short periods of time to evaluate how the perch were reacting to such mild temperatures once again. Would they be holed up in the deep feature swims or starting to group up and moving about?

By the time Martin arrived I had caught several small perch, plus a good fish of 2¼lb and as many jack pike on the statutory ledgered lobworms from no fewer than seven different swims, and had blanks in a further two. So few conclusions could be drawn, except that if we were going to get amongst some whoppers, with the river being so clear (a two- to three-foot visibility and so different from when we fished together here last March when it was in heavy flood), it would happen during the last two hours before dusk. And that's exactly how it turned out.

On arrival Martin moved into the long straight where he recently caught the big fish while I decided to spend the rest of the day in a swim that I had always fancied for some really big perch, due to its immense promise provided by a depth of six feet running close beside a thick bed of sedges, which ran right to left downstream along my own bank for over forty yards. Several past sessions however had produced just one 3lb perch and little else in the way of bites. Nevertheless something made me feel extremely confident as I settled in presenting the quiver tip rod worm close beside the sedges on a long cast, and the second in midstream just ten yards away. After clipping the ledger bobbin indicator between reel and butt ring on the second rod, my Heritage Avon quiver tip, I catapulted out a dozen or so broken lobworms (which I obtain through the post from the aptly named Wiggly Wigglers on a next-day service) and sat back to wait events, every so often adding the extra worm or two. At around 3 pm up went the ledger bobbin and the soft tip of the Heritage Avon curved over into that satisfying throbbing, head-shaking power arc produced only by big perch. This particular rod has been instrumental I'm certain in my landing an exceptionally high percentage of big perch hooked, due to the soft tip, allowing me both to enjoy a powerful fight and then draw safely over the net perch in which the hook is barely set or is held in by a mere sliver of skin.

The first fish weighed 3lb 2oz, shortly followed by a massive stripy of 3lb 15oz, only an ounce below that magical four-pound barrier. This was quite unreal perch fishing but there was more to come. In the space of an amazing forty-five-minute spell prior to dusk falling, the big boys went on a real feeding rampage for my continual supply of broken lobs. I feared that Martin would become cheesed off leaving his swim to help weigh my catches but he was equally as excited as I put monsters of 4lb 3oz, 4lb 4½oz and 4lb 8oz (my personal best) into the weigh net. Surely that was it for the day? But no, on the very next cast I did the unthinkable and bumped off the hook another whopper. After this sport died for a while followed by several small fish in the eight-ounce area which had moved in over the carpet of worms once the big boys had vacated the swim. One more bite immediately before darkness set in produced a perch of 2¼lb, and then all action in the swim ceased.

ABOVE Five huge Upper Ouse perch totalling 20lb ½oz, which included specimens of 4lb 3oz, 4lb 4½oz, and 4lb 8oz, my largest ever.

Martin had anticipated that a serious photography session was in order with such a catch while we could still see the fish without a torch and had walked up to my swim. He duly obliged using my new camera, a Nikon F100, coupled to a 2.8, 20-35mm CPU autofocus lens and SB28 speedlight flash gun, and ran off a couple of rolls of Fuji 100 Provia film. I recently splashed out on such an outfit specifically to overcome the inconsistency problems with fill-in flash that I have experienced over the years with my old Nikon 301 cameras. And I must say that due to the speedlight firing a series of imperceptible preflashes which are detected by the F100 camera's five-segment TTL multi sensor and then analysed for brightness and contrast, exposure problems with flash are for me a thing of the past, even out in the field when you are tingling with excitement and it's getting darker by the second.

I really did assume that my catch of six perch for 23lb 15oz (that contained four over four pounds) and which I detailed back in October 1998 was a one-off but here, just a few months later, the Upper Ouse had provided me with yet another haul destined to rewrite the record books: five perch for 20lb ½oz – and what magical beauties they were too. Massively deep bodied and in fair bristling condition, they were absolutely scale and fin perfect. I was even happy about making the long drive home and content about managing to achieve some unprecedented hauls of monster perch. I haven't spent much time on the domestic scene in recent years due to commitments with foreign fishing. For instance during the past two winters I have visited the upper reaches of the Great Ouse specifically to catch perch on a total of just seventeen days, which is hardly blanket fishing.

Having now caught no fewer than eleven four-pound plus perch during that time, with Martin on a score of six, and Richard Bowler with two, I can only ponder what the future holds for the river now that we have taken the perch record list apart. Will all these monsters grow on to be five pounders or are we (which is why I have fished so hard for them) at the very peak of this remarkable era? After all it's got to stop somewhere. Adult specimens do eventually stop growing, prior to their imminent death. Nothing lasts for ever as all experienced anglers know full well and I'm just thankful that I have been around to experience this truly amazing and unprecedented fishing not only for river perch but for perch from any type of water.

That exceptional perch catch was in fact the last I recorded as the 1998/99 river season came to an end. I fished in the company of Martin and Richard for the last two days but the Ouse had risen almost to flood level again and was thickly coloured. However while Richard and I could attract only small perch and the occasional pike to our lobworms, Martin really finished on a wonderful high note by taking from the same swim, which produced a 4lb 7oz perch for me a few weeks before, a magnificent brace weighing 4lb 3oz and 4lb 11oz. What an unbelievable year's perching we three had enjoyed, accounting between us for no fewer than twenty-one perch over that magical four-pound mark.

It is perhaps only fitting that the very last fishing experience recorded in this autobiography concerns a return trip to the very place on earth I love most save for my home in Norfolk, and that is southern India. I couldn't possibly choose a better time to place a full stop at the end of my fifty years as a fisherman. Even better, my old mate, Andy Davison, with whom I had first experienced the mighty mahseer of the Cauvery River eleven years ago, had now left the oil industry and was to accompany me to southern India during the last two weeks of March.

We were met in Bangalore by our old friend, Susheel Gyanchand, and driven to his farm to chill out for a day prior to a couple of early morning wild boar shoots before we borrowed his four-wheel drive, Mahindra – a cook and handyman – and headed for the river. Now Susheel knows full well we both love pig shooting and had organized a dawn start in a beautiful valley a three-hour drive north of Bangalore which meant two already knackered travellers rising at 3.30 am.

Alas it was all to no avail because at the climax of three different beats the boar always broke too far away from the guns. However, towards the end of the final beat I was treated to a wonderful sight as a small herd of black buck, which are around the same size as our roe deer, came jumping through the thorn scrub directly to where I stood stock still in the shade of a large bush, not daring to move so much as an eyelid. Shooting boar is not just about helping farmers to cull wild animals that do so much damage to their crops, with the added bonus of a delicious meal thrown in. It is also about appreciating all the other animals and birds you see during the course of a beat. I felt privileged to study the dozen or so black buck that came literally to within twenty yards of where I stood. For perhaps thirty seconds they all looked directly at me with a mixture of curiosity and fear, before suddenly bounding off through the scrub as quickly as they had appeared. I felt compassion for the thirty or so villagers and peasant farmers who turned out and literally ran their legs off along a steep-sided valley over a mile wide and two miles long, thickly covered in thorn scrub and eucalyptus trees, in the hope they would be eating meat. That rare treat was withheld from them this time.

For us however it didn't matter because from his freezer Susheel stacked on to the barbecue the largest boar chops that turned out to be the most delicious I've ever eaten in my life. They were equal in size to the biggest T-bone steaks you can possibly buy. For the first time in three nights we slept like babies.

The following morning, however, it was another early call and a long drive in order to get the guns into position at various points along a wide valley before dawn broke. Susheel insisted that Andy and I be put in prime positions where the boar usually broke early well ahead of the beaters, which resulted in our bagging three each. There was thus more than enough meat to go around between the farmers and villagers who were so unashamedly grateful for our presence. It's perhaps difficult for us to understand that a single rampant elephant or a herd of wild boar can in a single night completely destroy a peasant farmer's work for an entire year.

On day three we finally made the sixty-mile journey south to the river in good time to meet up with old friends Bola, Chick Ragu and Boss Ragu, and that first sight of the Cauvery River valley as we descended around hairpin bends towards Sangham village was as magical as when I first clapped my eyes on it over a decade ago. Tall parched brown hills bordered along the floor of the wide flood plain with the bright green of trees nourished by monsoon rains contrasted starkly with the blue of the river itself. With black eagles, ospreys, fish eagle and kites working the thermals high overhead, and dusky terns noisily protecting the turbulent shallows, it was as though the valley had not changed at all. Immediately I felt as I always have in this hot, harsh and beautiful land. I felt I had returned home.

The river itself, however, was not in the best order for mahseer. Due to the next state downstream of Tamil Nadu requiring extra water for their paddy fields, a dam

way upstream near Mysore had released a large quantity of water, thus lowering the temperature of the Cauvery River and adding around two feet to the height of what we expected for the end of March – and it was still rising. Worse still, it was to rise throughout our week's stay. Nevertheless we were of good heart and made camp at Haira, our favourite location, from the provisions Susheel had provided and quickly had a pot of boiling water going to make a batch of ragi bait.

Earlier on I mentioned that to be successful when fishing the Upper Ouse for big perch or chub you need to be always alert and concentrate as though you have just missed a bite and are expecting another. Mahseer fishing is no different; only the circumstances and location are changed. With buttocks perched uncomfortably around jagged rocks and one knee raised to support the rod against the unbelievable force of the current, you patiently wait with a ledgered duck-egg-size ball of ragi paste or a six-ounce deadbait cast downstream and across, conveniently caught with a small spiral of lead, amongst the rocks in the middle of the river. You wait for those thick rubbery lips of the mahseer's cavernous mouth to vacuum the bait up and belt off downstream, thus almost hooking itself in a similar fashion to how our European barbel bites. In the meantime your mind greedily drinks in all the wonders of the river valley.

You hear the distinct, did-de-do-it, did-de-do-it of the red watled lapwing as it mobs an eagle or crow venturing above its nest. You watch the inquisitive Indian otter at play or an elderly woman cow herder scold her buffalos as they graze on coarse grasses provided by the life blood of India – the monsoon rains. Only yesterday evening we were treated to the kind of experience that still may not happen were you to spend a month of Sundays bird spotting in Scotland. Fishing just above our camp down a long turbulent pool for over twenty minutes we watched an osprey searching the shallows along the opposite bank. Every now and then it would hover in that strange wing-flapping leant-back stance with talons outstretched, not unlike a goose coming in to land, before plummeting down to grab its prey, which turned out to be a mahseer of around a pound and a half. What a truly majestic sight! It then flew upstream almost opposite us as if to say, 'I've done it' before slowly flying with its meal down the valley to its nest.

It is now lunchtime, we've just had a swim to cool off following a fruitless morning's session, so Andy and I have only one day left to hit the big time. In almost a week we have taken just one thirty-pounder each plus a couple of babies – much more meagre results than we had expected. Our camp cook, Purusho, has just served up two great platefuls of dahl and pallya with several deep-fried pureés to scoop it all up, and we're about to wash it down with a slug of Hercules brand XXX rum and litchi juice to which the same quantity of water has been added. Wonderful . . . then we'll have a snooze until this evening's session.

Just beyond the folding camp table the shoreline slopes down to the water's edge, thickly carpeted in clumps of tussock grass to which our coracle is tied. In its shade are hundreds of large water skaters and as my eyes look up and across the 300-yard-wide expanse of the Cauvery at our campsite my mind suddenly ponders that top surfcasters in the UK, like my old mate, Neil Mackellow, actually put a 5oz lead out the same distance, yet sitting here it seems impossible. I wonder how Jo is managing at home. It's two o'clock Indian time and so, being five hours behind in the UK, she'll no doubt be walking our four dogs around the lakes after breakfast. As the coarse fishing season is now closed, soon we'll be feeding up the carp in our two lakes so they'll be in tip-top condition when spawning times comes around. And some of those same carp that were caught by syndicate members just a few weeks ago will soon be accepting bread scraps from our hands from the bridge connecting the two lakes.

Bola our faithful guide is doing everything in his power to ensure Andy and I hit into the stamp of mahseer we have enjoyed on all past visits. But I fear he is trying in vain. We have concentrated on all the favourite pools and rapids that have produced countless hour-long battles with fifty- and sixty-pounders over the past decade, plus the seventies and eighties, and even ninety-pound monsters. But right now we must rely upon cherished memories of past encounters. For the present we cannot buy a bite. So whether we finally manage to do the business in the next twenty-four hours before returning to the UK remains to be seen. Personally I doubt it. But should you ever see me along the river bank, you can always enquire. I must say that I have derived tremendous enjoyment from still being able to jump about over the rocks and swim across the river here in India with less than four years to go to my sixtieth birthday.

Fishing is indeed an ongoing cycle which for me thankfully never stops. It has provided me with an exciting, memorable and wonderfully healthy life spanning these last fifty years, starting at the age of five, when I first saw those glistening silver-bellied sticklebacks and redthroats in the bottom of Dad's net. I've always

RIGHT It's no good asking for chicken tikka masala in the Indian jungle. Curried catfish, though, is a possibility. Our campsite beside the Cauvery River at Haira.

endeavoured to live life to the full and have been most fortunate in realizing many personal ambitions through angling which has taken me to wet a line in over sixty different countries. The pinnacle unquestionably has been that rare opportunity of actually creating a piece of natural history by designing and excavating my very own gravel-pit fishery. It was and is a most fulfilling exercise, and a privilege. But there are many goals still to achieve. I should love to catch a three-pound roach for instance, and, at the other end of the scale, perhaps a marlin or really huge shark. There are river systems in Asia, Australasia and in South America which I hope one day to explore, so I doubt my passion will ever wain.

I do worry about the British Isles and the pressure on it. It may lead to there being far fewer anglers in the future. The computerized, televized world has much to answer for and it's difficult to encourage youngsters out into the countryside with so many distractions at home on the small screen through CD Roms, DVDs and the ever-increasing material obtainable via satellite and cable television. But as long as we pull together with those participants in other field sports and place conservation high upon our list of priorities, there will always be a clean-flowing river along which to trot a float for those who have the passion.

POSTSCRIPT

Well, you didn't really think I could end this book with me and Andy blanking, did you? Lo and behold on the last morning (of course it had to happen on our last morning) the river actually started to drop with a noticeable increase in air temperature, though clarity seemed the same. From one of our favourite pools at Kangal I banged into a thirty-five-pounder first cast and missed only the fourth bite of the week, while Andy hit the jackpot with a superb golden mahseer of exactly 70lb which led him and Bola a merry song and dance in the coracle for a full forty-five minutes. What a wonderful ending, which highlighted the fact that no one can ever succeed and enjoy success without the help of others. That is for certain.

BELOW Andy and Bola gently cradle mahseer of 70lb and 35lb. The river gave up its fruits on our last day's fishing.

My All-Time Big Fish List
Freshwater

Barbel	12lb 12oz	River Wensum, Norfolk
Barbel (Southern)	6lb 3oz	River Ebro, Spain
Bass (Big mouth)	4lb 2oz	Dam, Morocco
Bream	13lb 14oz	Forgotten Lake, Norfolk
Bream (Red bellied)	2lb 6oz	Zambezi River, Zimbabwe
Bream (Robustos)	4lb 8oz	Zambezi River, Zimbabwe
Carp (Carnatic)	5lb 0oz	Cauvery River, India
Carp – common	24lb 2oz	Red River, Canada
Carp – crucian	3lb 14oz	Karlstad Lake, Sweden
Carp – grass	21lb 5oz	Lakeside, Norfolk
Carp – mirror	33lb 1oz	Estate Lake, Norfolk
Catfish (Barbel)	18lb 3oz	Lake Kariba, Zimbabwe
Catfish (Bullhead)	3lb 0oz	Red River, Canada
Catfish (Channel)	32lb 8oz	Red River, Canada
Catfish (Electric)	6lb 0oz (est)	Lake Nasser, Egypt
Catfish (Flathead)	9lb 0oz	Rufigi River, Tanzania
Catfish (Silver)	4lb 4oz	Cauvery River, India
Catfish (Vundu)	95lb 0oz	Lake Kariba, Zimbabwe
Catfish (wels)	22lb 8oz	Jimmy's Lake, Essex
Catfish (Yellow)	3lb 0oz	Cauvery River, India
Chub	6lb 7oz	Gravel Pit, Norfolk
Dace	1lb 2oz	River Kennet, Berkshire
Dourado (Golden)	18lb 8oz	Paraná River, Brazil
Drum	9lb 3oz	Red River, Canada
Eel	5lb 2oz	Lakeside, Norfolk
Golden orfe	6lb 6oz	Lakeside, Norfolk
Grayling	3lb ½oz	River Frome, Dorset
Grayling (Arctic)	3lb 3oz	Kazan River, Canada
Ide – golden	4lb 12oz	Klaralven River, Sweden
Mahseer (Black)	44lb 0oz	Cauvery River, India
Mahseer (Golden)	92lb 0oz	Cauvery River, India
Mahseer (Silver)	23lb 8oz	Cauvery River, India
Manyame salmon	5lb 1oz	Zambezi River, Zimbabwe
Murrell	6lb 0oz	Cauvery River, India
Nile perch	120lb 0oz	Lake Nasser, Egypt
Perch	4lb 8oz	Great Ouse, Buckinghamshire
Pike	30lb 13oz	Somerton Broad, Norfolk
Roach	2lb 14½oz	River Wensum, Norfolk
Roach/bream hybrid	5lb 1oz	Gravel Pit, Norfolk
Roach/rudd hybrid	3lb 15oz	Forgotten Lake, Norfolk
Rudd	3lb 8oz	Elstowe Pit, Bedfordshire
Salmon	10lb 6oz	River Bann, Northern Ireland
Salmon (Pink)	5lb 0oz	Copper River, Canada
Sik	3lb 2oz	Klaralven River, Sweden
Tench	8lb 0oz	Sywell Reservoir, Northamptonshire
Trout – brook	8lb 8oz	Kamastastin Lake, Canada
Trout – brown	9lb 2oz	River Kennet, Berkshire
Trout – cheeta	3lb 3oz	Avington
Trout – lake	26lb 9oz	Kazan River, Canada
Trout – rainbow	12lb 8oz	Blackwool Farm, Sussex
Trout – sea	9lb 4oz	Morrum River, Sweden
Trout – steelhead	14lb 11oz	Copper River, Canada
Trout – tiger	5lb 8oz	Chalksprings, Sussex
Tiger fish	14lb 2oz	Zambezi River, Zimbabwe
Zander	11lb 3oz	Middle Level Drain, Norfolk

Sea

Amberjack	78lb 0oz	Islamorado Florida		Pollack	18lb 12oz	South Coast
Antarctic rock cod	5lb 12oz	Falklands				
				Rainbow runner	7lb 0oz	The Seychelles
Barracuda	32lb 0oz	The Gambia		Ray – eagle	65lb 0oz	Australia
Bass	11lb 4oz	Essex coast		Ray – small eyed	10lb 0oz	Channel Islands
Bastard halibut	4lb 3oz	The Gambia		Ray – spotted	4lb 8oz	Dorset coast
Black bream	4lb 1oz	Channel Islands		Ray sting	200lb-plus (est)	Barbados
Bonefish	7lb 0oz	Bahamas		Ray – thornback	11lb 6oz	South coast
Bonito	9lb 0oz	The Seychelles		Rubber lipped grouper	5lb 8oz	The Gambia
Bull huss	14lb 0oz	Weymouth				
				Sailfish	91lb 0oz	Mexico
Cassarva	12lb 0oz	The Gambia		Salmon – threadfin	12lb 0oz	The Gambia
Catfish – hardhead	31lb 0oz	The Gambia		Shark – black tipped	80lb 0oz	Fiji
Catfish – silver	8lb 0oz	Aden		Shark – blue	85lb 0oz	Bahamas
Coalfish	8lb 0oz	Denmark		Shark – hammerhead	300lb-plus (est)	Islamorada Florida
Cod	26lb 8oz	Sussex coast		Shark – lemon	300lb-plus	The Gambia
Conger eel	76lb 0oz	Sussex coast		Shark – leopard	21lb 0oz	San Francisco
Crevalle jack	12lb 0oz	Barbados		Shark – nurse	20lb 0oz	Tonga
				Shark – oceanic	180lb 0oz	Mauritius
Dorado	43lb 0oz	The Seychelles		Smoothound	8lb 0oz	Essex coast
				Snapper – cubera	35lb 0oz	The Gambia
Flathead	7lb 0oz	Australia		Snapper – red	21lb 8oz	New Zealand
				Snook	9lb 6oz	Barbados
Garfish	1lb 10oz	Channel Islands		Spotted seatrout	5lb 0oz	Morocco
Green jobfish	15lb 0oz	The Seychelles		Spurdog	11lb 8oz	Ireland
Guitarfish	35lb 0oz	Morocco				
Gurnard – tub	6lb 8oz	New Zealand		Tarpon	130lb 0oz	Islamorada Florida
				Tomato hind	6lb 0oz	The Seychelles
Houndfish	6lb 0oz	The Seychelles		Tope	42lb 0oz	Ireland
				Trevally – blue spotted	18lb 0oz	The Seychelles
Ladyfish	9lb 12oz	The Gambia		Tuna – big eyed	220lb 0oz	Madeira
Ling	30lb 0oz	Denmark		Tuna – black fin	12lb 0oz	Mauritius
Ling cod	7lb 8oz	Canada		Tuna – blue fin	30lb 0oz	Australia
				Tuna – skipjack	7lb 0oz	Madeira
Mackerel – king	26lb 0oz	Kenya		Tuna – yellow fin	42lb 0oz	The Seychelles
Mackerel – Spanish	8lb 6oz	Barbados				
Moontail sea bass	11lb 0oz	The Seychelles		Wahoo	43lb 0oz	Kenya
Moray eel	8lb 0oz	Barbados				
Mullet (Grey thick lipped)	4lb 2oz	Weymouth				

Index